AERO

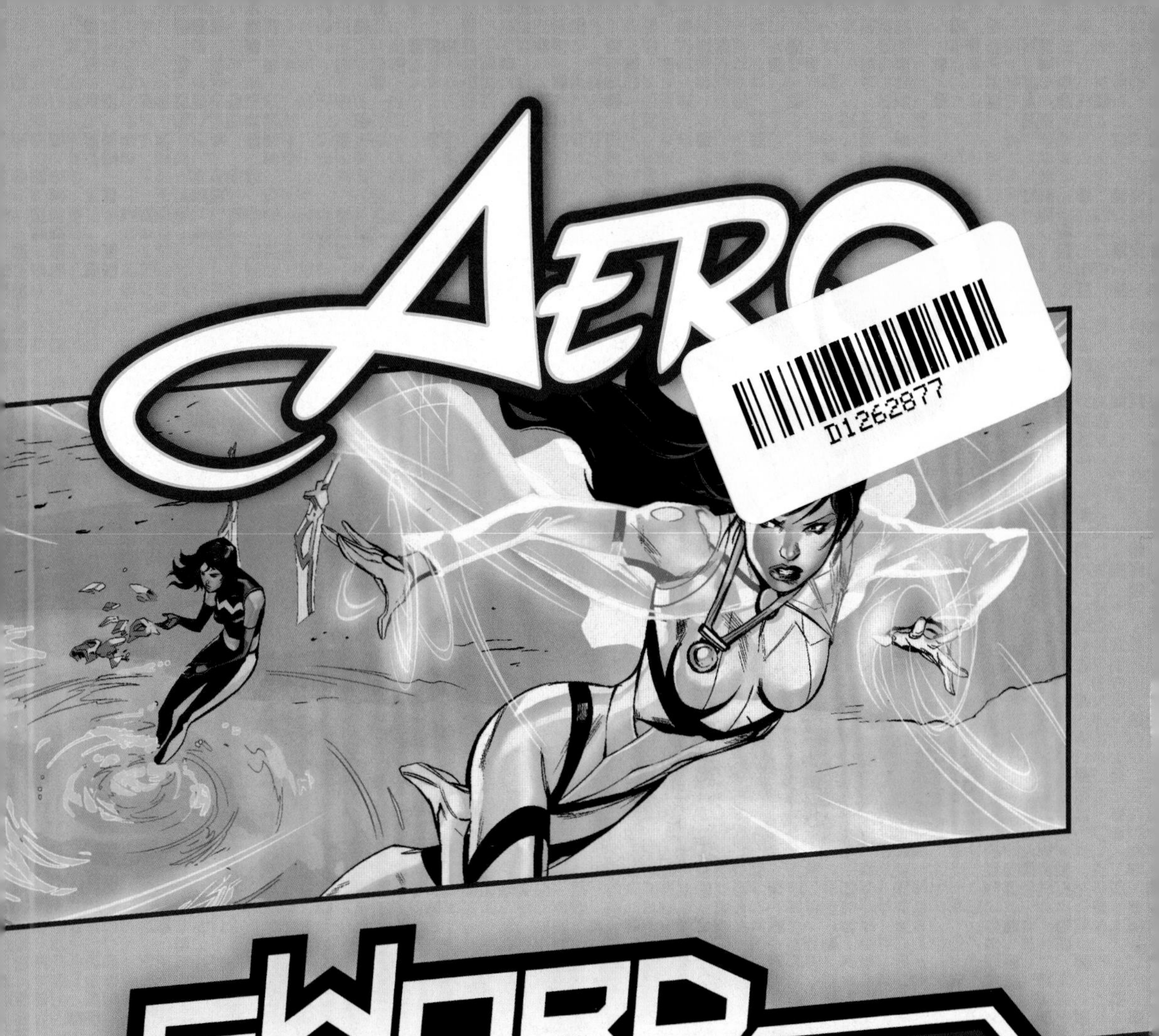

SWORD MASTER

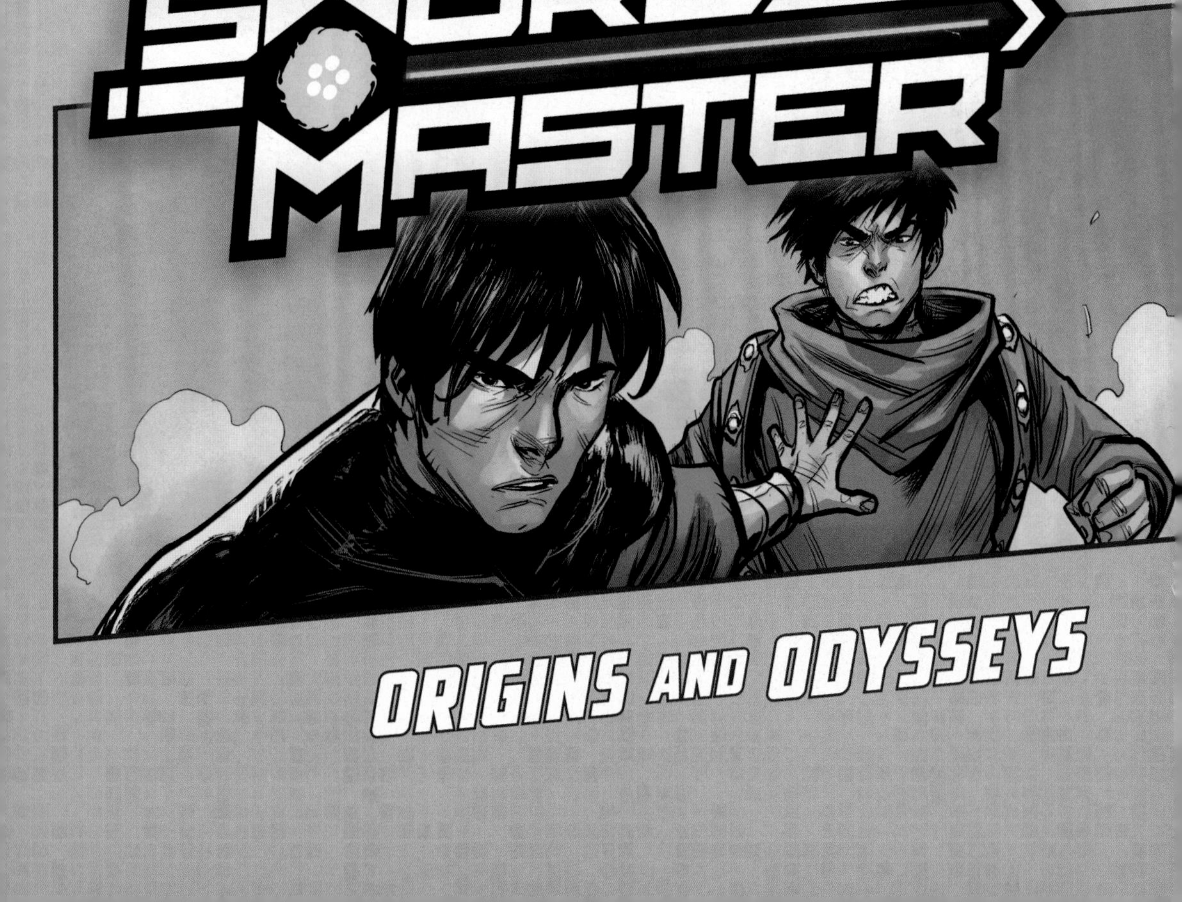

ORIGINS AND ODYSSEYS

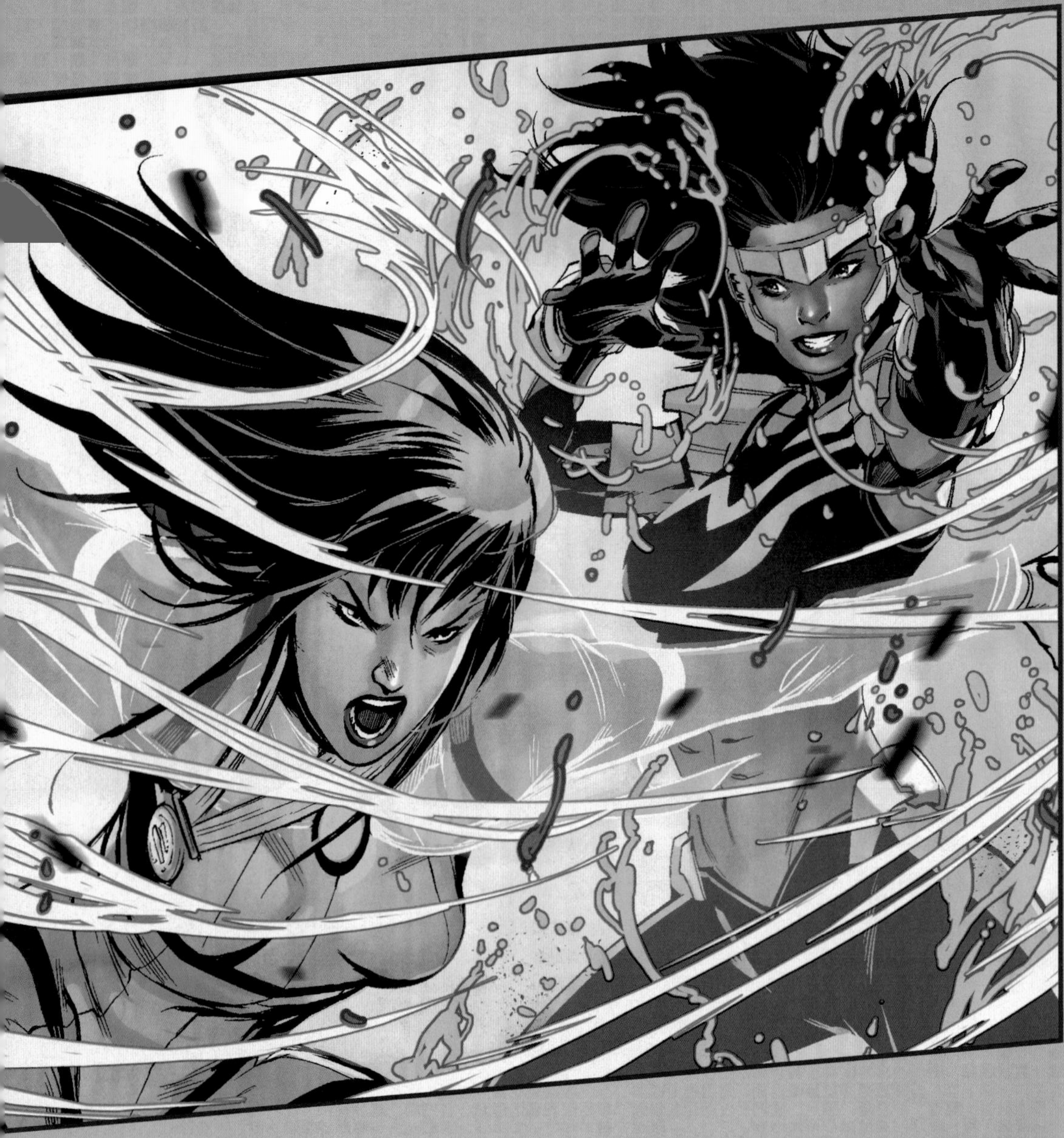

COLLECTION EDITOR: **Jennifer Grünwald**
ASSISTANT MANAGING EDITOR: **Maia Loy**
ASSISTANT MANAGING EDITOR: **Lisa Montalbano**
EDITOR, SPECIAL PROJECTS: **Mark D. Beazley**

VP PRODUCTION & SPECIAL PROJECTS: **Jeff Youngquist**
BOOK DESIGNER: **Adam Del Re**
SVP PRINT, SALES & MARKETING: **David Gabriel**
EDITOR IN CHIEF: **C.B. Cebulski**

AERO & SWORD MASTER: ORIGINS AND ODYSSEYS. Contains material originally published in magazine form as AERO (2019) #1-6 and SWORD MASTER (2019) #1-6. First printing 2020. ISBN 978-1-302-92261-0. Published by MARVEL WORLDWIDE, INC., a subsidiary of MARVEL ENTERTAINMENT, LLC. OFFICE OF PUBLICATION: 1290 Avenue of the Americas, New York, NY 10104. © 2020 MARVEL No similarity between any of the names, characters, persons, and/or institutions in this magazine with those of any living or dead person or institution is intended, and any such similarity which may exist is purely coincidental. **Printed in Canada.** KEVIN FEIGE, Chief Creative Officer; DAN BUCKLEY, President, Marvel Entertainment; JOHN NEE, Publisher; JOE QUESADA, EVP & Creative Director; TOM BREVOORT, SVP of Publishing; DAVID BOGART, Associate Publisher & SVP of Talent Affairs; Publishing & Partnership; DAVID GABRIEL, VP of Print & Digital Publishing; JEFF YOUNGQUIST, VP of Production & Special Projects; DAN CARR, Executive Director of Publishing Technology; ALEX MORALES, Director of Publishing Operations; DAN EDINGTON, Managing Editor; SUSAN CRESPI, Production Manager; STAN LEE, Chairman Emeritus. For information regarding advertising in Marvel Comics or on Marvel.com, please contact Vit DeBellis, Custom Solutions & Integrated Advertising Manager, at vdebellis@marvel.com. For Marvel subscription inquiries, please call 888-511-5480. **Manufactured between 6/26/2020 and 7/28/2020 by SOLISCO PRINTERS, SCOTT, QC, CANADA.**

10 9 8 7 6 5 4 3 2 1

AERO & WAVE: ORIGINS & DESTINIES

WRITERS:
GREG PAK (PARTS 1-6) & **ALYSSA WONG** (PARTS 2-6)

ARTIST:
POP MHAN

COLOR ARTIST:
FEDERICO BLEE

LETTERER:
VC's JOE CARAMAGNA

COVER ART:
Jay Anacleto & Rain Beredo

SWORD MASTER & SHANG-CHI: MASTER CLASS

WRITERS:
GREG PAK (PARTS 1-6) & **FONDA LEE** (PARTS 4-6)

ARTIST:
ARIO ANINDITO

COLOR ARTIST:
RACHELLE ROSENBERG

LETTERER:
VC's TRAVIS LANHAM

COVER ART:
Billy Tan & **Haining** of Tan Studios

ASSISTANT EDITORS:
Tom Groneman & Lindsey Cohick

EDITOR:
Mark Paniccia

SPECIAL THANKS TO
Winni Woo & Yifan Jiang

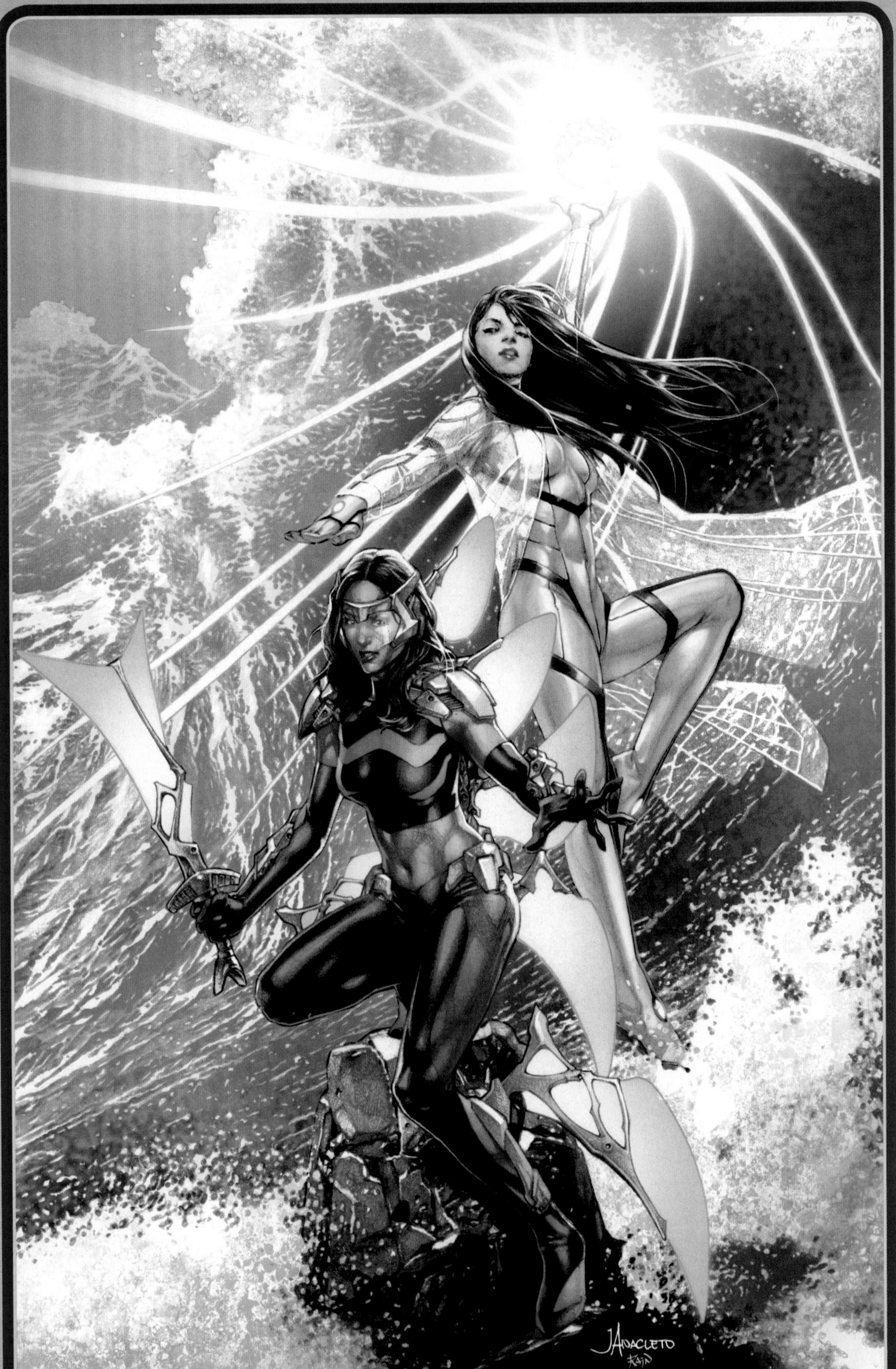

AERO & WAVE: ORIGINS & DESTINIES

Aero & Wave: Origins & Destinies Part One

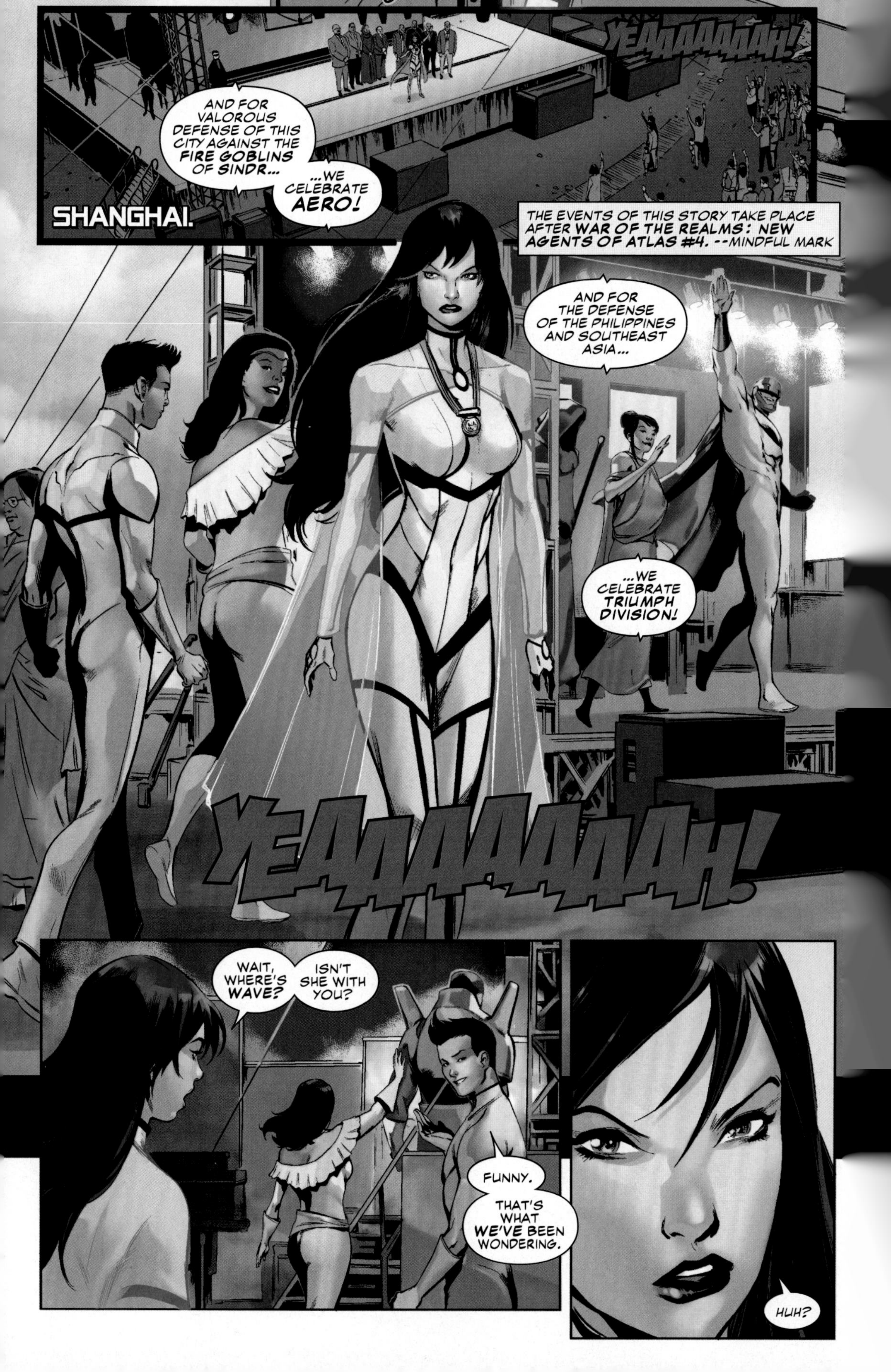
SHANGHAI.
AND FOR VALOROUS DEFENSE OF THIS CITY AGAINST THE FIRE GOBLINS OF SINDR...
...WE CELEBRATE AERO!
YEAAAAAAAH!
THE EVENTS OF THIS STORY TAKE PLACE AFTER WAR OF THE REALMS: NEW AGENTS OF ATLAS #4. --MINDFUL MARK
AND FOR THE DEFENSE OF THE PHILIPPINES AND SOUTHEAST ASIA...
...WE CELEBRATE TRIUMPH DIVISION!
YEAAAAAAAH!
WAIT, WHERE'S WAVE?
ISN'T SHE WITH YOU?
FUNNY.
THAT'S WHAT WE'VE BEEN WONDERING.
HUH?

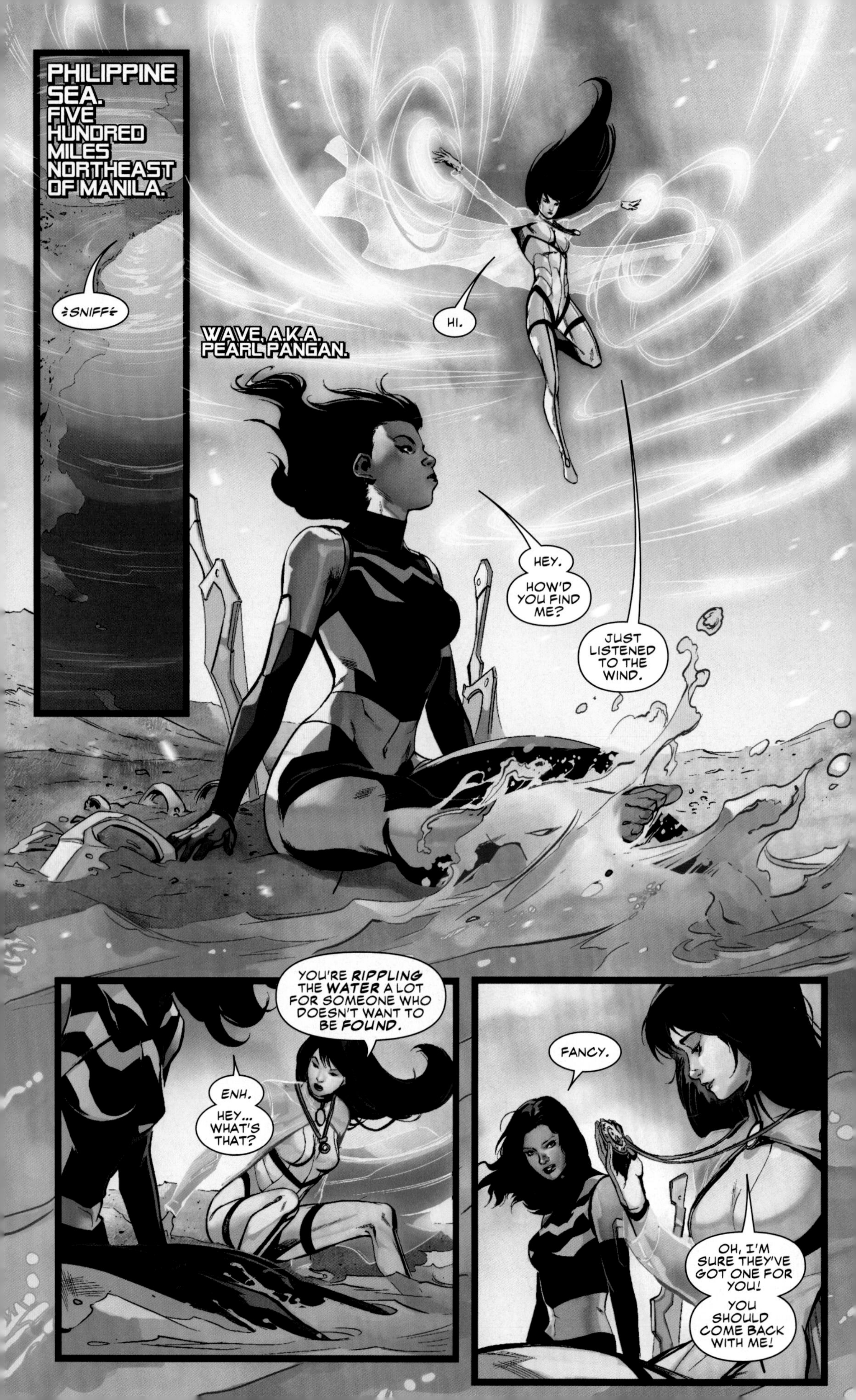
PHILIPPINE SEA. FIVE HUNDRED MILES NORTHEAST OF MANILA.
≷SNIFF≶
HI.
WAVE, A.K.A. PEARL PANGAN.
HEY.
HOW'D YOU FIND ME?
JUST LISTENED TO THE WIND.
YOU'RE RIPPLING THE WATER A LOT FOR SOMEONE WHO DOESN'T WANT TO BE FOUND.
ENH.
HEY... WHAT'S THAT?
FANCY.
OH, I'M SURE THEY'VE GOT ONE FOR YOU!
YOU SHOULD COME BACK WITH ME!

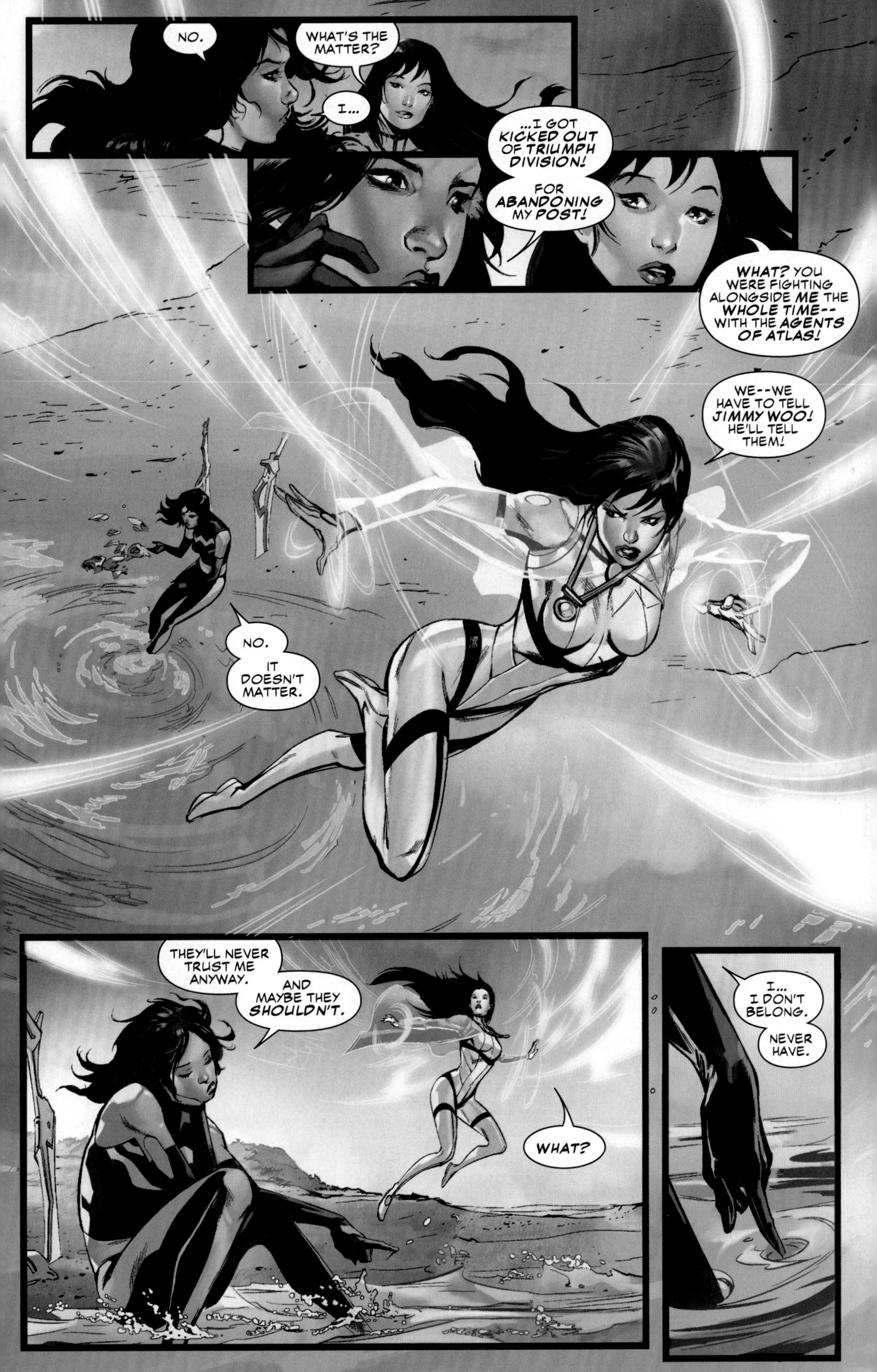
NO.
WHAT'S THE MATTER?
I...
...I GOT KICKED OUT OF TRIUMPH DIVISION!
FOR ABANDONING MY POST!
WHAT? YOU WERE FIGHTING ALONGSIDE ME THE WHOLE TIME--WITH THE AGENTS OF ATLAS!
WE--WE HAVE TO TELL JIMMY WOO! HE'LL TELL THEM!
NO.
IT DOESN'T MATTER.
THEY'LL NEVER TRUST ME ANYWAY.
AND MAYBE THEY SHOULDN'T.
WHAT?
I... I DON'T BELONG.
NEVER HAVE.

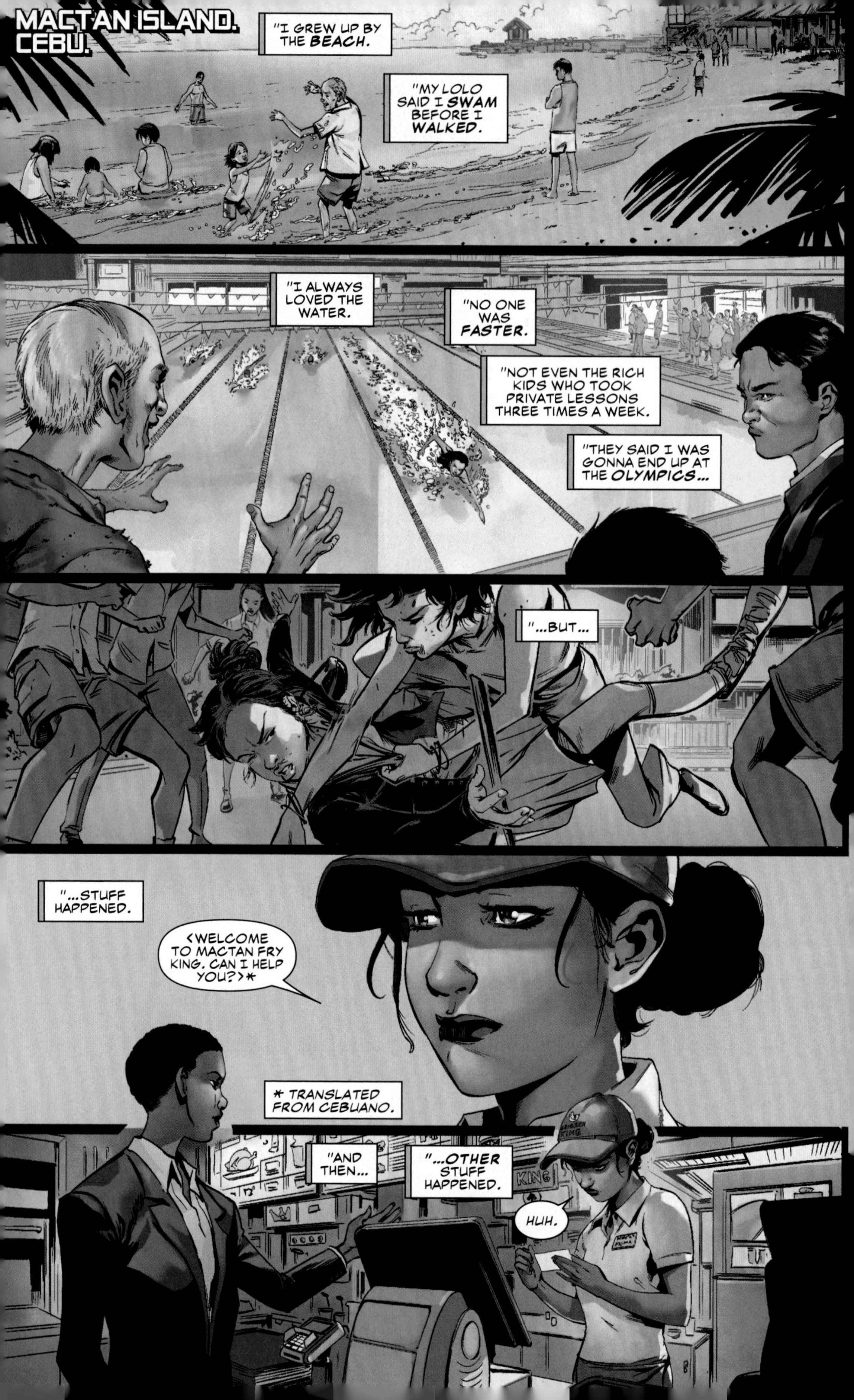
MACTAN ISLAND. CEBU.
"I GREW UP BY THE BEACH.
"MY LOLO SAID I SWAM BEFORE I WALKED.
"I ALWAYS LOVED THE WATER.
"NO ONE WAS FASTER.
"NOT EVEN THE RICH KIDS WHO TOOK PRIVATE LESSONS THREE TIMES A WEEK.
"THEY SAID I WAS GONNA END UP AT THE OLYMPICS...
"...BUT...
"...STUFF HAPPENED.
<WELCOME TO MACTAN FRY KING. CAN I HELP YOU?>*
* TRANSLATED FROM CEBUANO.
"AND THEN...
"...OTHER STUFF HAPPENED.
HUH.

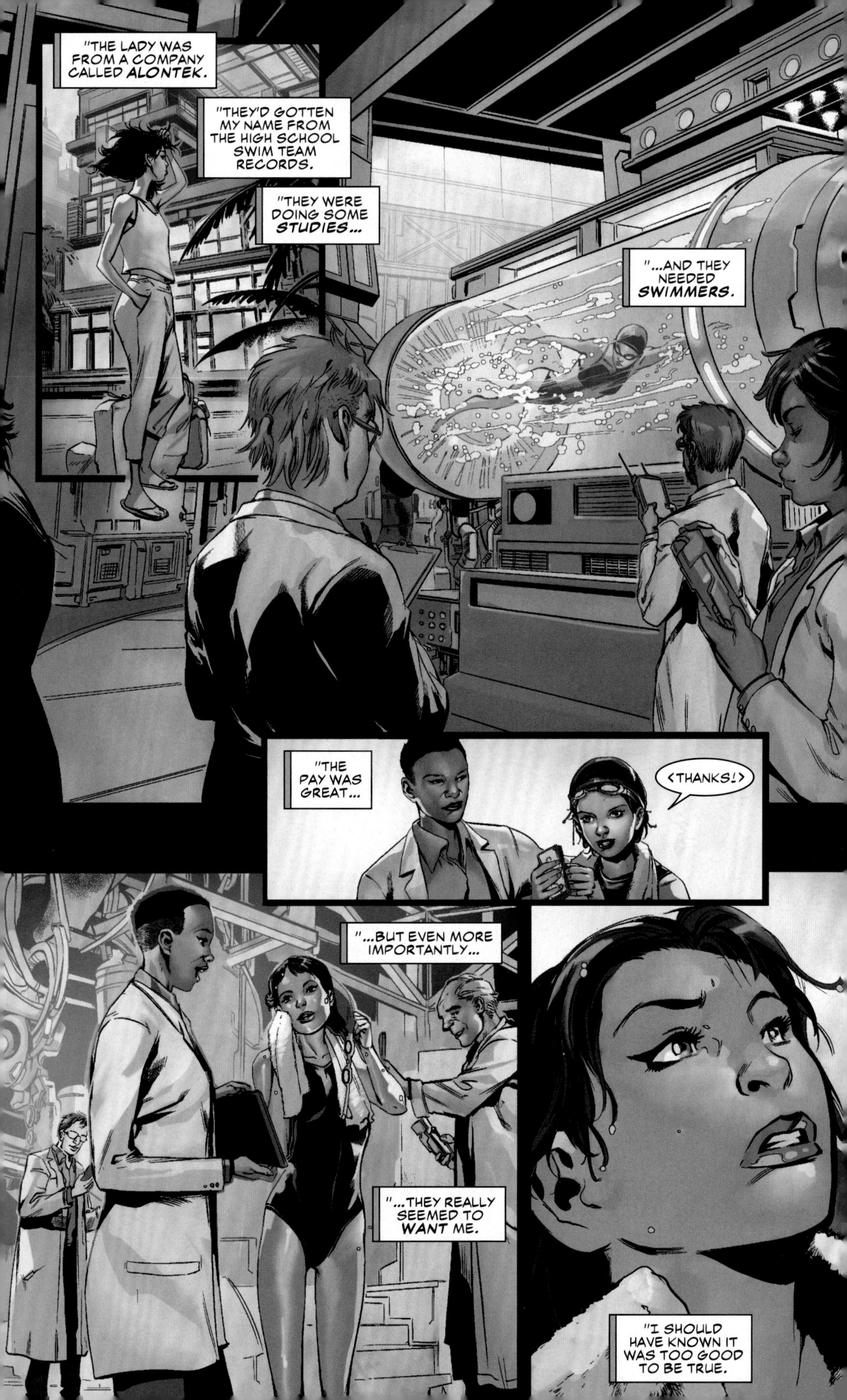
"THE LADY WAS FROM A COMPANY CALLED ALONTEK.
"THEY'D GOTTEN MY NAME FROM THE HIGH SCHOOL SWIM TEAM RECORDS.
"THEY WERE DOING SOME STUDIES...
"...AND THEY NEEDED SWIMMERS.
"THE PAY WAS GREAT...
<THANKS!>
"...BUT EVEN MORE IMPORTANTLY...
"...THEY REALLY SEEMED TO WANT ME.
"I SHOULD HAVE KNOWN IT WAS TOO GOOD TO BE TRUE.

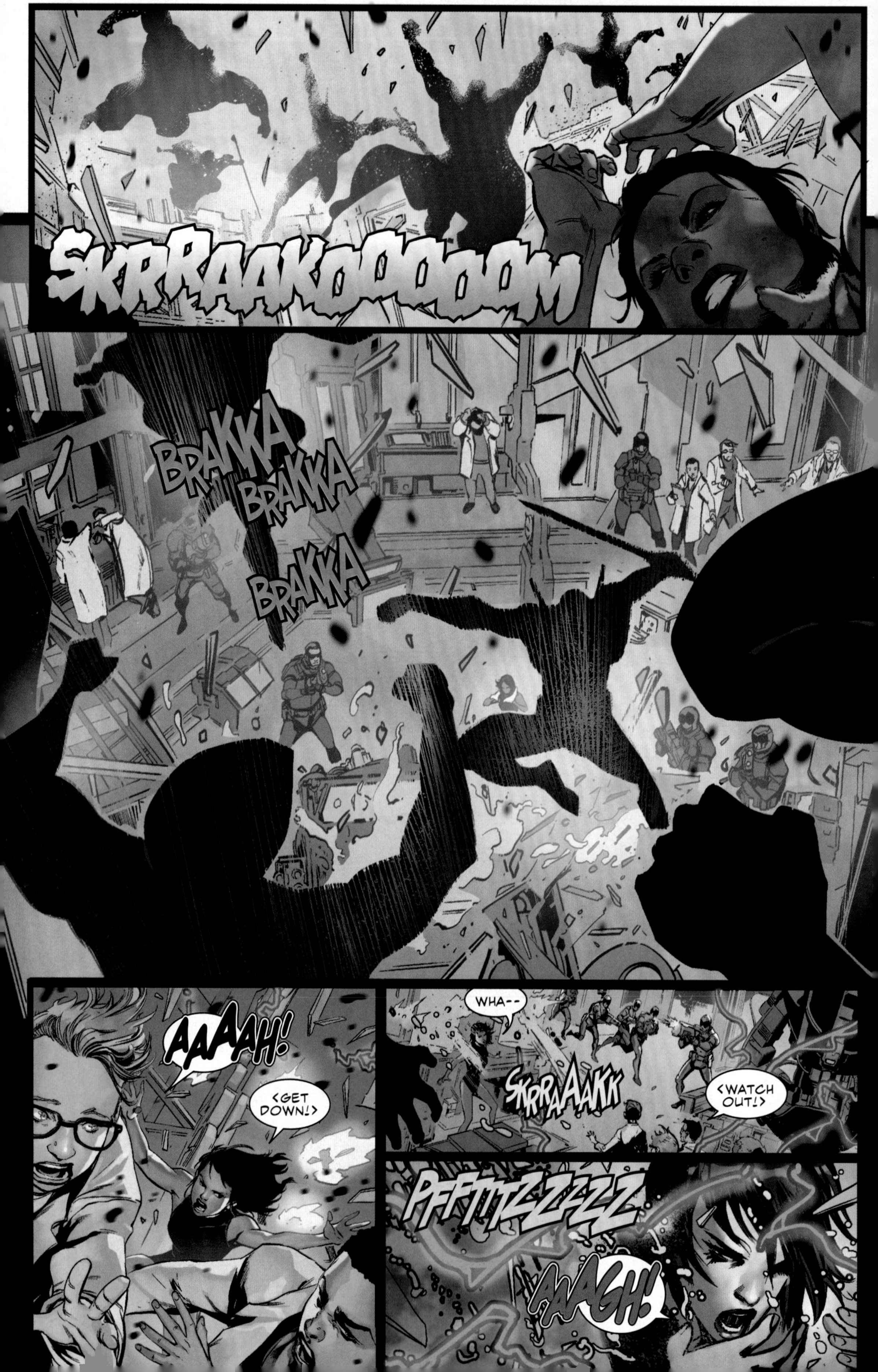

SKRRAAKOOOOOM
BRAKKA
BRAKKA
BRAKKA
AAAAH!
<GET DOWN!>
WHA--
SKRRAAAKK
<WATCH OUT!>
PFFTTTZZZZZ
AAAGH!

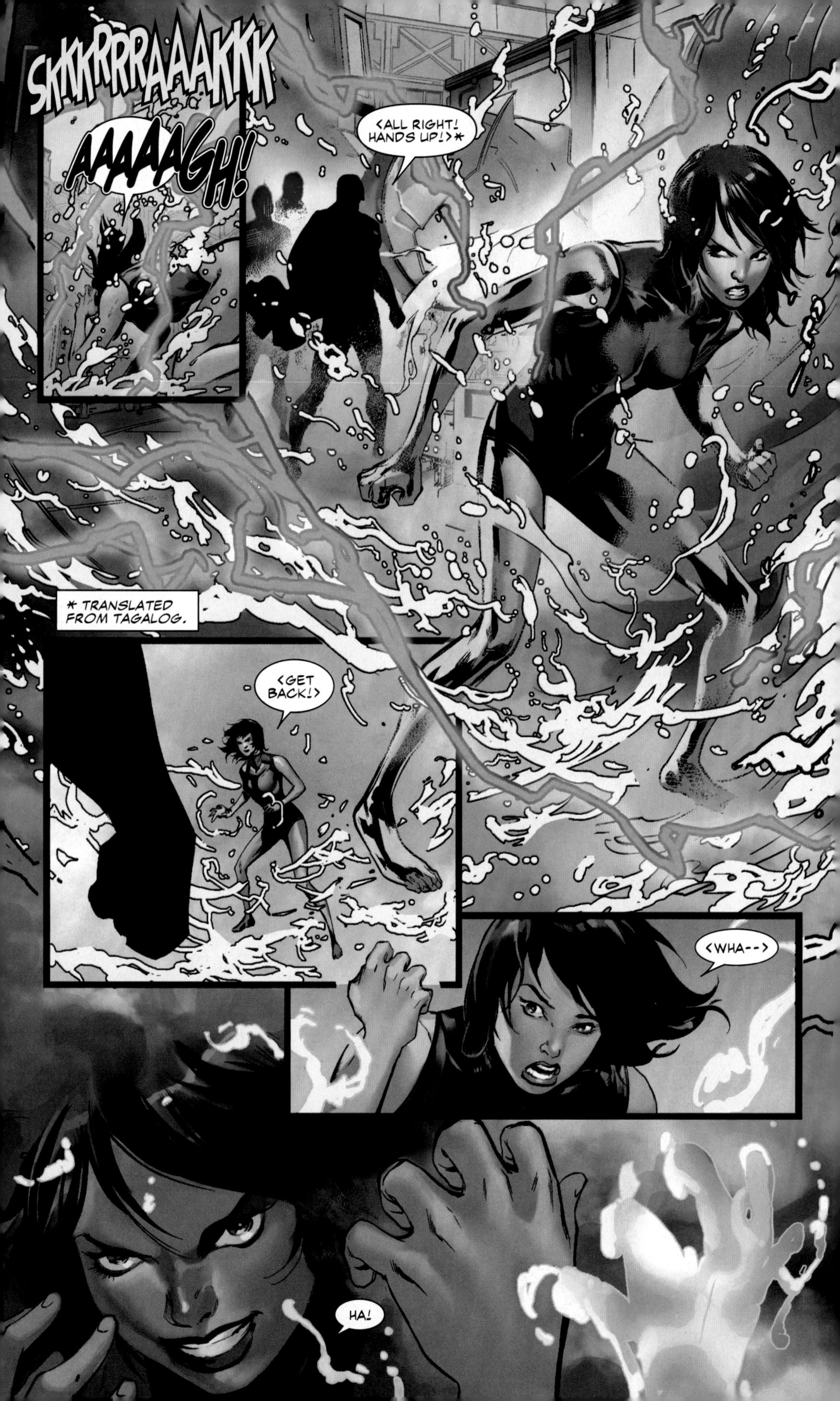

SKKKRRRAAAKKK
AAAAAGH!
<ALL RIGHT! HANDS UP!>*
* TRANSLATED FROM TAGALOG.
<GET BACK!>
<WHA-->
HA!

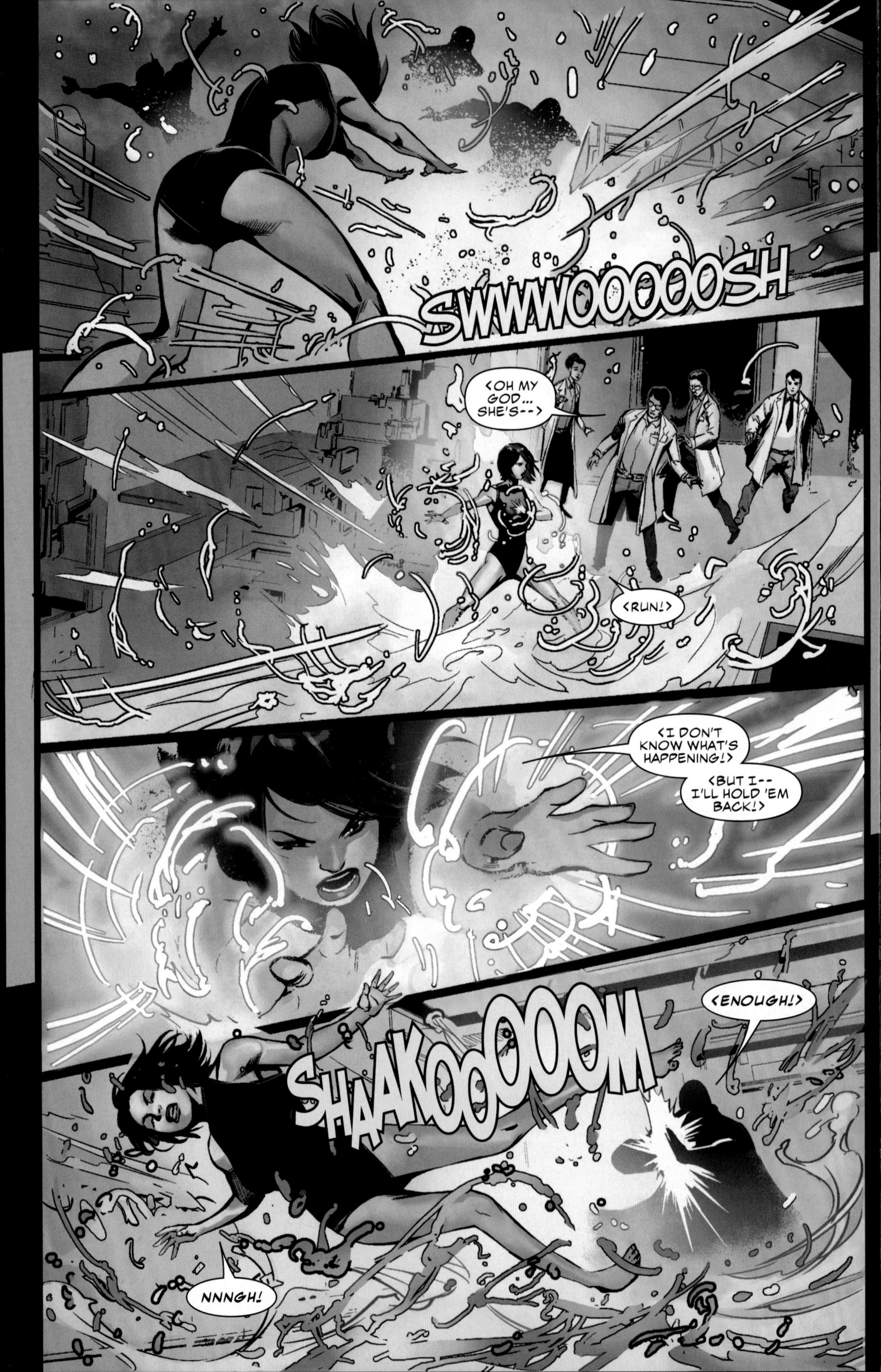
SWWWOOOOOSH
<OH MY GOD... SHE'S-->
<RUN!>
<I DON'T KNOW WHAT'S HAPPENING!>
<BUT I-- I'LL HOLD 'EM BACK!>
<ENOUGH!>
SHAAKOOOOOM
NNNGH!

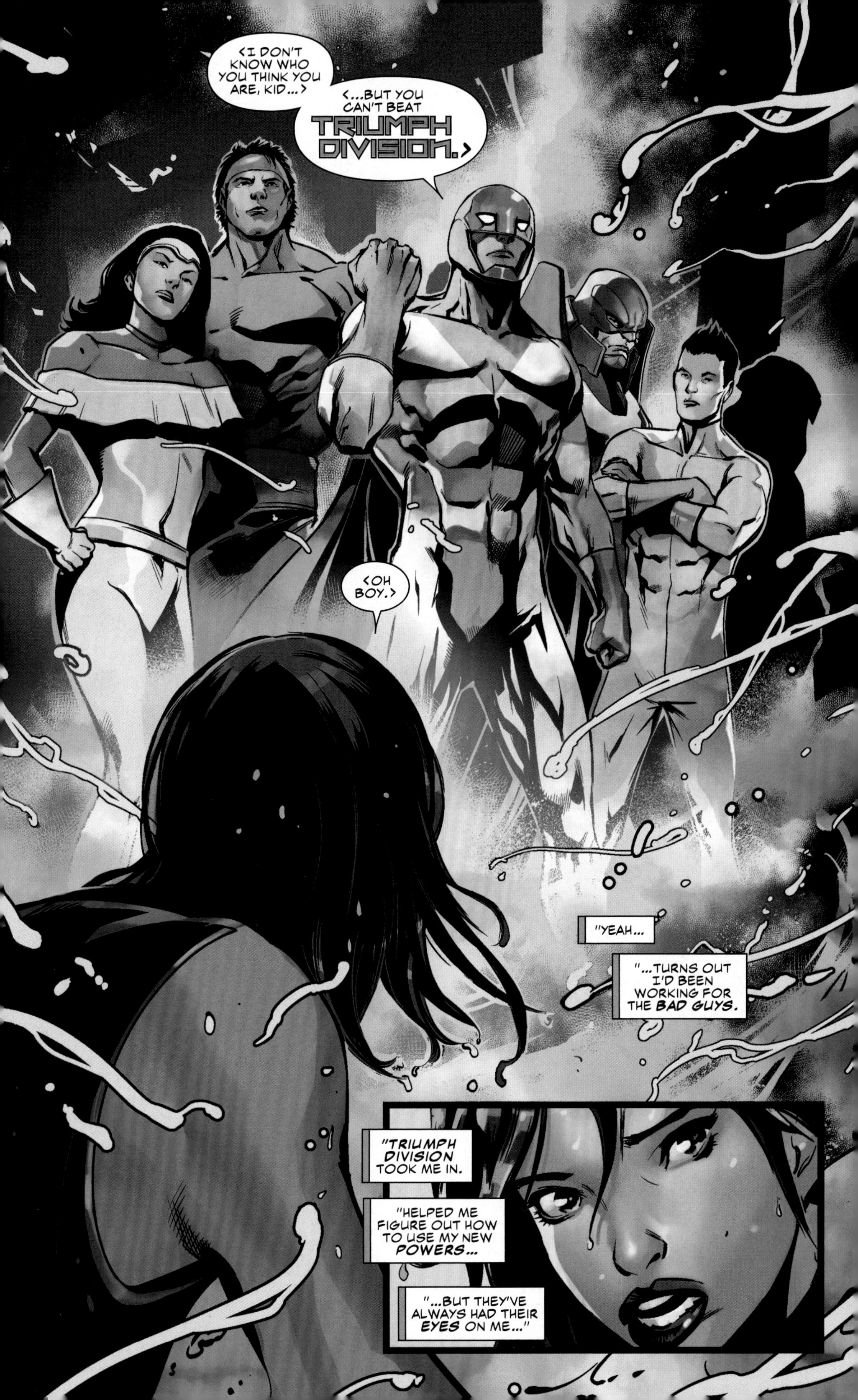
<I DON'T KNOW WHO YOU THINK YOU ARE, KID...>
<...BUT YOU CAN'T BEAT TRIUMPH DIVISION.>
<OH BOY.>
"YEAH...
"...TURNS OUT I'D BEEN WORKING FOR THE BAD GUYS.
"TRIUMPH DIVISION TOOK ME IN.
"HELPED ME FIGURE OUT HOW TO USE MY NEW POWERS...
"...BUT THEY'VE ALWAYS HAD THEIR EYES ON ME..."

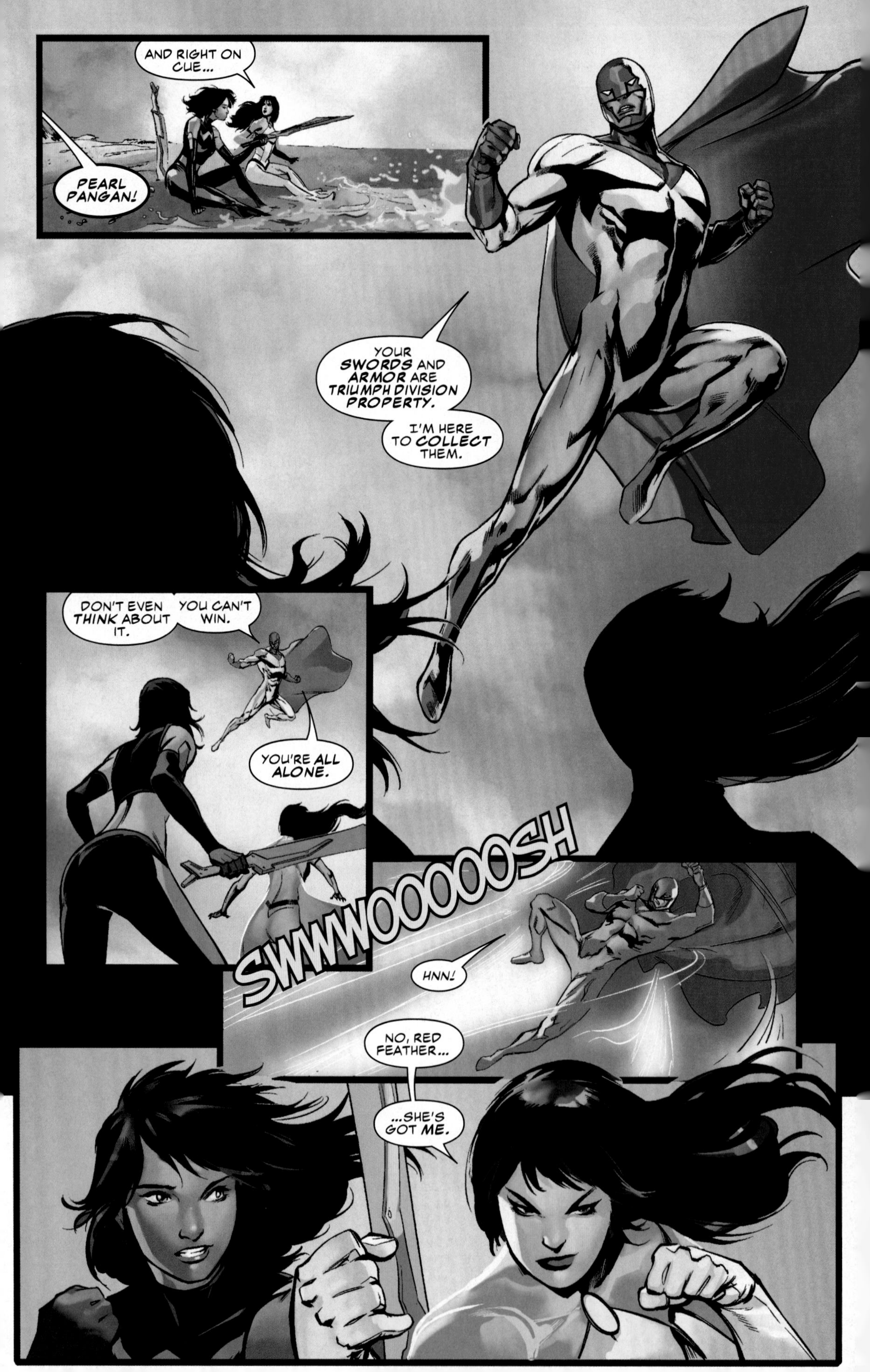

AND RIGHT ON CUE...
PEARL PANGAN!
YOUR SWORDS AND ARMOR ARE TRIUMPH DIVISION PROPERTY.
I'M HERE TO COLLECT THEM.
DON'T EVEN THINK ABOUT IT.
YOU CAN'T WIN.
YOU'RE ALL ALONE.
SWWWOOOOOOSH
HNN!
NO, RED FEATHER...
...SHE'S GOT ME.

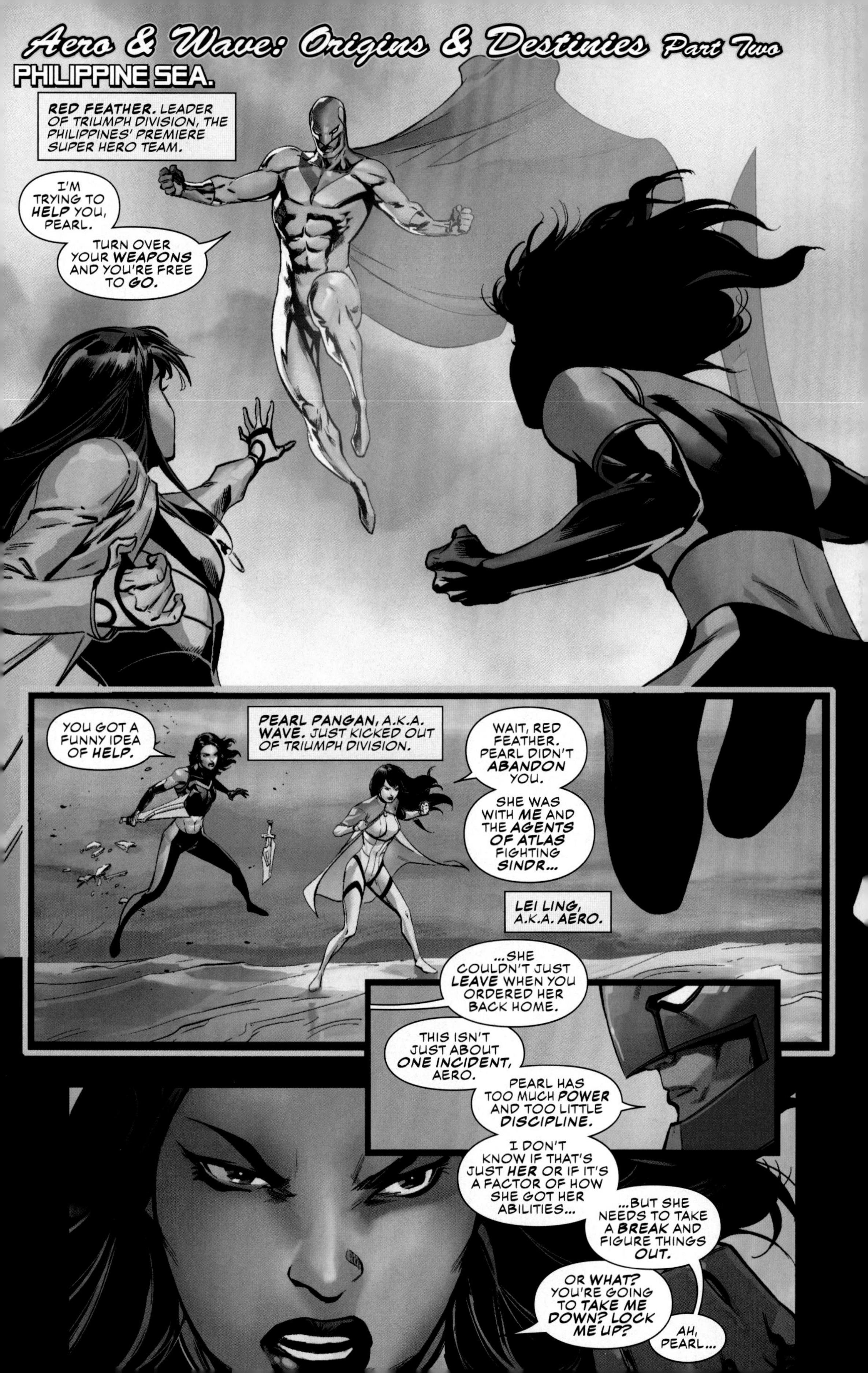
Aero & Wave: Origins & Destinies Part Two
PHILIPPINE SEA.
RED FEATHER. LEADER OF TRIUMPH DIVISION, THE PHILIPPINES' PREMIERE SUPER HERO TEAM.
I'M TRYING TO HELP YOU, PEARL.
TURN OVER YOUR WEAPONS AND YOU'RE FREE TO GO.
YOU GOT A FUNNY IDEA OF HELP.
PEARL PANGAN, A.K.A. WAVE. JUST KICKED OUT OF TRIUMPH DIVISION.
WAIT, RED FEATHER. PEARL DIDN'T ABANDON YOU.
SHE WAS WITH ME AND THE AGENTS OF ATLAS FIGHTING SINDR...
LEI LING, A.K.A. AERO.
...SHE COULDN'T JUST LEAVE WHEN YOU ORDERED HER BACK HOME.
THIS ISN'T JUST ABOUT ONE INCIDENT, AERO.
PEARL HAS TOO MUCH POWER AND TOO LITTLE DISCIPLINE.
I DON'T KNOW IF THAT'S JUST HER OR IF IT'S A FACTOR OF HOW SHE GOT HER ABILITIES...
...BUT SHE NEEDS TO TAKE A BREAK AND FIGURE THINGS OUT.
OR WHAT? YOU'RE GOING TO TAKE ME DOWN? LOCK ME UP?
AH, PEARL...

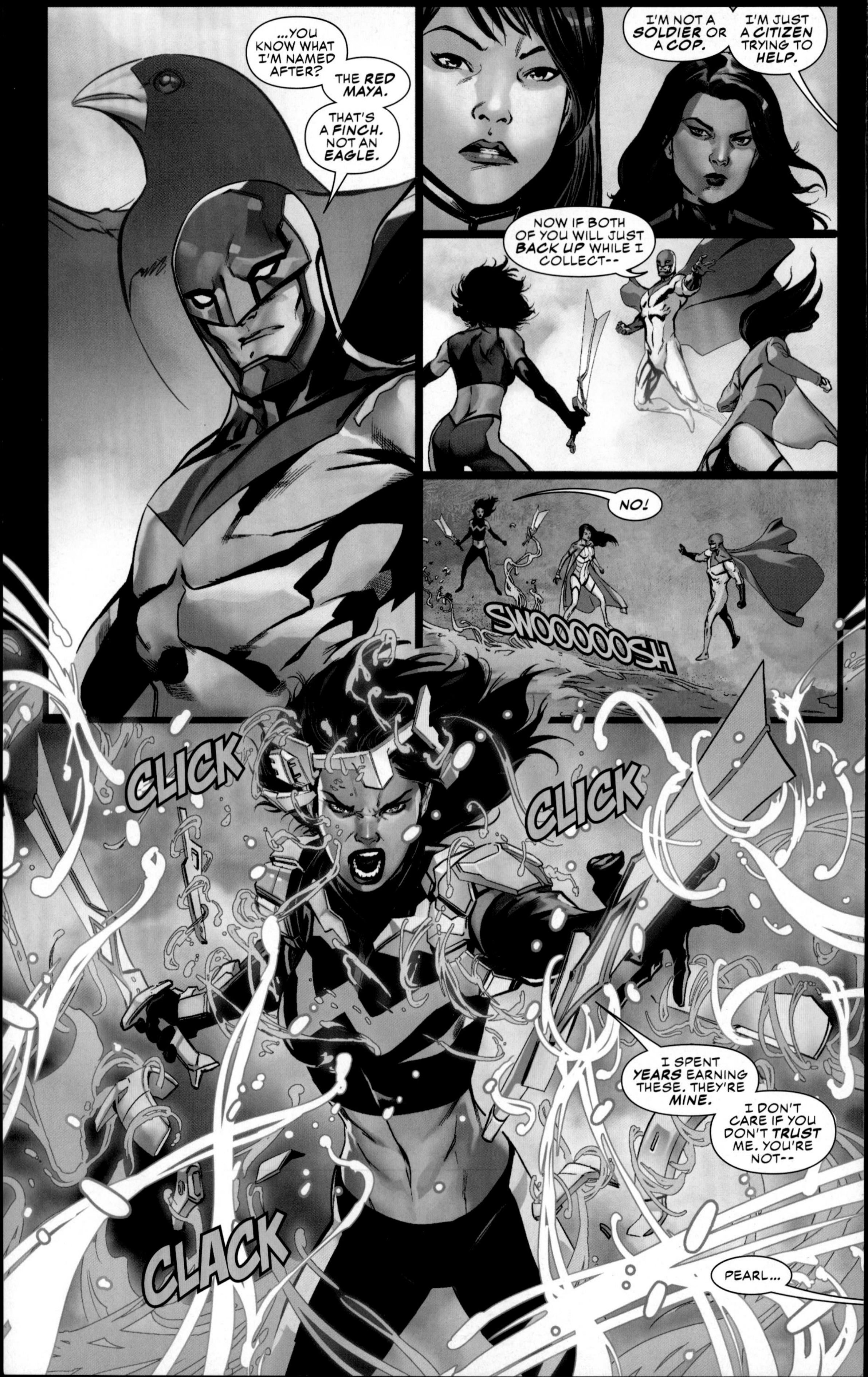
...YOU KNOW WHAT I'M NAMED AFTER?
THE RED MAYA.
THAT'S A FINCH. NOT AN EAGLE.
I'M NOT A SOLDIER OR A COP.
I'M JUST A CITIZEN TRYING TO HELP.
NOW IF BOTH OF YOU WILL JUST BACK UP WHILE I COLLECT--
NO!
SWOOOOOSH
CLICK
CLICK
CLACK
I SPENT YEARS EARNING THESE. THEY'RE MINE.
I DON'T CARE IF YOU DON'T TRUST ME. YOU'RE NOT--
PEARL...

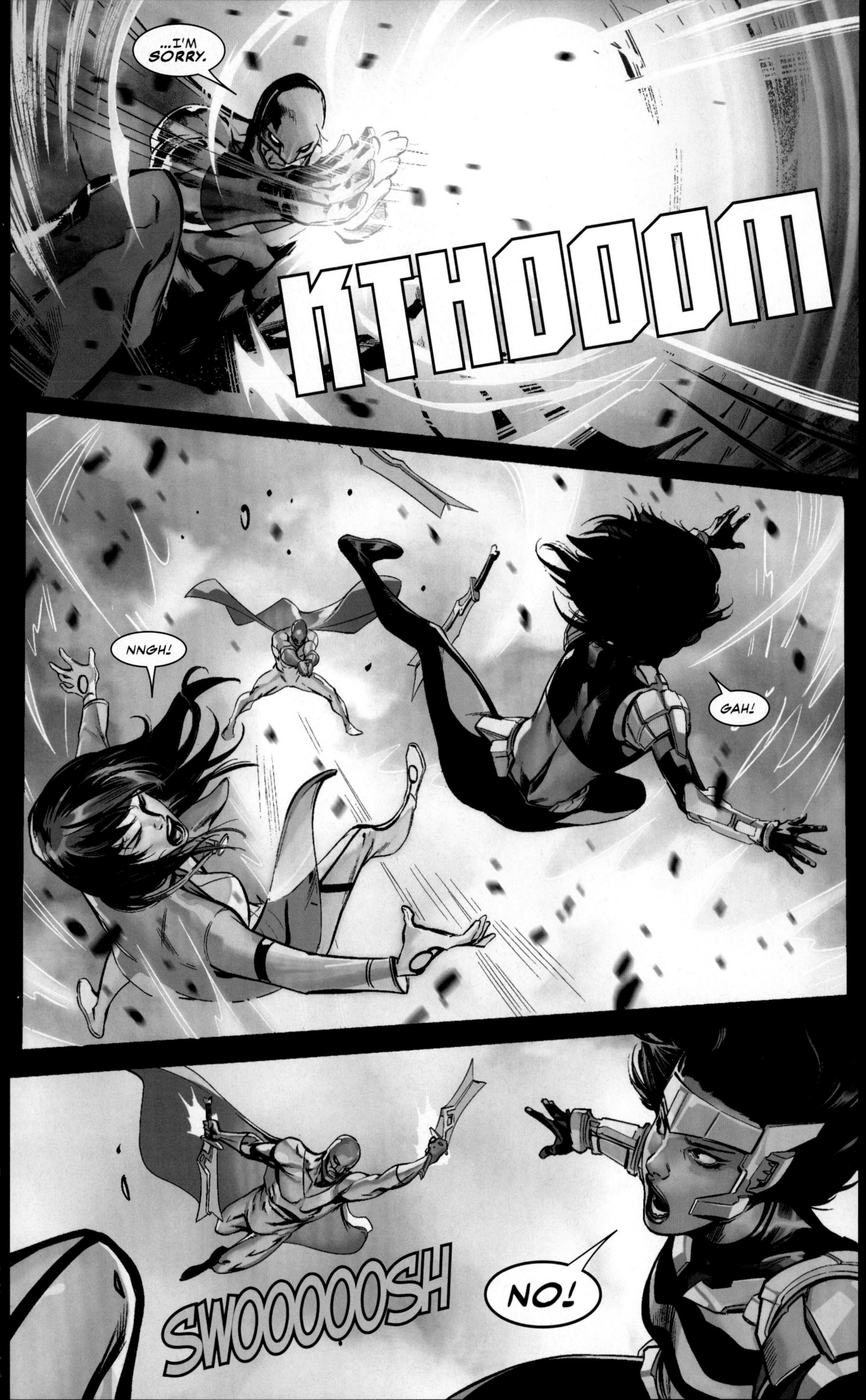
...I'M SORRY.
KTHOOOM
NNGH!
GAH!
SWOOOOOSH
NO!

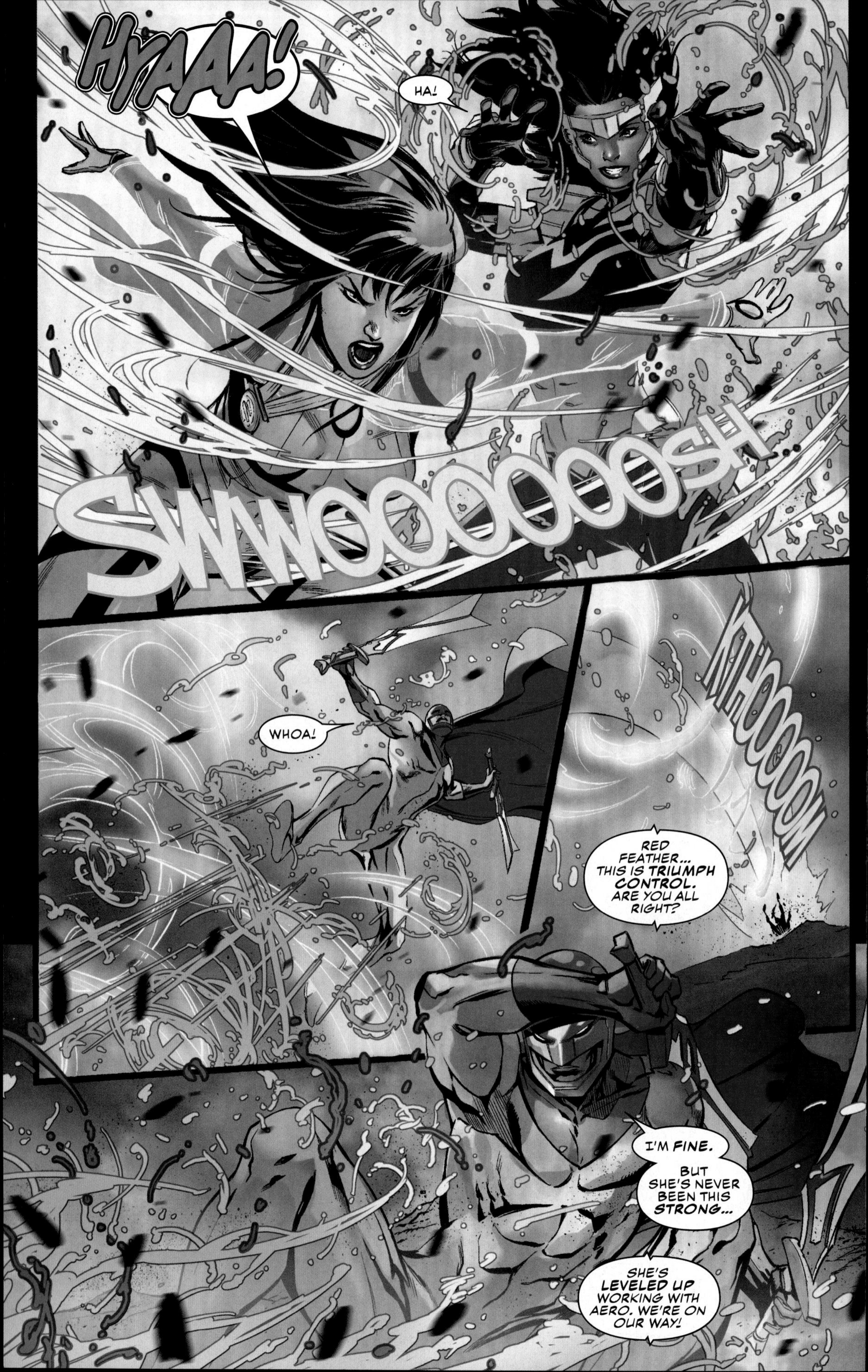
HYAAA!
HA!
SWWOOOOOOOSH...
WHOA!
KTHOOOOOM
RED FEATHER... THIS IS TRIUMPH CONTROL. ARE YOU ALL RIGHT?
I'M FINE.
BUT SHE'S NEVER BEEN THIS STRONG...
SHE'S LEVELED UP WORKING WITH AERO. WE'RE ON OUR WAY!

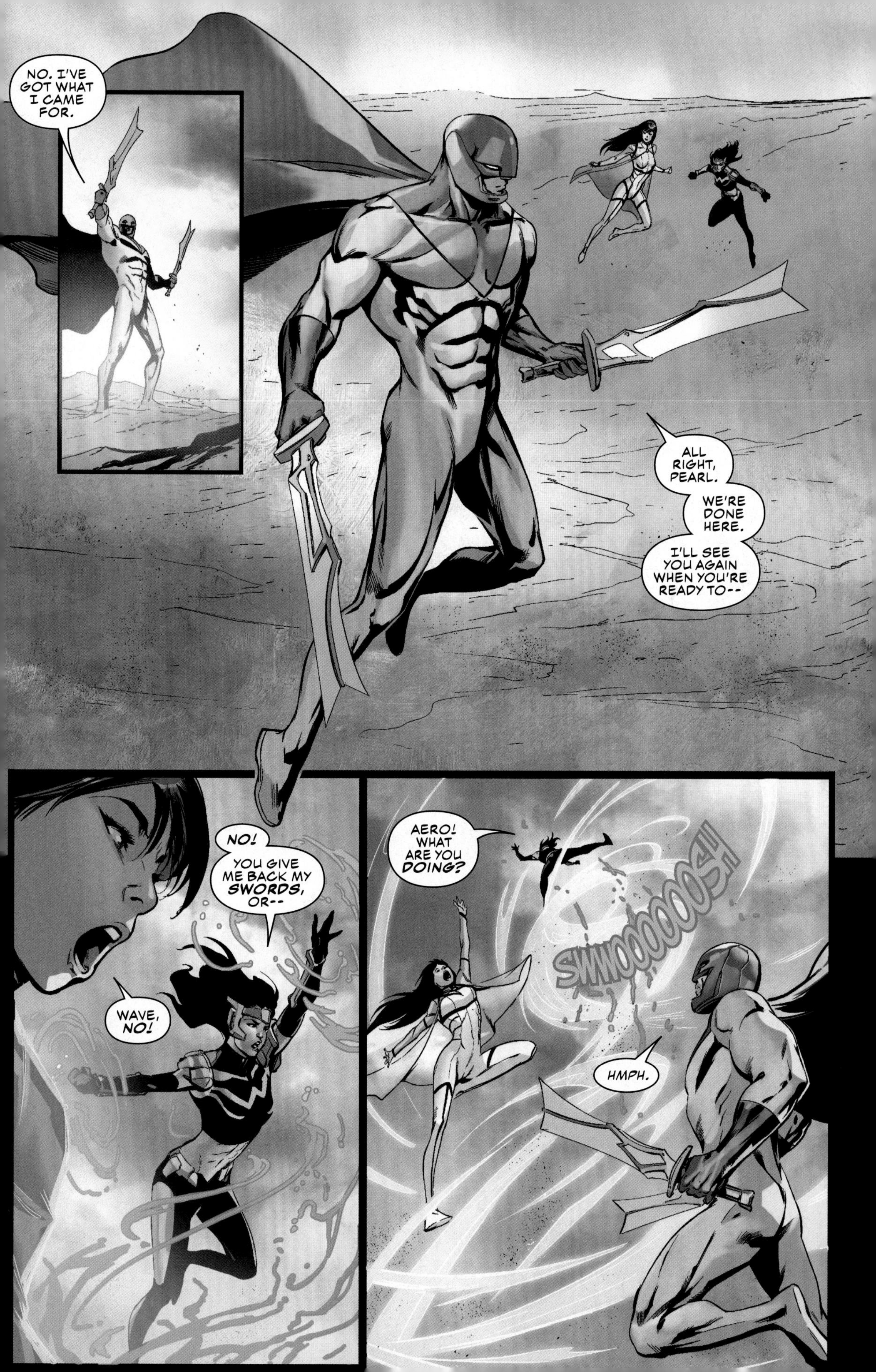
NO. I'VE GOT WHAT I CAME FOR.
ALL RIGHT, PEARL.
WE'RE DONE HERE.
I'LL SEE YOU AGAIN WHEN YOU'RE READY TO--
NO!
YOU GIVE ME BACK MY SWORDS, OR--
WAVE, NO!
AERO! WHAT ARE YOU DOING?
SWOOOOOOOSH!
HMPH.

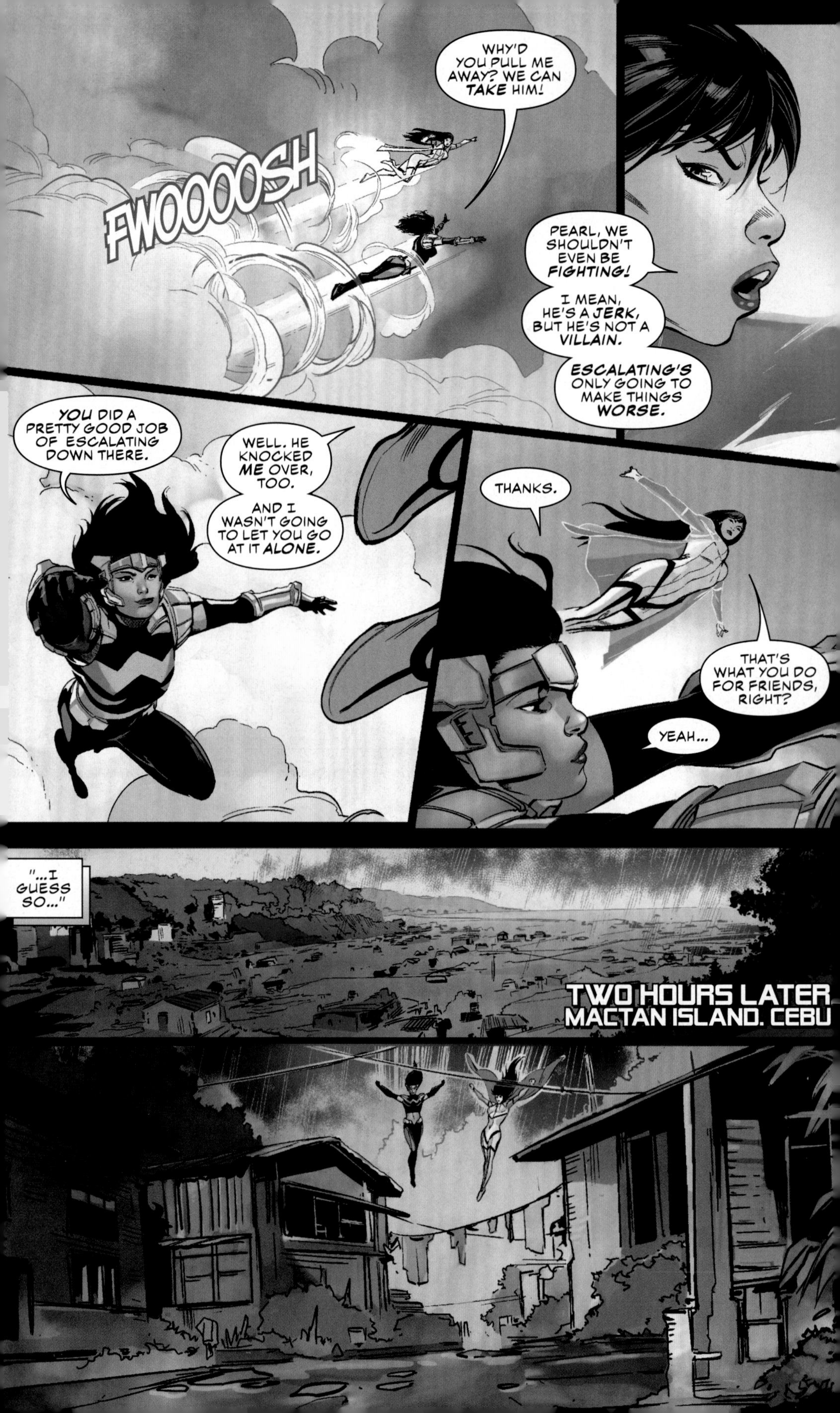
WHY'D YOU PULL ME AWAY? WE CAN TAKE HIM!
FWOOOOSH
PEARL, WE SHOULDN'T EVEN BE FIGHTING!
I MEAN, HE'S A JERK, BUT HE'S NOT A VILLAIN.
ESCALATING'S ONLY GOING TO MAKE THINGS WORSE.
YOU DID A PRETTY GOOD JOB OF ESCALATING DOWN THERE.
WELL. HE KNOCKED ME OVER, TOO.
AND I WASN'T GOING TO LET YOU GO AT IT ALONE.
THANKS.
THAT'S WHAT YOU DO FOR FRIENDS, RIGHT?
YEAH...
"...I GUESS SO..."
TWO HOURS LATER
MACTAN ISLAND. CEBU

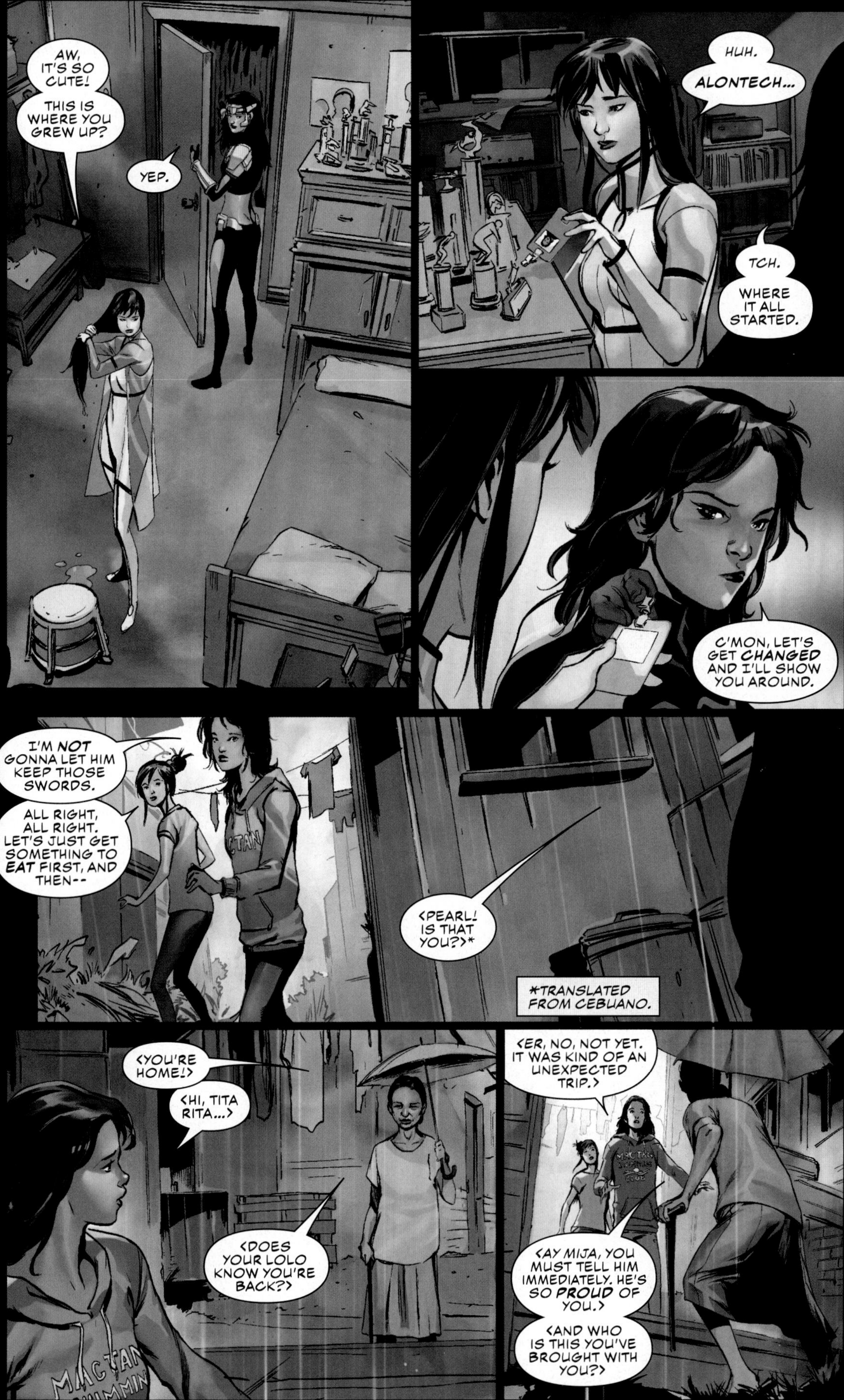
AW, IT'S SO CUTE!
THIS IS WHERE YOU GREW UP?
YEP.
HUH. ALONTECH...
TCH. WHERE IT ALL STARTED.
C'MON, LET'S GET CHANGED AND I'LL SHOW YOU AROUND.
I'M NOT GONNA LET HIM KEEP THOSE SWORDS.
ALL RIGHT, ALL RIGHT. LET'S JUST GET SOMETHING TO EAT FIRST, AND THEN--
<PEARL! IS THAT YOU?>*
*TRANSLATED FROM CEBUANO.
<YOU'RE HOME!>
<HI, TITA RITA...>
<DOES YOUR LOLO KNOW YOU'RE BACK?>
<ER, NO, NOT YET. IT WAS KIND OF AN UNEXPECTED TRIP.>
<AY MIJA, YOU MUST TELL HIM IMMEDIATELY. HE'S SO PROUD OF YOU.>
<AND WHO IS THIS YOU'VE BROUGHT WITH YOU?>

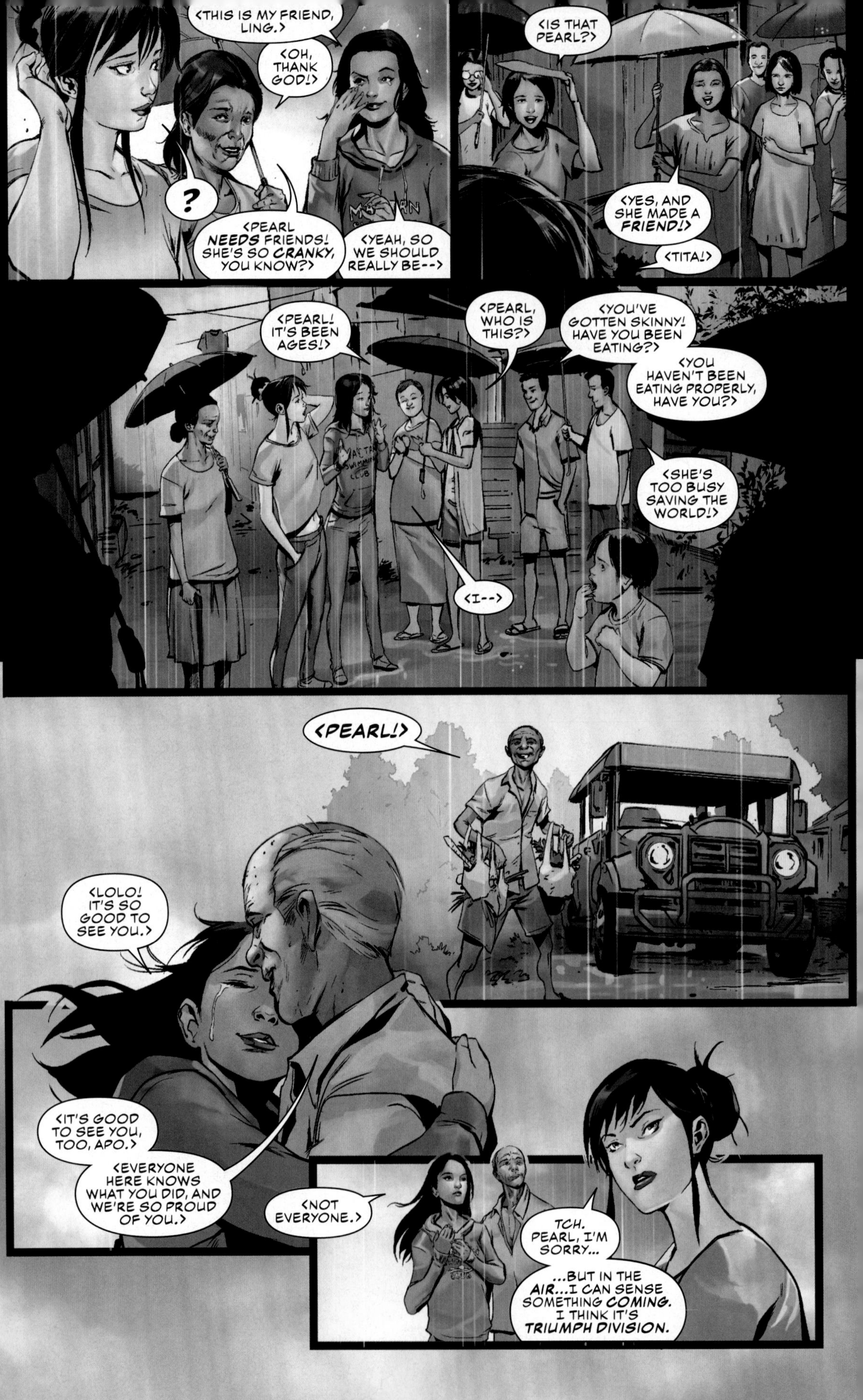

<THIS IS MY FRIEND, LING.>
<OH, THANK GOD!>
?
<PEARL NEEDS FRIENDS! SHE'S SO CRANKY, YOU KNOW?>
<YEAH, SO WE SHOULD REALLY BE-->
<IS THAT PEARL?>
<YES, AND SHE MADE A FRIEND!>
<TITA!>
<PEARL! IT'S BEEN AGES!>
<PEARL, WHO IS THIS?>
<YOU'VE GOTTEN SKINNY! HAVE YOU BEEN EATING?>
<YOU HAVEN'T BEEN EATING PROPERLY, HAVE YOU?>
<SHE'S TOO BUSY SAVING THE WORLD!>
<I-->
<PEARL!>
<LOLO! IT'S SO GOOD TO SEE YOU.>
<IT'S GOOD TO SEE YOU, TOO, APO.>
<EVERYONE HERE KNOWS WHAT YOU DID, AND WE'RE SO PROUD OF YOU.>
<NOT EVERYONE.>
TCH. PEARL, I'M SORRY...
...BUT IN THE AIR...I CAN SENSE SOMETHING COMING. I THINK IT'S TRIUMPH DIVISION.

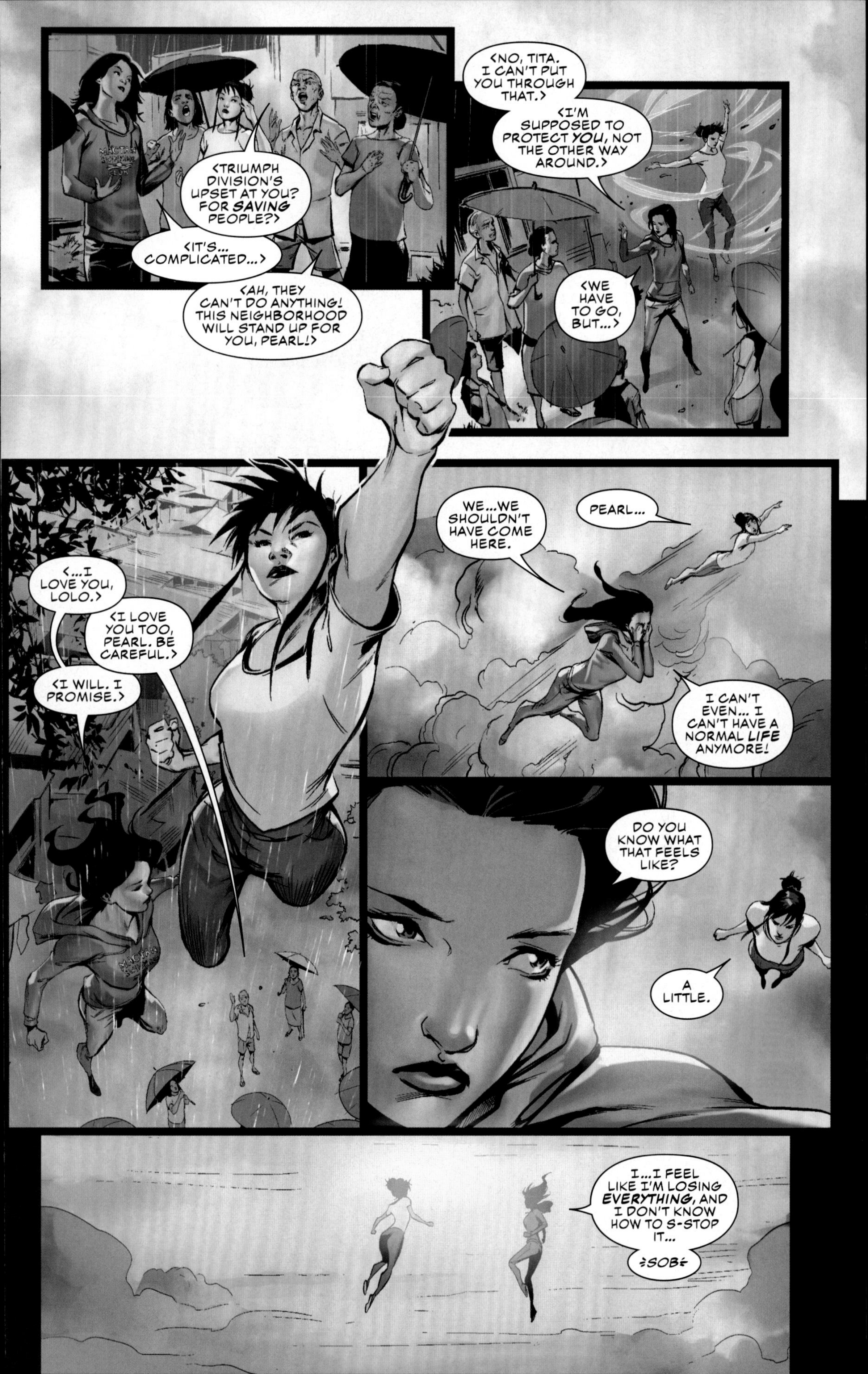
<TRIUMPH DIVISION'S UPSET AT YOU? FOR SAVING PEOPLE?>
<IT'S... COMPLICATED...>
<AH, THEY CAN'T DO ANYTHING! THIS NEIGHBORHOOD WILL STAND UP FOR YOU, PEARL!>
<NO, TITA. I CAN'T PUT YOU THROUGH THAT.>
<I'M SUPPOSED TO PROTECT YOU, NOT THE OTHER WAY AROUND.>
<WE HAVE TO GO, BUT...>
<...I LOVE YOU, LOLO.>
<I LOVE YOU TOO, PEARL. BE CAREFUL.>
<I WILL. I PROMISE.>
WE...WE SHOULDN'T HAVE COME HERE.
PEARL...
I CAN'T EVEN... I CAN'T HAVE A NORMAL LIFE ANYMORE!
DO YOU KNOW WHAT THAT FEELS LIKE?
A LITTLE.
I...I FEEL LIKE I'M LOSING EVERYTHING, AND I DON'T KNOW HOW TO S-STOP IT...
SOB

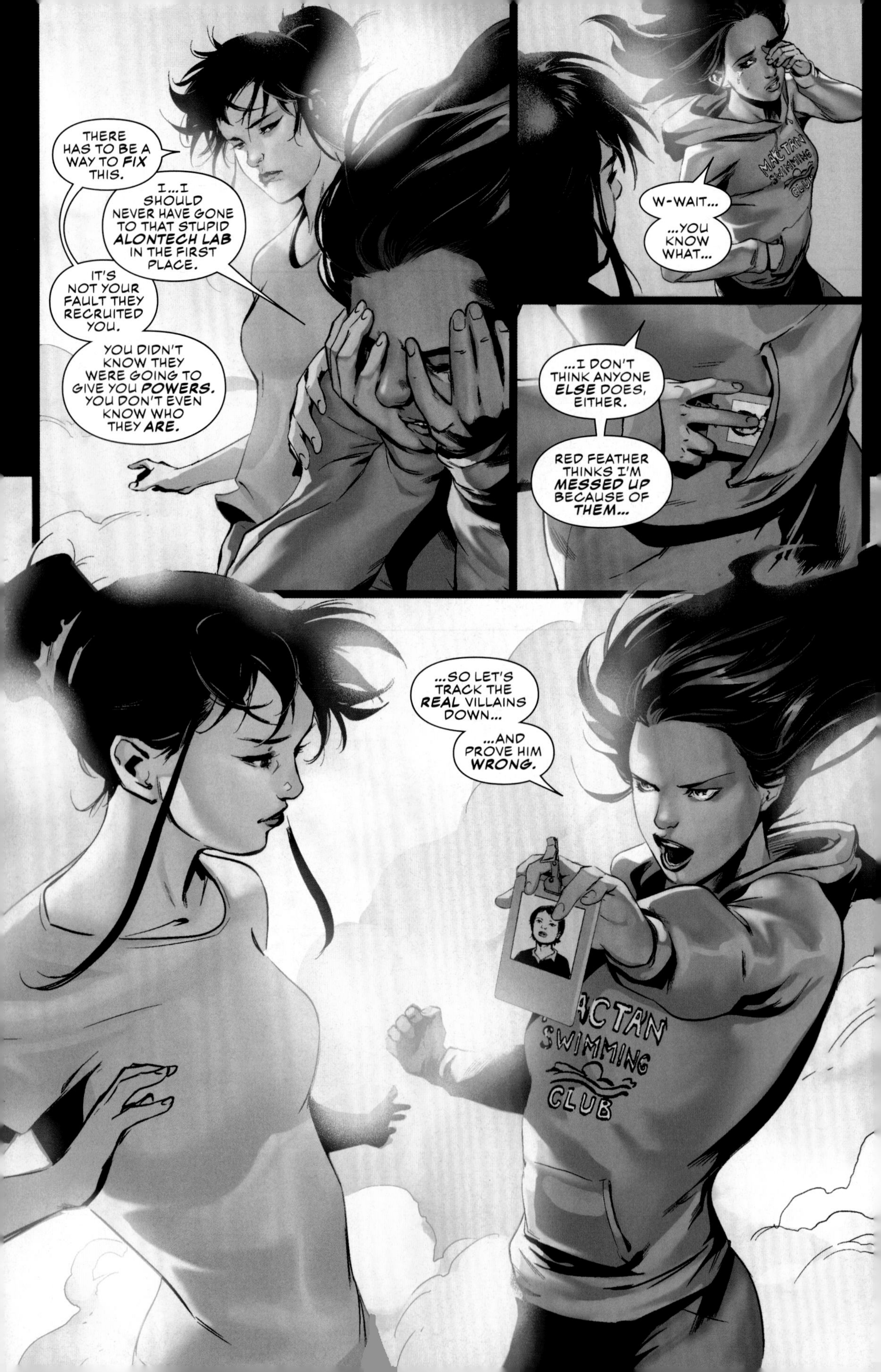
THERE HAS TO BE A WAY TO FIX THIS.
I...I SHOULD NEVER HAVE GONE TO THAT STUPID ALONTECH LAB IN THE FIRST PLACE.
IT'S NOT YOUR FAULT THEY RECRUITED YOU.
YOU DIDN'T KNOW THEY WERE GOING TO GIVE YOU POWERS. YOU DON'T EVEN KNOW WHO THEY ARE.
MACTAN SWIMMING CLUB
W-WAIT...
...YOU KNOW WHAT...
...I DON'T THINK ANYONE ELSE DOES, EITHER.
RED FEATHER THINKS I'M MESSED UP BECAUSE OF THEM...
...SO LET'S TRACK THE REAL VILLAINS DOWN...
...AND PROVE HIM WRONG.
MACTAN SWIMMING CLUB

Aero & Wave: Origins & Destinies Part Three

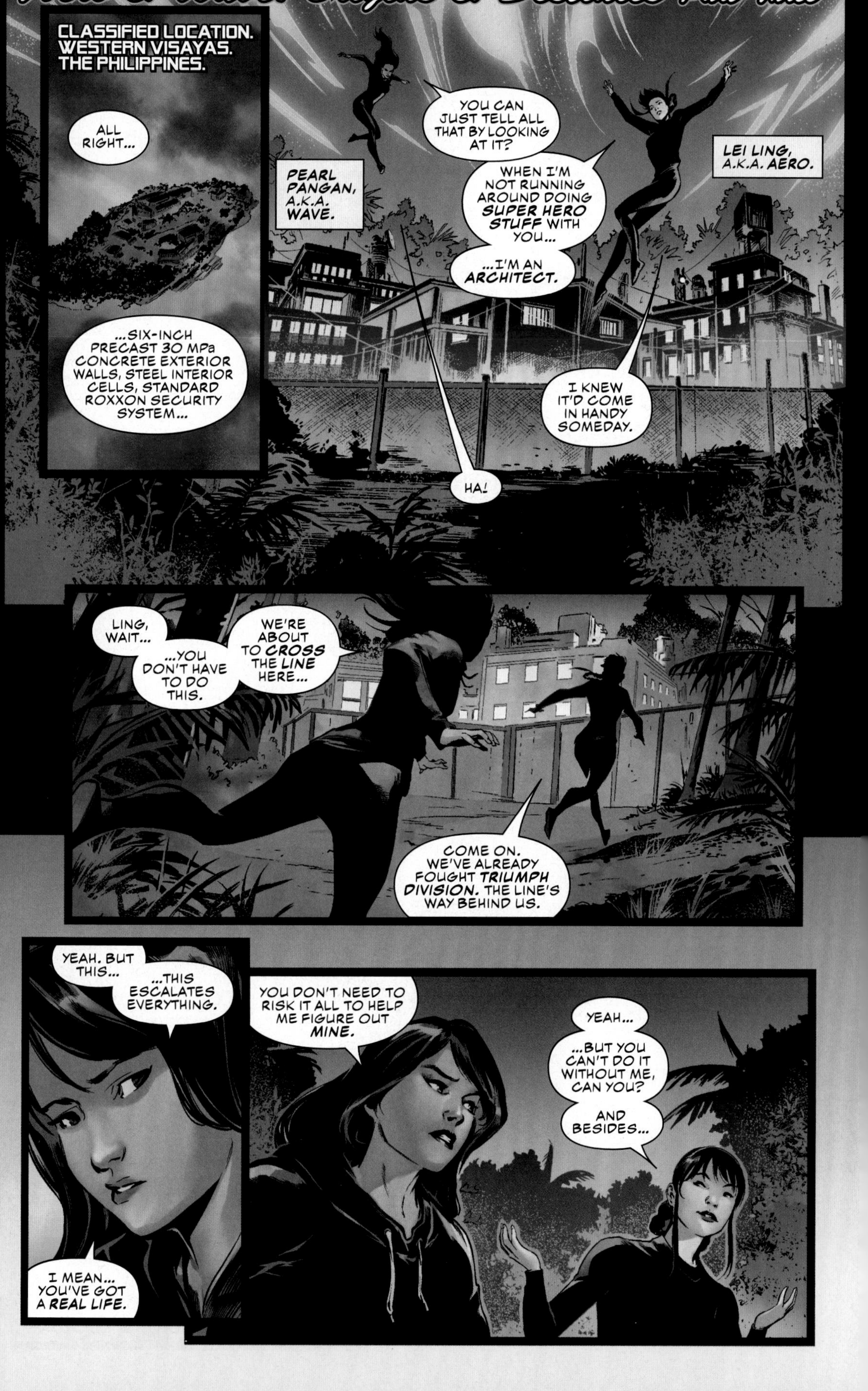
CLASSIFIED LOCATION. WESTERN VISAYAS. THE PHILIPPINES.
ALL RIGHT...
...SIX-INCH PRECAST 30 MPa CONCRETE EXTERIOR WALLS, STEEL INTERIOR CELLS, STANDARD ROXXON SECURITY SYSTEM...
PEARL PANGAN, A.K.A. WAVE.
YOU CAN JUST TELL ALL THAT BY LOOKING AT IT?
WHEN I'M NOT RUNNING AROUND DOING SUPER HERO STUFF WITH YOU...
...I'M AN ARCHITECT.
LEI LING, A.K.A. AERO.
I KNEW IT'D COME IN HANDY SOMEDAY.
HA!
LING, WAIT...
...YOU DON'T HAVE TO DO THIS.
WE'RE ABOUT TO CROSS THE LINE HERE...
COME ON. WE'VE ALREADY FOUGHT TRIUMPH DIVISION. THE LINE'S WAY BEHIND US.
YEAH. BUT THIS...
...THIS ESCALATES EVERYTHING.
I MEAN... YOU'VE GOT A REAL LIFE.
YOU DON'T NEED TO RISK IT ALL TO HELP ME FIGURE OUT MINE.
YEAH...
...BUT YOU CAN'T DO IT WITHOUT ME, CAN YOU?
AND BESIDES...

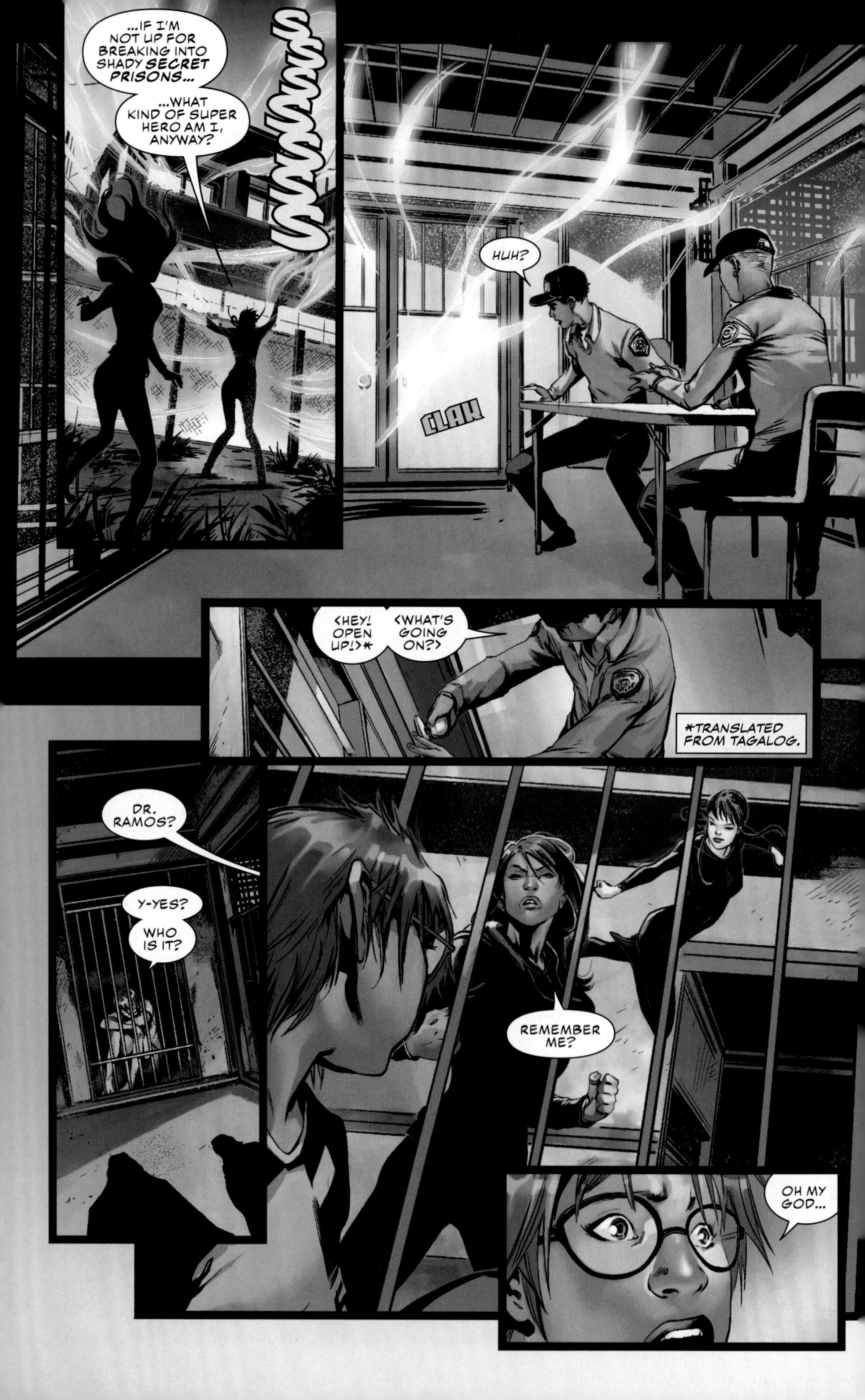

...IF I'M NOT UP FOR BREAKING INTO SHADY SECRET PRISONS...
...WHAT KIND OF SUPER HERO AM I, ANYWAY?
SSSSSSHWOOSH
HUH?
CLAK
<HEY! OPEN UP!>*
<WHAT'S GOING ON?>
*TRANSLATED FROM TAGALOG.
DR. RAMOS?
Y-YES?
WHO IS IT?
REMEMBER ME?
OH MY GOD...

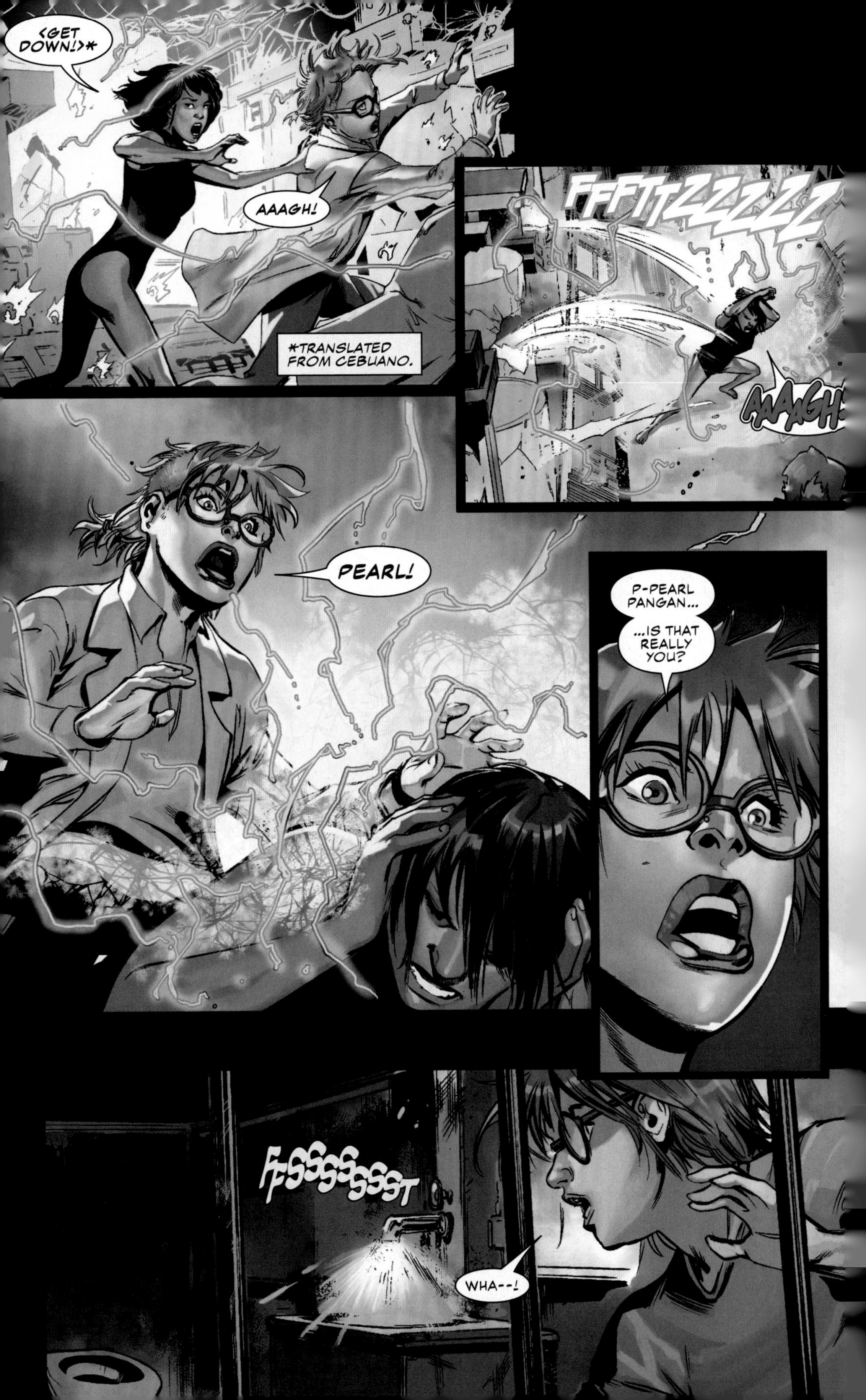
<GET DOWN!>*
AAAGH!
*TRANSLATED FROM CEBUANO.
FFFTTZZZZZZ
AAAAGH
PEARL!
P-PEARL PANGAN...
...IS THAT REALLY YOU?
FFSSSSSSST
WHA--!

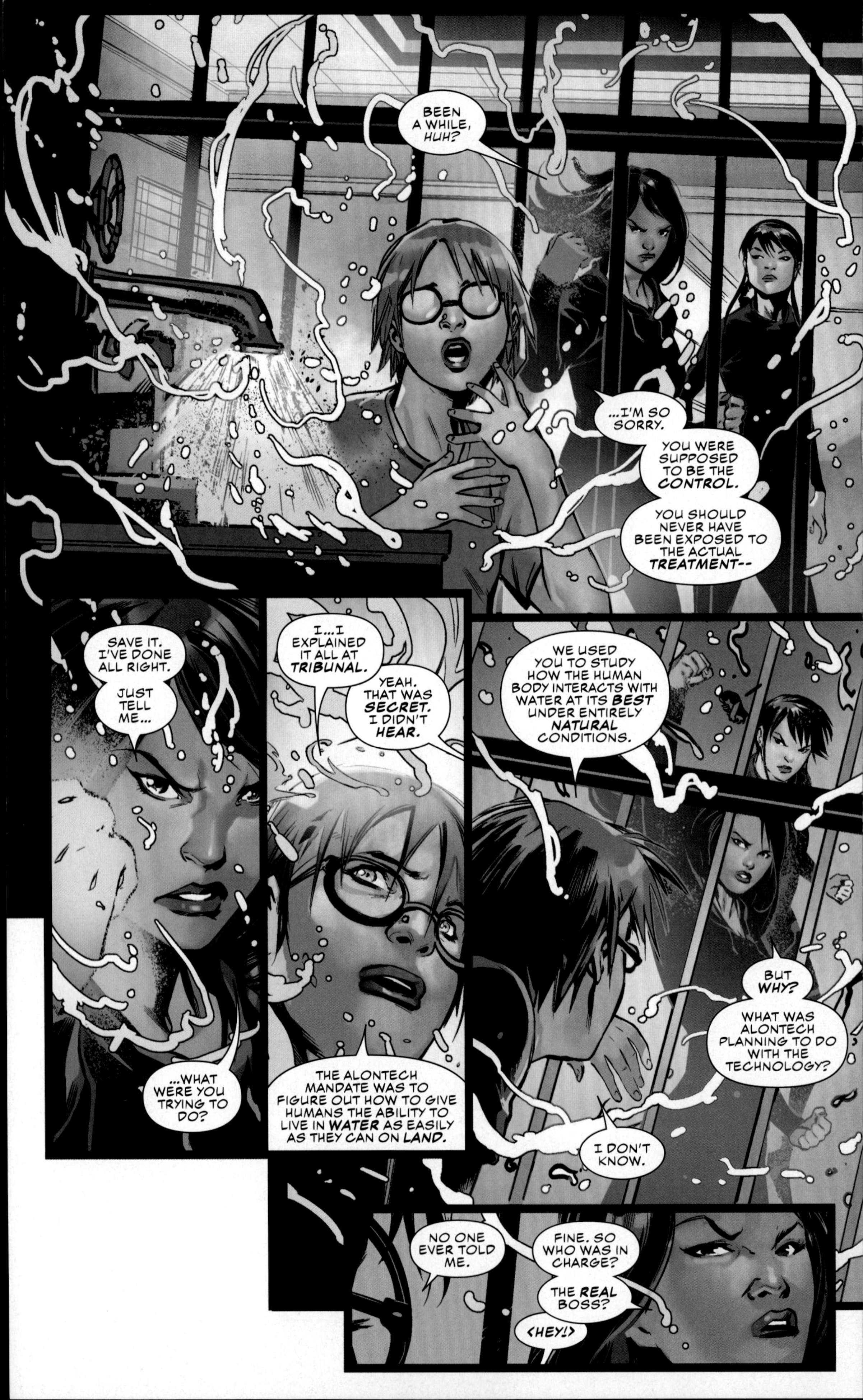

BEEN A WHILE, HUH?
...I'M SO SORRY.
YOU WERE SUPPOSED TO BE THE CONTROL.
YOU SHOULD NEVER HAVE BEEN EXPOSED TO THE ACTUAL TREATMENT--
SAVE IT. I'VE DONE ALL RIGHT.
JUST TELL ME...
...WHAT WERE YOU TRYING TO DO?
I...I EXPLAINED IT ALL AT TRIBUNAL.
YEAH. THAT WAS SECRET. I DIDN'T HEAR.
THE ALONTECH MANDATE WAS TO FIGURE OUT HOW TO GIVE HUMANS THE ABILITY TO LIVE IN WATER AS EASILY AS THEY CAN ON LAND.
WE USED YOU TO STUDY HOW THE HUMAN BODY INTERACTS WITH WATER AT ITS BEST UNDER ENTIRELY NATURAL CONDITIONS.
BUT WHY?
WHAT WAS ALONTECH PLANNING TO DO WITH THE TECHNOLOGY?
I DON'T KNOW.
NO ONE EVER TOLD ME.
FINE. SO WHO WAS IN CHARGE?
THE REAL BOSS?
<HEY!>

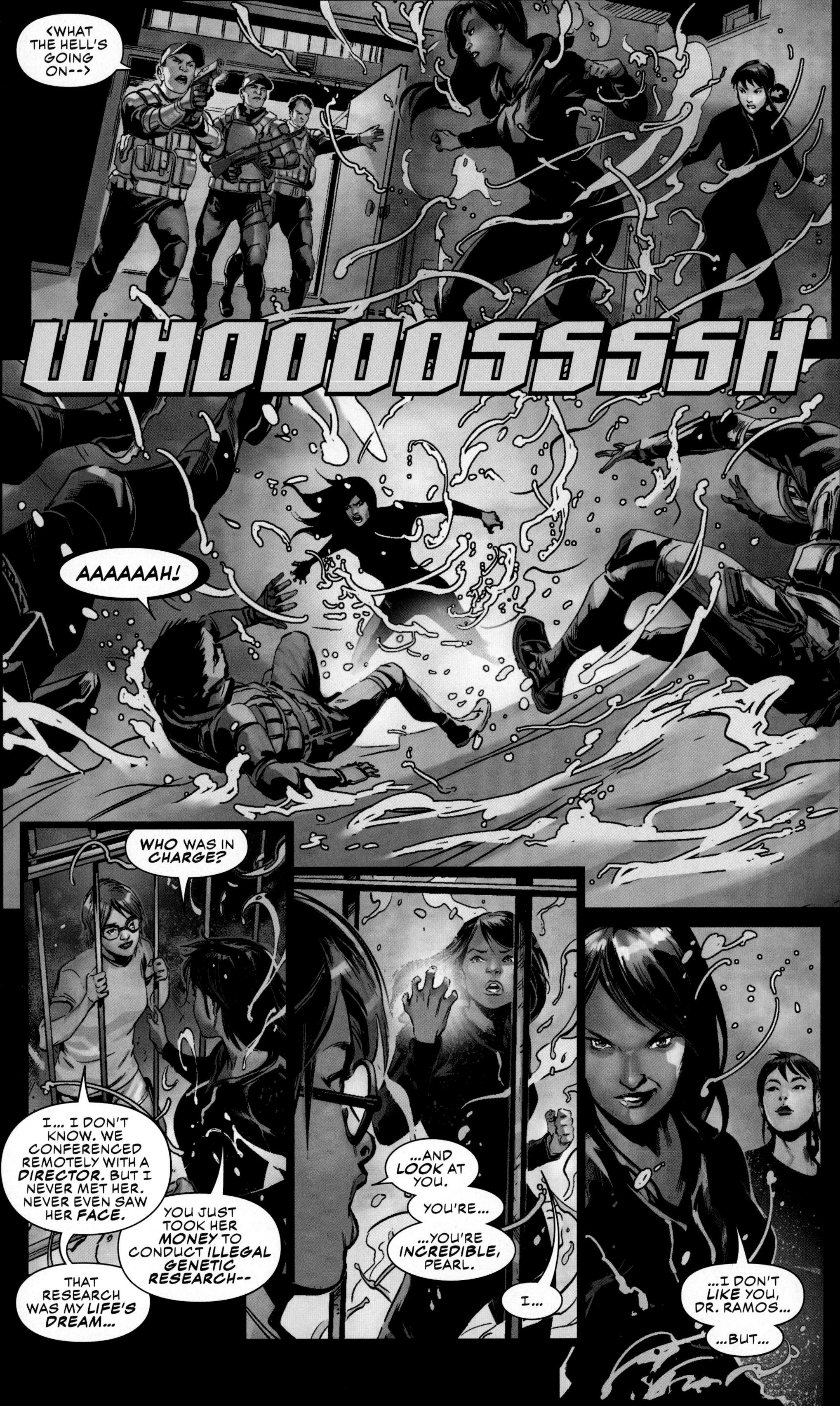

<WHAT THE HELL'S GOING ON-->
WHOOOOSSSSH
AAAAAAH!
WHO WAS IN CHARGE?
I... I DON'T KNOW. WE CONFERENCED REMOTELY WITH A DIRECTOR. BUT I NEVER MET HER. NEVER EVEN SAW HER FACE.
YOU JUST TOOK HER MONEY TO CONDUCT ILLEGAL GENETIC RESEARCH--
THAT RESEARCH WAS MY LIFE'S DREAM...
...AND LOOK AT YOU.
YOU'RE...
...YOU'RE INCREDIBLE, PEARL.
I...
...I DON'T LIKE YOU, DR. RAMOS...
...BUT...

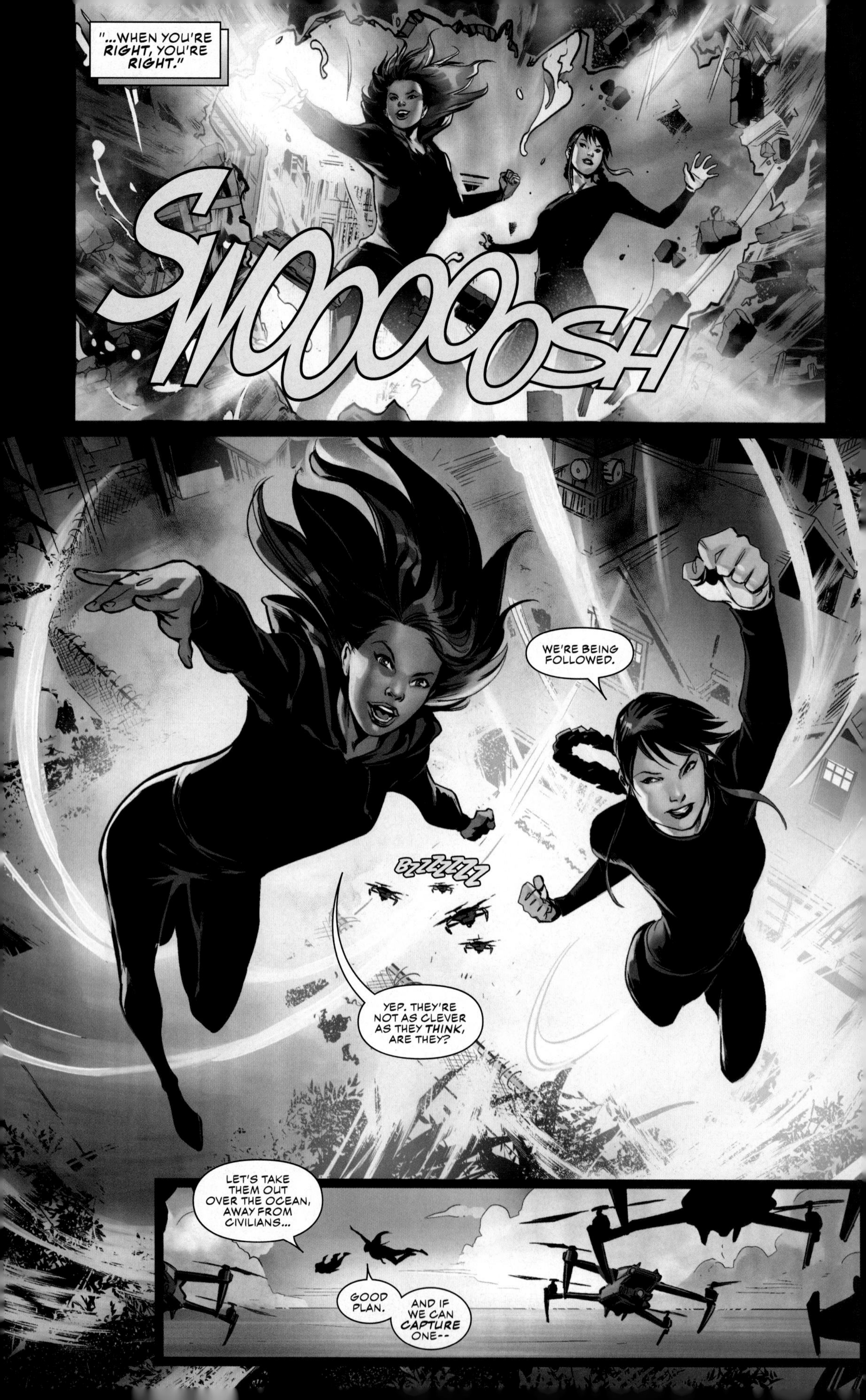
"...WHEN YOU'RE RIGHT, YOU'RE RIGHT."
SWOOOOSH
WE'RE BEING FOLLOWED.
BZZZZZZZ
YEP. THEY'RE NOT AS CLEVER AS THEY THINK, ARE THEY?
LET'S TAKE THEM OUT OVER THE OCEAN, AWAY FROM CIVILIANS...
GOOD PLAN.
AND IF WE CAN CAPTURE ONE--

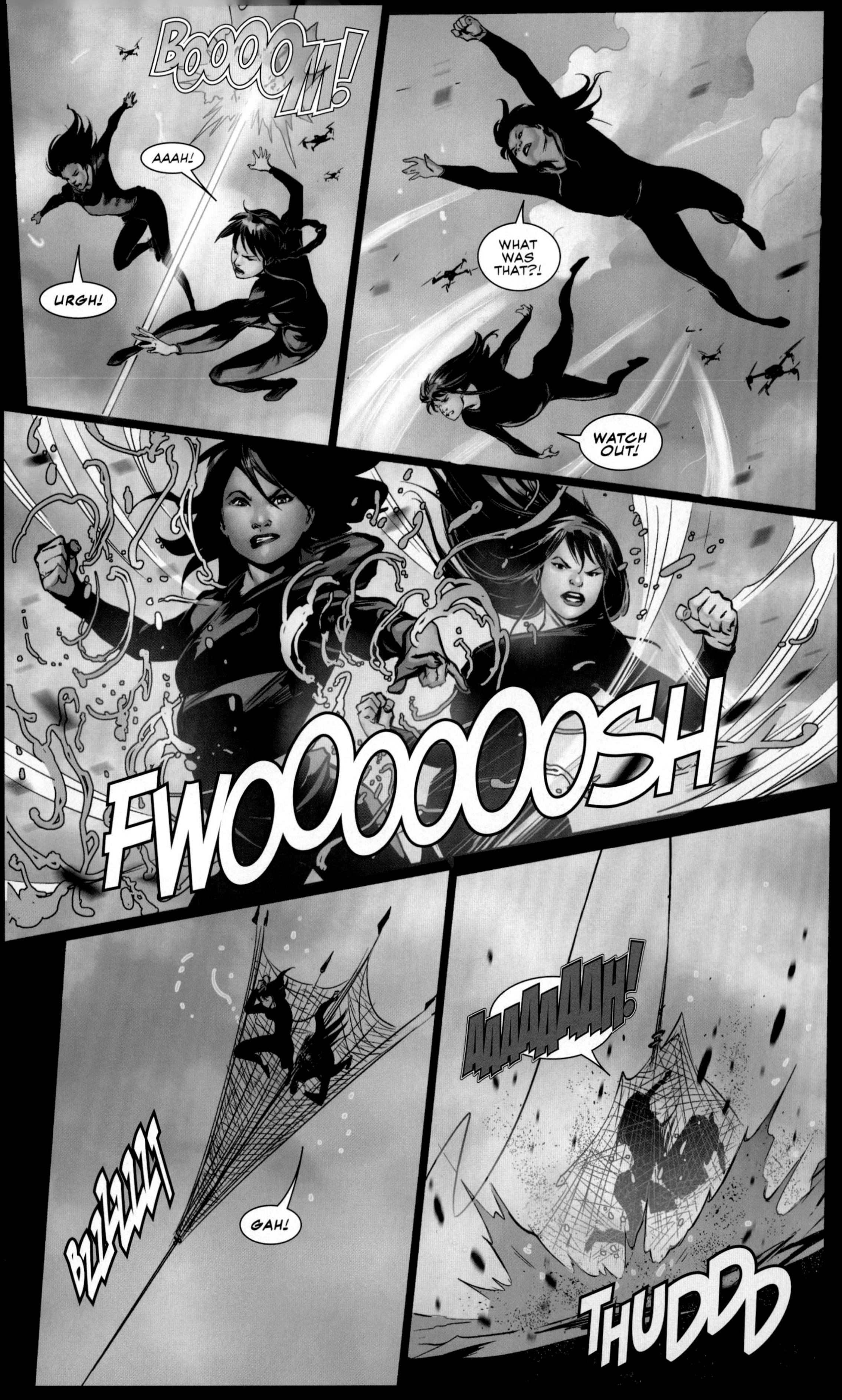
BOOOOM!
AAAH!
URGH!
WHAT WAS THAT?!
WATCH OUT!
FWOOOOOOSH
GAH!
BZZZZZT
AAAAAAAH!
THUDDD

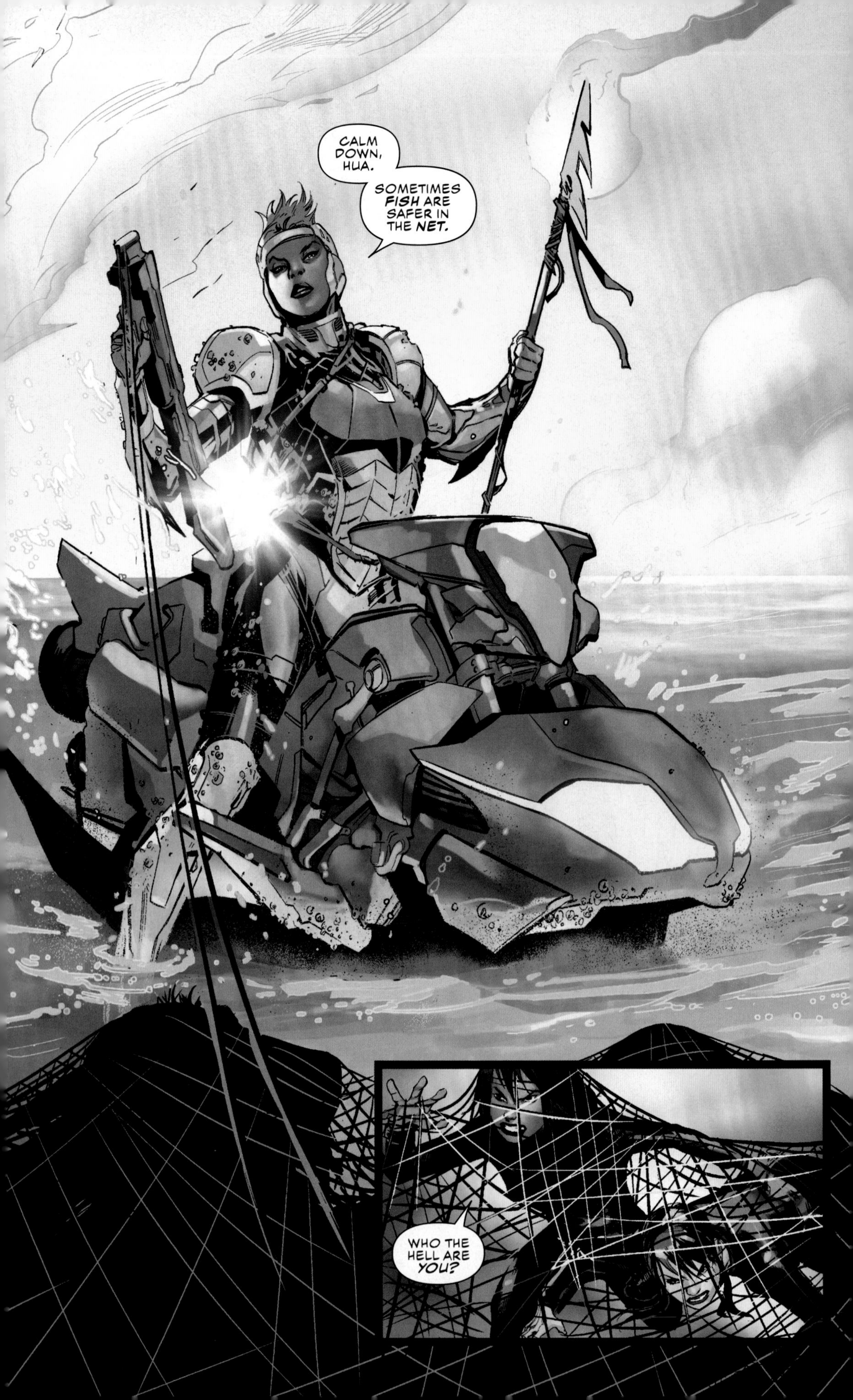
CALM DOWN, HUA.
SOMETIMES FISH ARE SAFER IN THE NET.
WHO THE HELL ARE YOU?

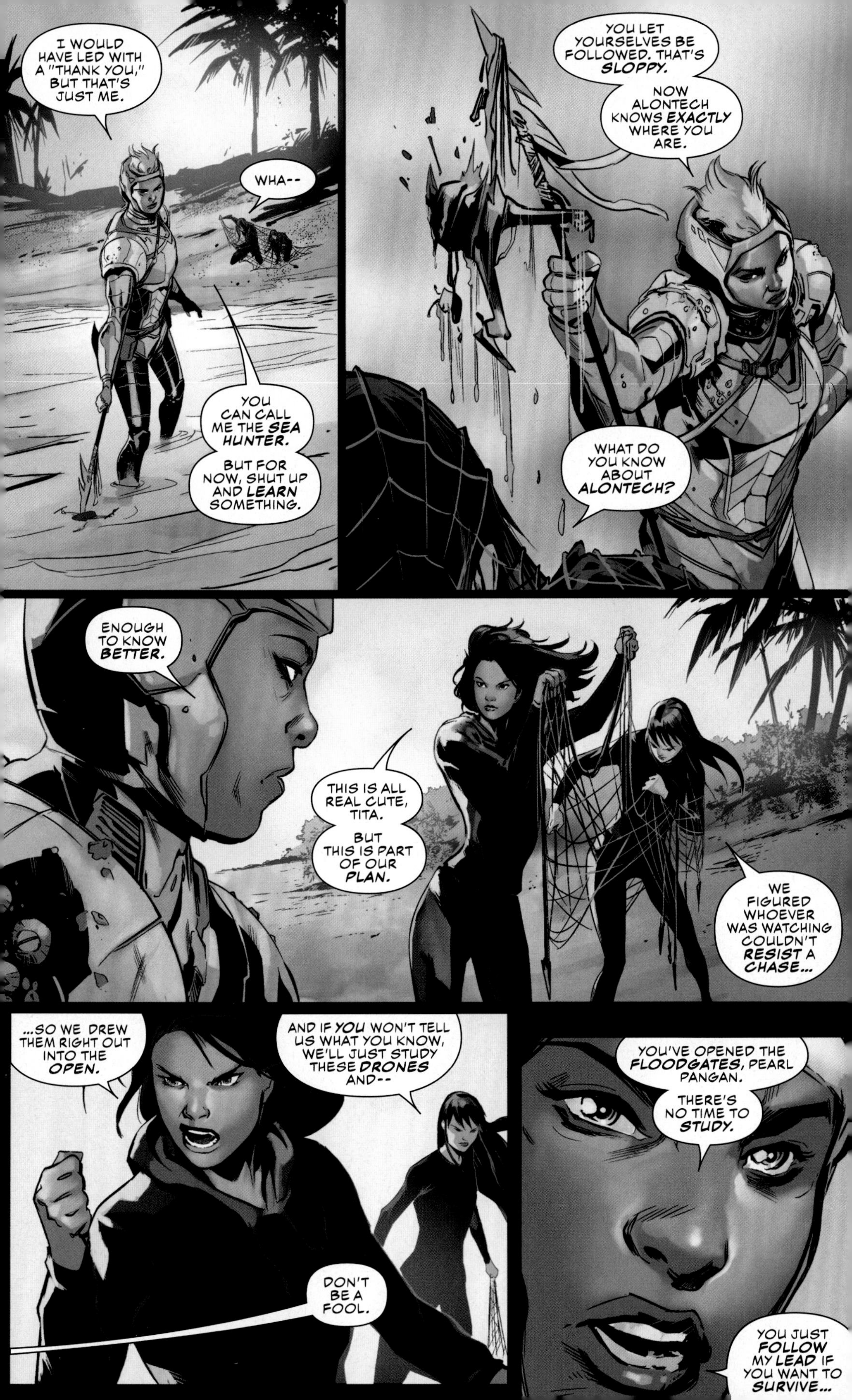
I WOULD HAVE LED WITH A "THANK YOU," BUT THAT'S JUST ME.
WHA--
YOU CAN CALL ME THE SEA HUNTER.
BUT FOR NOW, SHUT UP AND LEARN SOMETHING.
YOU LET YOURSELVES BE FOLLOWED. THAT'S SLOPPY.
NOW ALONTECH KNOWS EXACTLY WHERE YOU ARE.
WHAT DO YOU KNOW ABOUT ALONTECH?
ENOUGH TO KNOW BETTER.
THIS IS ALL REAL CUTE, TITA.
BUT THIS IS PART OF OUR PLAN.
WE FIGURED WHOEVER WAS WATCHING COULDN'T RESIST A CHASE...
...SO WE DREW THEM RIGHT OUT INTO THE OPEN.
AND IF YOU WON'T TELL US WHAT YOU KNOW, WE'LL JUST STUDY THESE DRONES AND--
DON'T BE A FOOL.
YOU'VE OPENED THE FLOODGATES, PEARL PANGAN.
THERE'S NO TIME TO STUDY.
YOU JUST FOLLOW MY LEAD IF YOU WANT TO SURVIVE...

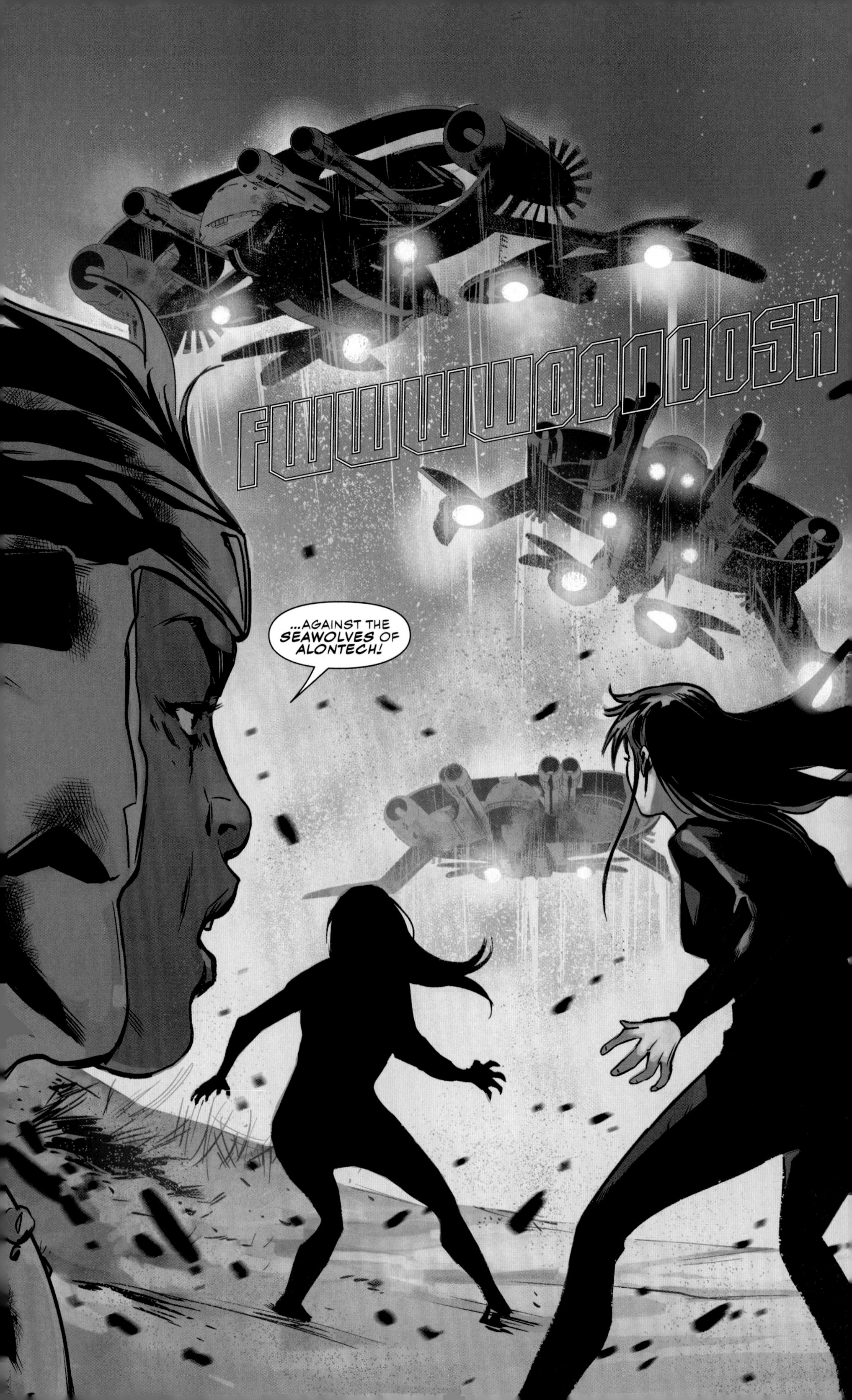
FWWWWOOOOOOSH
...AGAINST THE SEAWOLVES OF ALONTECH!

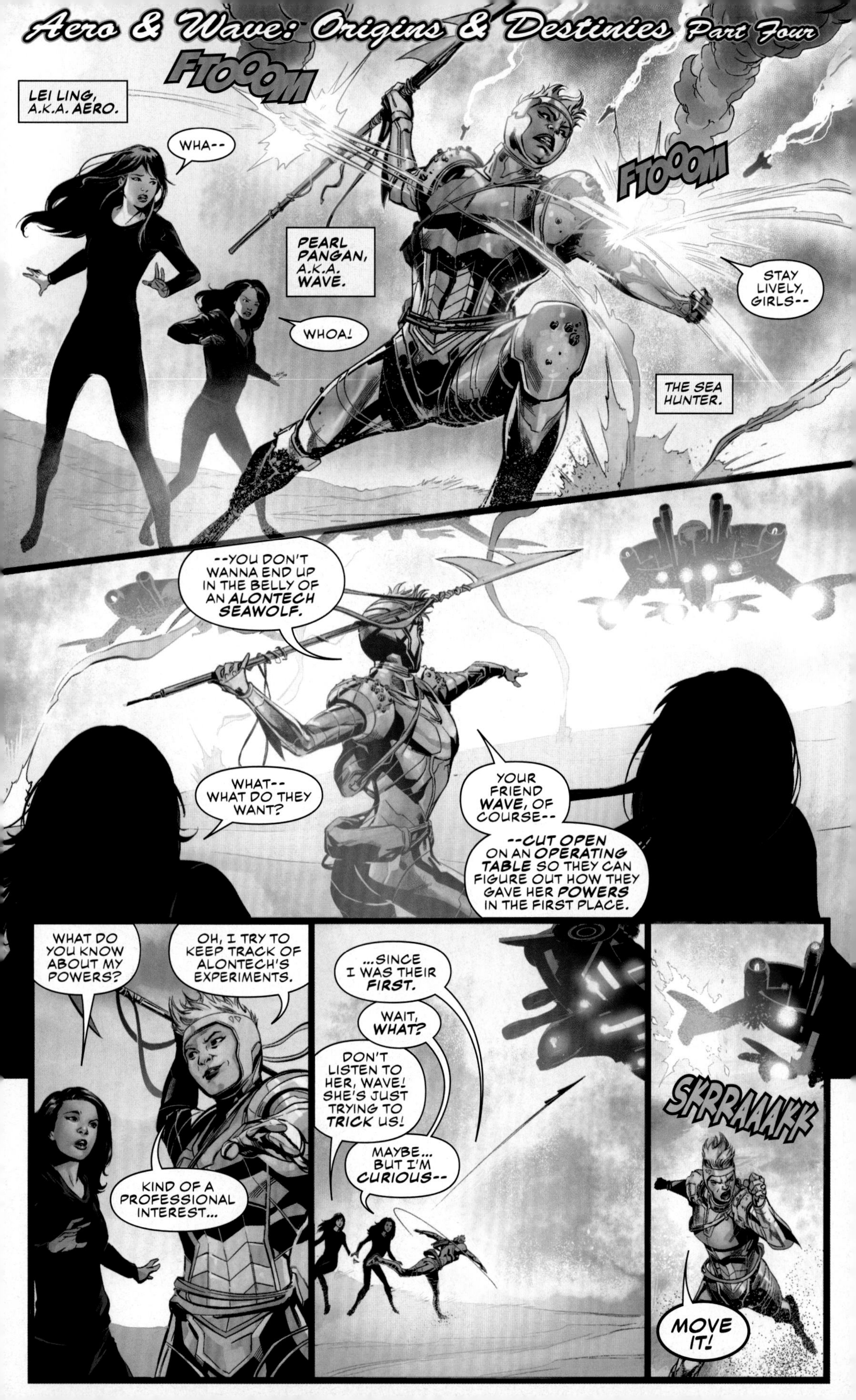
Aero & Wave: Origins & Destinies Part Four
FTOOOM
LEI LING, A.K.A. AERO.
WHA--
PEARL PANGAN, A.K.A. WAVE.
WHOA!
FTOOOM
STAY LIVELY, GIRLS--
THE SEA HUNTER.
--YOU DON'T WANNA END UP IN THE BELLY OF AN ALONTECH SEAWOLF.
WHAT-- WHAT DO THEY WANT?
YOUR FRIEND WAVE, OF COURSE--
--CUT OPEN ON AN OPERATING TABLE SO THEY CAN FIGURE OUT HOW THEY GAVE HER POWERS IN THE FIRST PLACE.
WHAT DO YOU KNOW ABOUT MY POWERS?
OH, I TRY TO KEEP TRACK OF ALONTECH'S EXPERIMENTS.
KIND OF A PROFESSIONAL INTEREST...
...SINCE I WAS THEIR FIRST.
WAIT, WHAT?
DON'T LISTEN TO HER, WAVE! SHE'S JUST TRYING TO TRICK US!
MAYBE... BUT I'M CURIOUS--
SKRRAAAKK
MOVE IT!

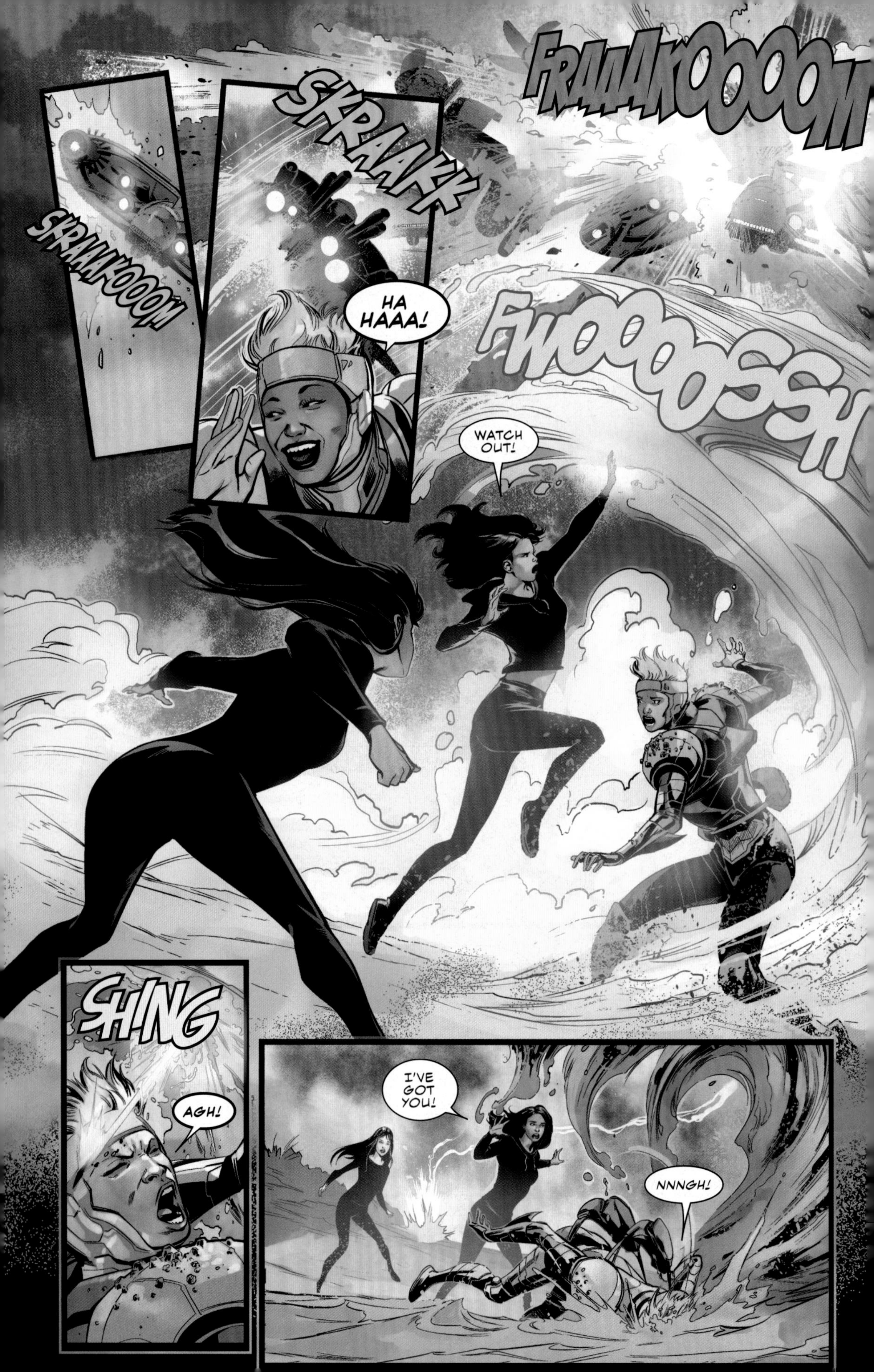
SKRAAAKOOOOM
SKRAAKK
HA HAAA!
FRAAAKOOOOM
FWOOOOSSH
WATCH OUT!
SHING
AGH!
I'VE GOT YOU!
NNNGH!

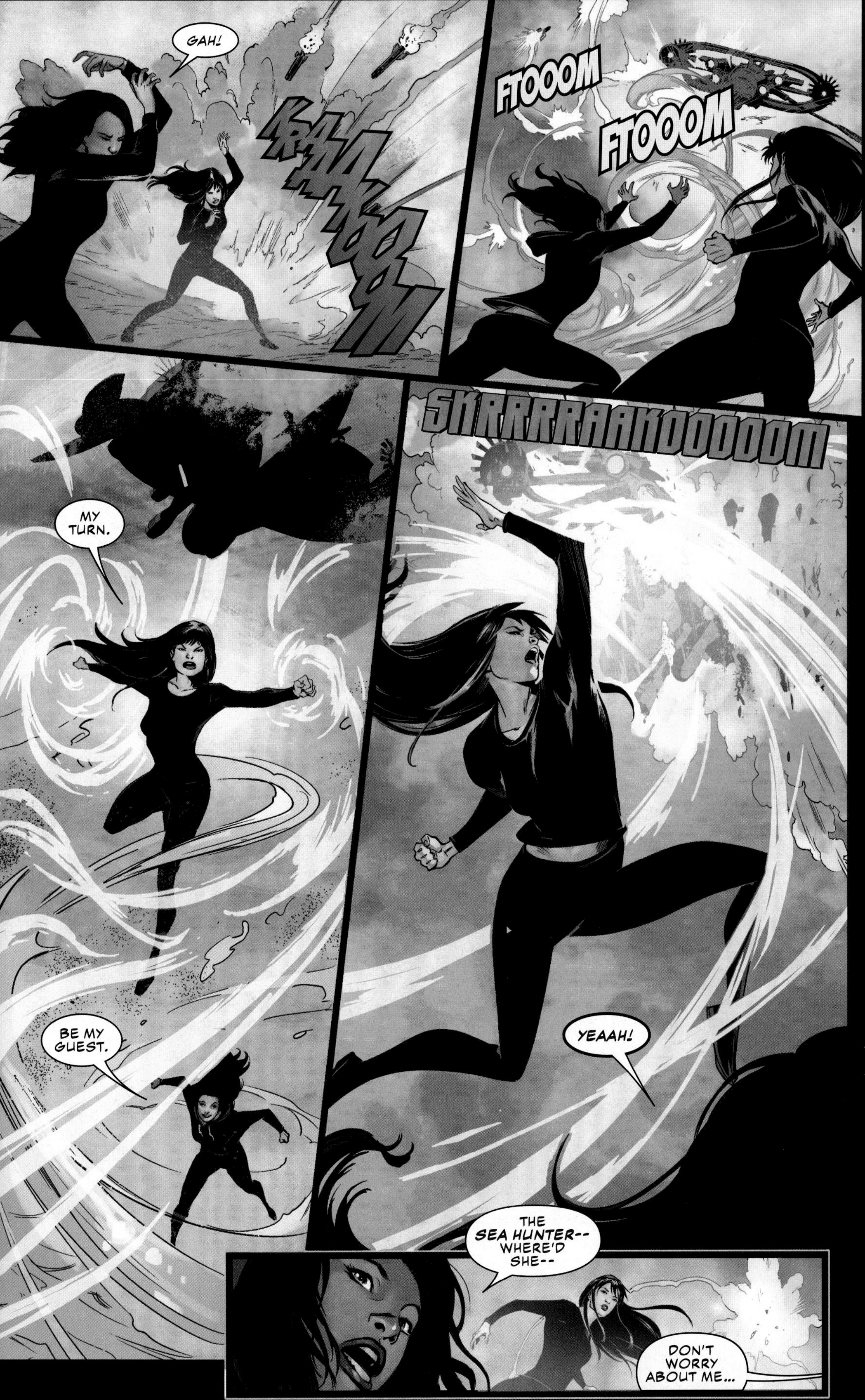
GAH!
KRAAKOOM
FTOOOM
FTOOOM
SKRRRRAAKOOOOOM
MY TURN.
BE MY GUEST.
YEAAH!
THE SEA HUNTER-- WHERE'D SHE--
DON'T WORRY ABOUT ME...

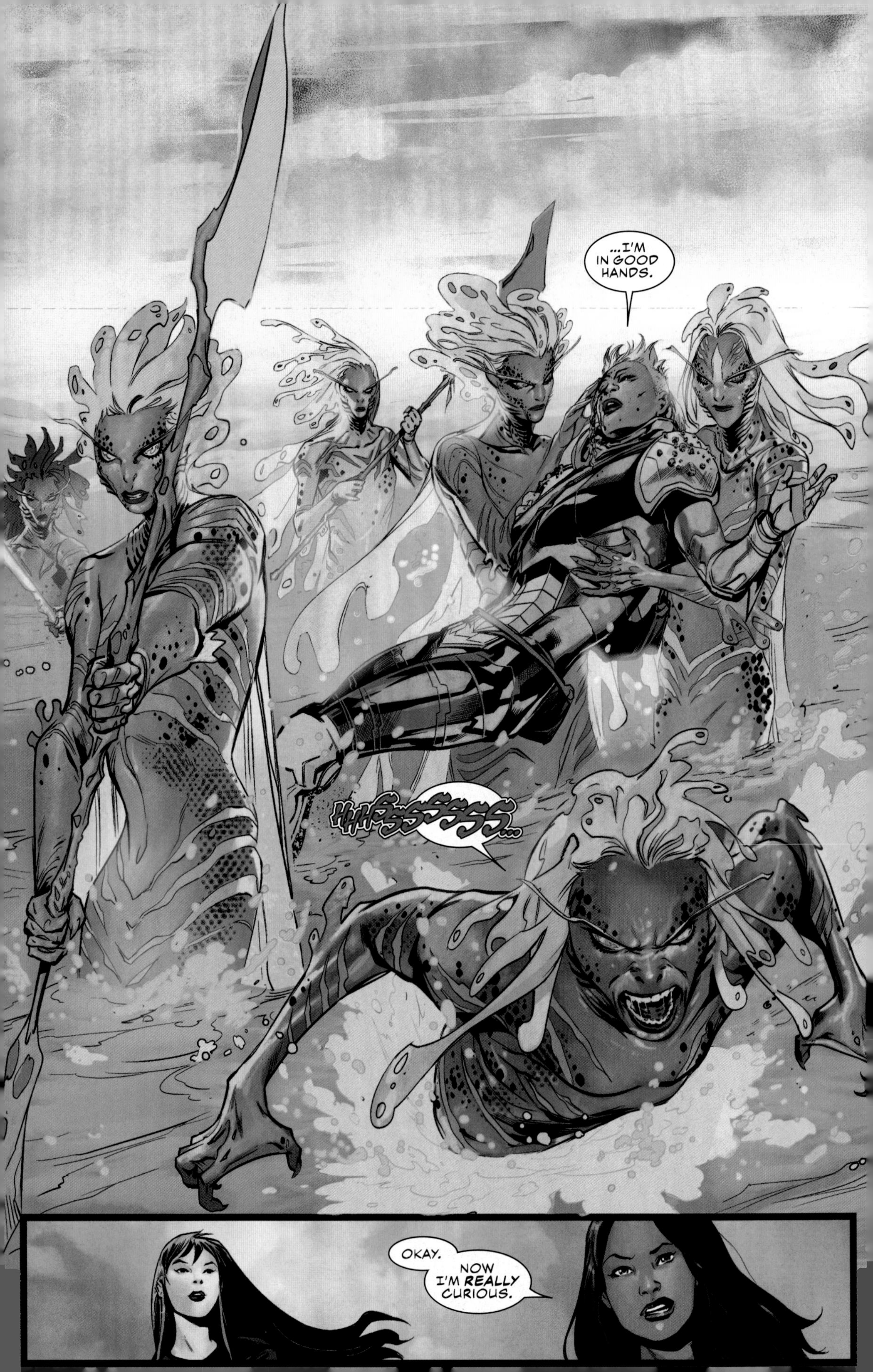
...I'M IN GOOD HANDS.
HHHSSSSSS...
OKAY.
NOW I'M REALLY CURIOUS.

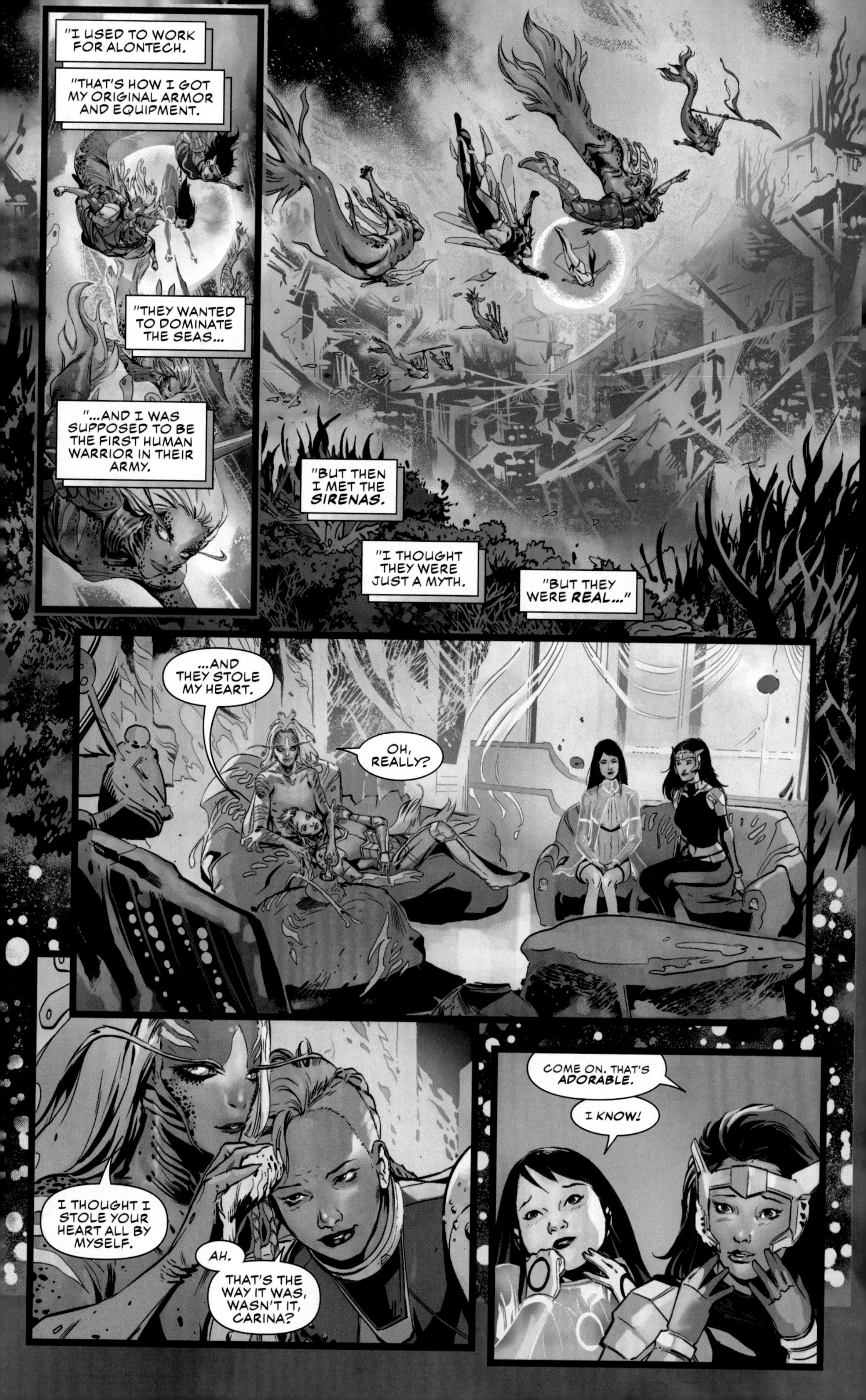
"I USED TO WORK FOR ALONTECH.
"THAT'S HOW I GOT MY ORIGINAL ARMOR AND EQUIPMENT.
"THEY WANTED TO DOMINATE THE SEAS...
"...AND I WAS SUPPOSED TO BE THE FIRST HUMAN WARRIOR IN THEIR ARMY.
"BUT THEN I MET THE SIRENAS.
"I THOUGHT THEY WERE JUST A MYTH.
"BUT THEY WERE REAL..."
...AND THEY STOLE MY HEART.
OH, REALLY?
I THOUGHT I STOLE YOUR HEART ALL BY MYSELF.
AH.
THAT'S THE WAY IT WAS, WASN'T IT, CARINA?
COME ON. THAT'S ADORABLE.
I KNOW!

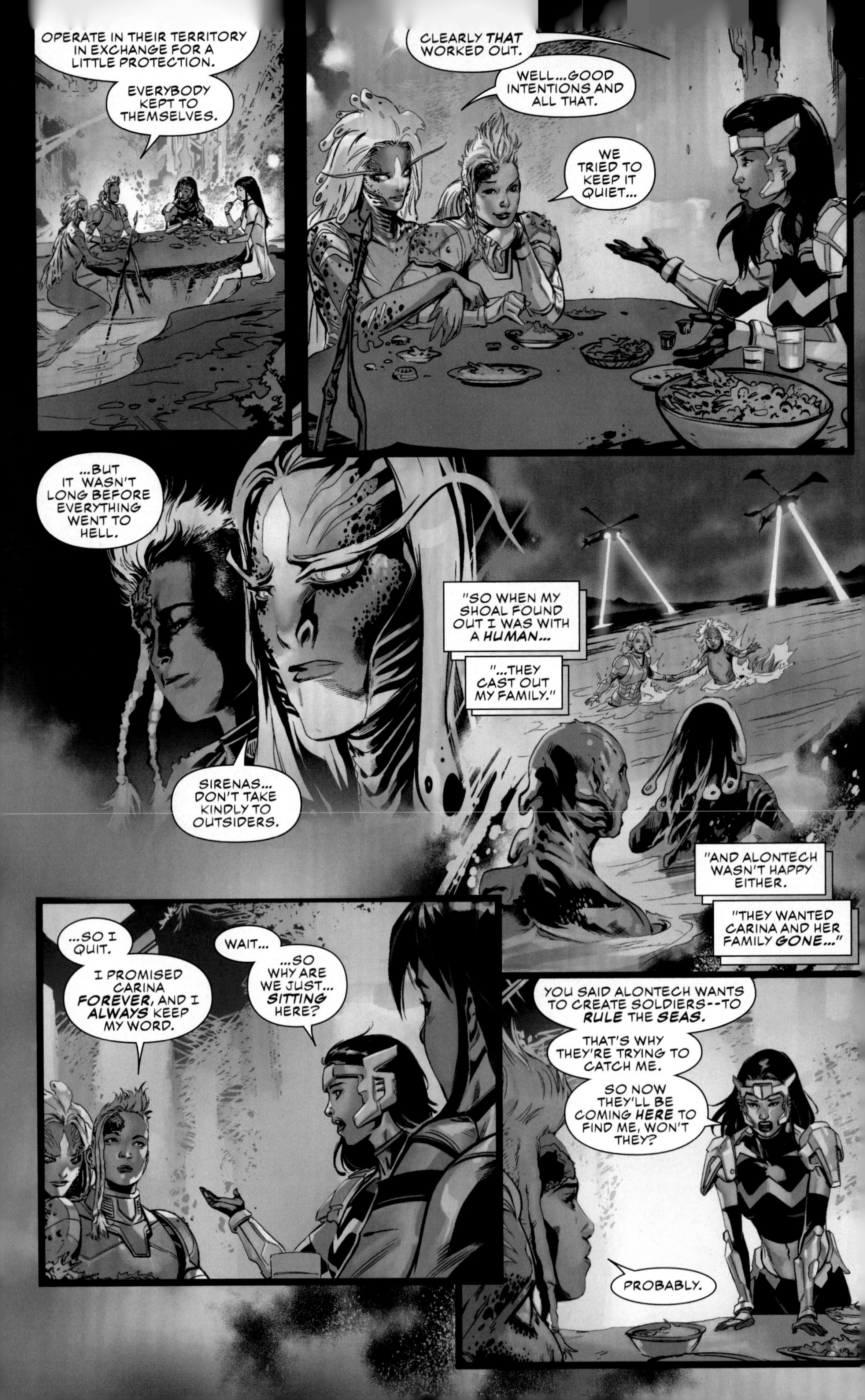
OPERATE IN THEIR TERRITORY IN EXCHANGE FOR A LITTLE PROTECTION.
EVERYBODY KEPT TO THEMSELVES.
CLEARLY THAT WORKED OUT.
WELL...GOOD INTENTIONS AND ALL THAT.
WE TRIED TO KEEP IT QUIET...
...BUT IT WASN'T LONG BEFORE EVERYTHING WENT TO HELL.
SIRENAS... DON'T TAKE KINDLY TO OUTSIDERS.
"SO WHEN MY SHOAL FOUND OUT I WAS WITH A HUMAN...
"...THEY CAST OUT MY FAMILY."
"AND ALONTECH WASN'T HAPPY EITHER.
"THEY WANTED CARINA AND HER FAMILY GONE..."
...SO I QUIT.
I PROMISED CARINA FOREVER, AND I ALWAYS KEEP MY WORD.
WAIT...
...SO WHY ARE WE JUST... SITTING HERE?
YOU SAID ALONTECH WANTS TO CREATE SOLDIERS--TO RULE THE SEAS.
THAT'S WHY THEY'RE TRYING TO CATCH ME.
SO NOW THEY'LL BE COMING HERE TO FIND ME, WON'T THEY?
PROBABLY.

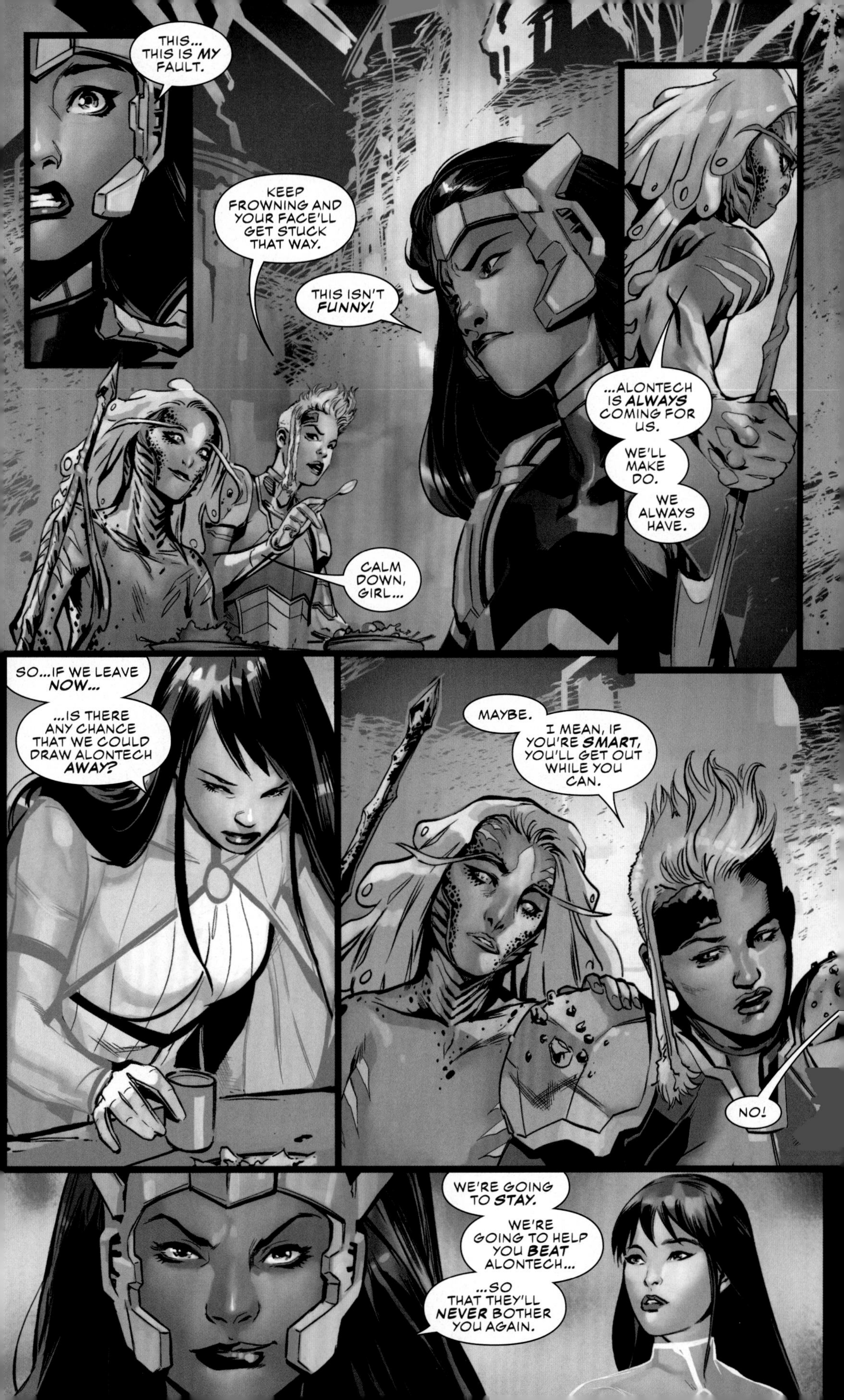
THIS... THIS IS MY FAULT.
KEEP FROWNING AND YOUR FACE'LL GET STUCK THAT WAY.
THIS ISN'T FUNNY!
CALM DOWN, GIRL...
...ALONTECH IS ALWAYS COMING FOR US.
WE'LL MAKE DO.
WE ALWAYS HAVE.
SO...IF WE LEAVE NOW...
...IS THERE ANY CHANCE THAT WE COULD DRAW ALONTECH AWAY?
MAYBE.
I MEAN, IF YOU'RE SMART, YOU'LL GET OUT WHILE YOU CAN.
NO!
WE'RE GOING TO STAY.
WE'RE GOING TO HELP YOU BEAT ALONTECH...
...SO THAT THEY'LL NEVER BOTHER YOU AGAIN.

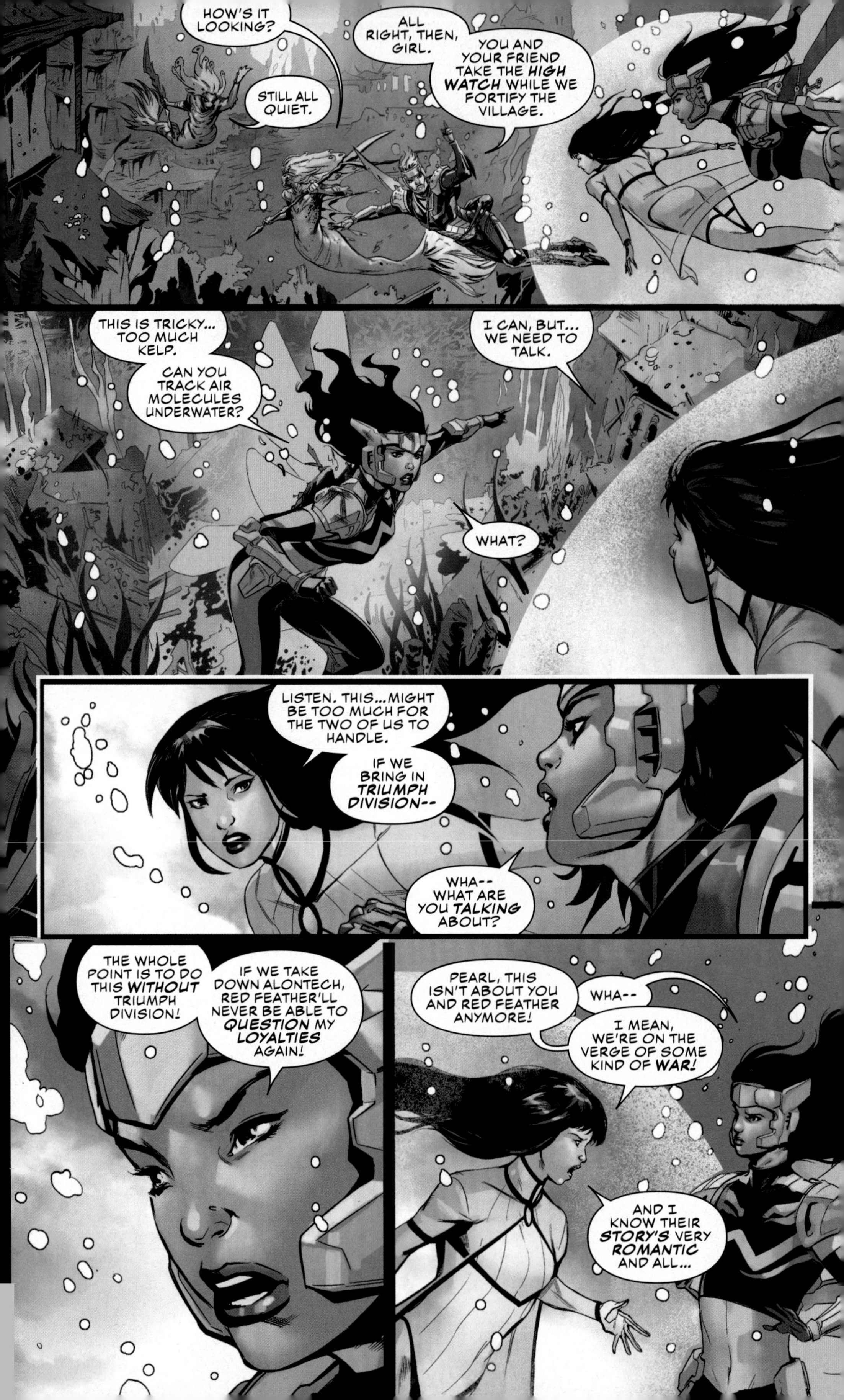
HOW'S IT LOOKING?
STILL ALL QUIET.
ALL RIGHT, THEN, GIRL.
YOU AND YOUR FRIEND TAKE THE HIGH WATCH WHILE WE FORTIFY THE VILLAGE.
THIS IS TRICKY... TOO MUCH KELP.
CAN YOU TRACK AIR MOLECULES UNDERWATER?
I CAN, BUT... WE NEED TO TALK.
WHAT?
LISTEN. THIS...MIGHT BE TOO MUCH FOR THE TWO OF US TO HANDLE.
IF WE BRING IN TRIUMPH DIVISION--
WHA-- WHAT ARE YOU TALKING ABOUT?
THE WHOLE POINT IS TO DO THIS WITHOUT TRIUMPH DIVISION!
IF WE TAKE DOWN ALONTECH, RED FEATHER'LL NEVER BE ABLE TO QUESTION MY LOYALTIES AGAIN!
PEARL, THIS ISN'T ABOUT YOU AND RED FEATHER ANYMORE!
WHA--
I MEAN, WE'RE ON THE VERGE OF SOME KIND OF WAR!
AND I KNOW THEIR STORY'S VERY ROMANTIC AND ALL...

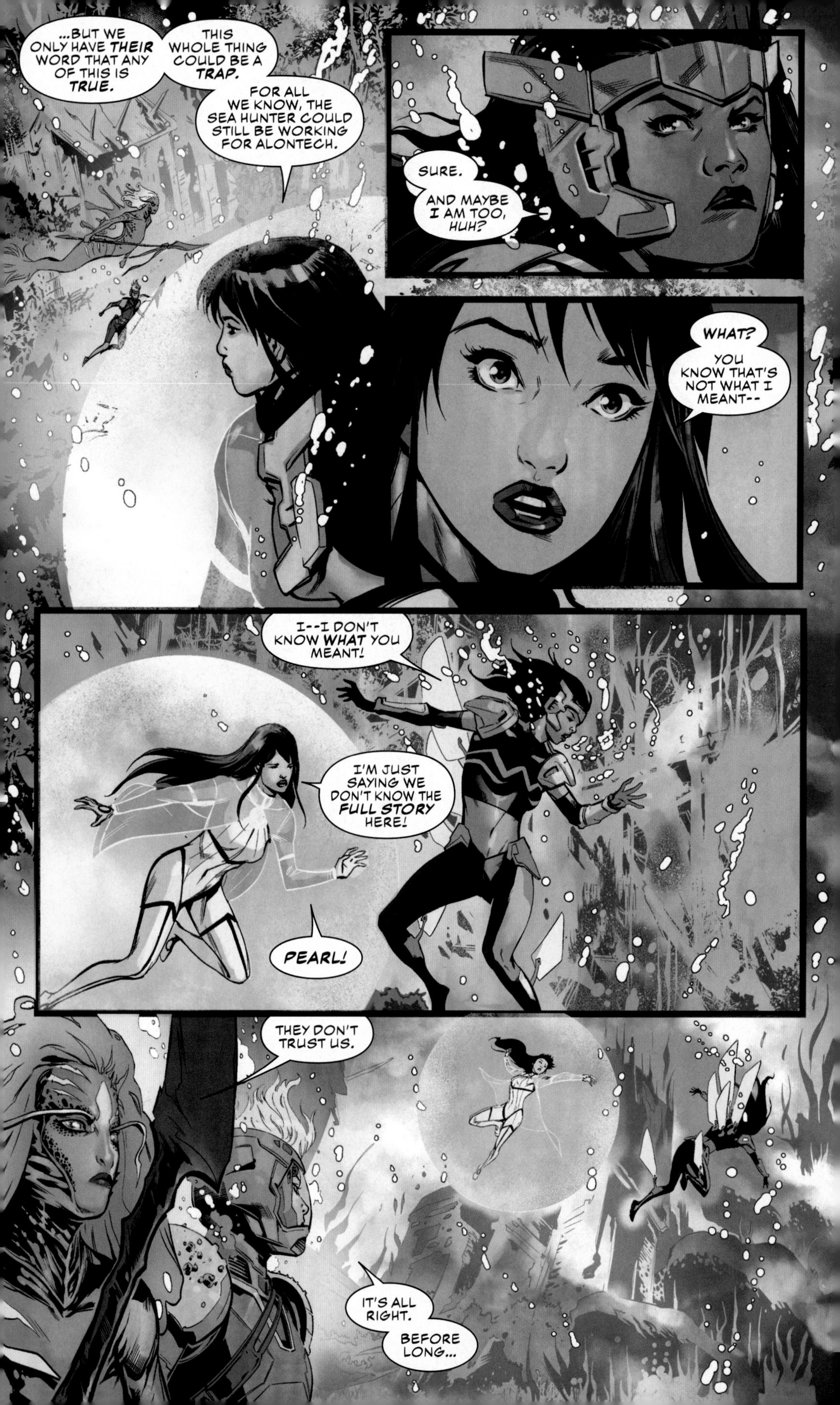

...BUT WE ONLY HAVE THEIR WORD THAT ANY OF THIS IS TRUE.
THIS WHOLE THING COULD BE A TRAP.
FOR ALL WE KNOW, THE SEA HUNTER COULD STILL BE WORKING FOR ALONTECH.
SURE.
AND MAYBE I AM TOO, HUH?
WHAT?
YOU KNOW THAT'S NOT WHAT I MEANT--
I--I DON'T KNOW WHAT YOU MEANT!
I'M JUST SAYING WE DON'T KNOW THE FULL STORY HERE!
PEARL!
THEY DON'T TRUST US.
IT'S ALL RIGHT.
BEFORE LONG...

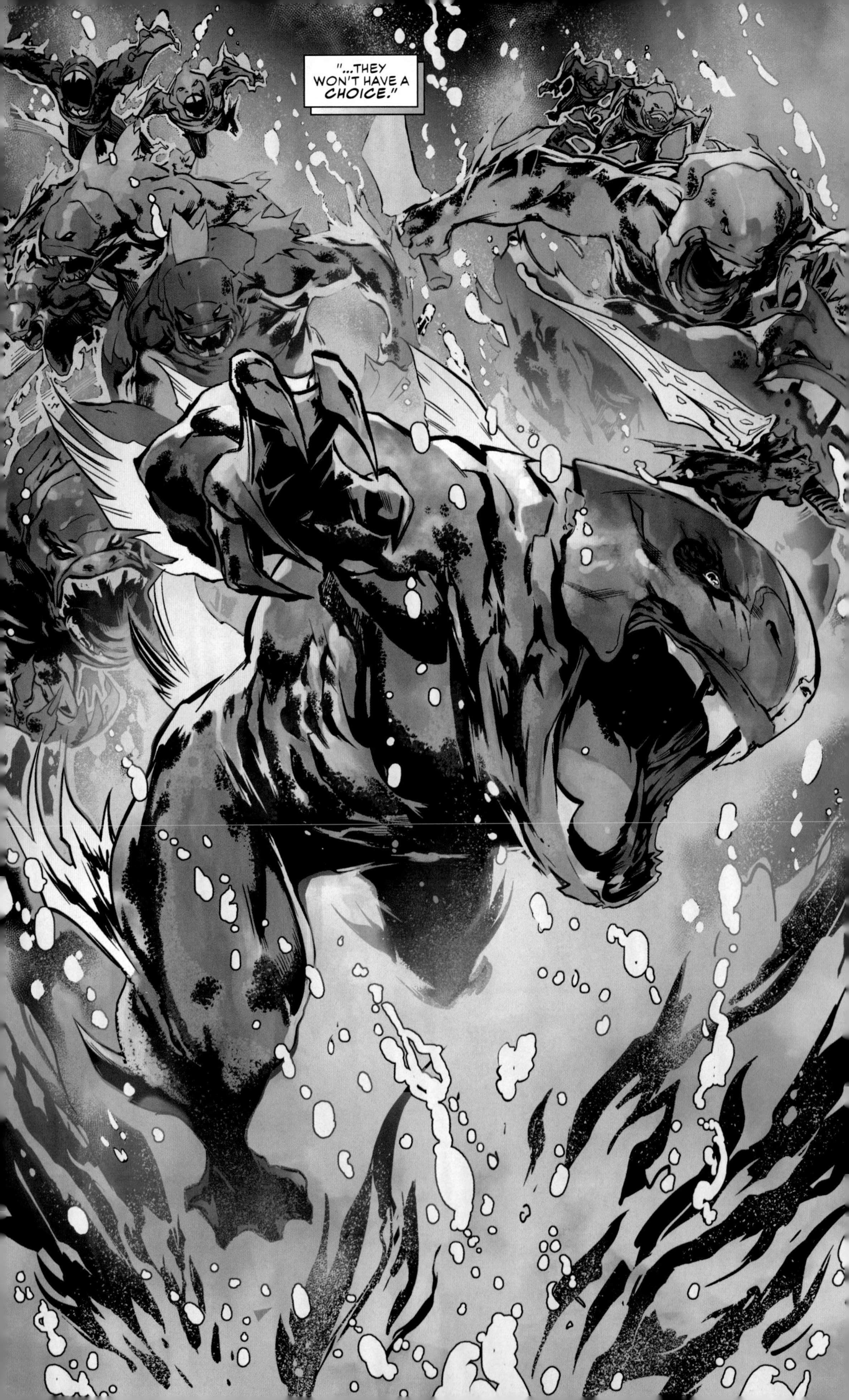
"...THEY WON'T HAVE A CHOICE."

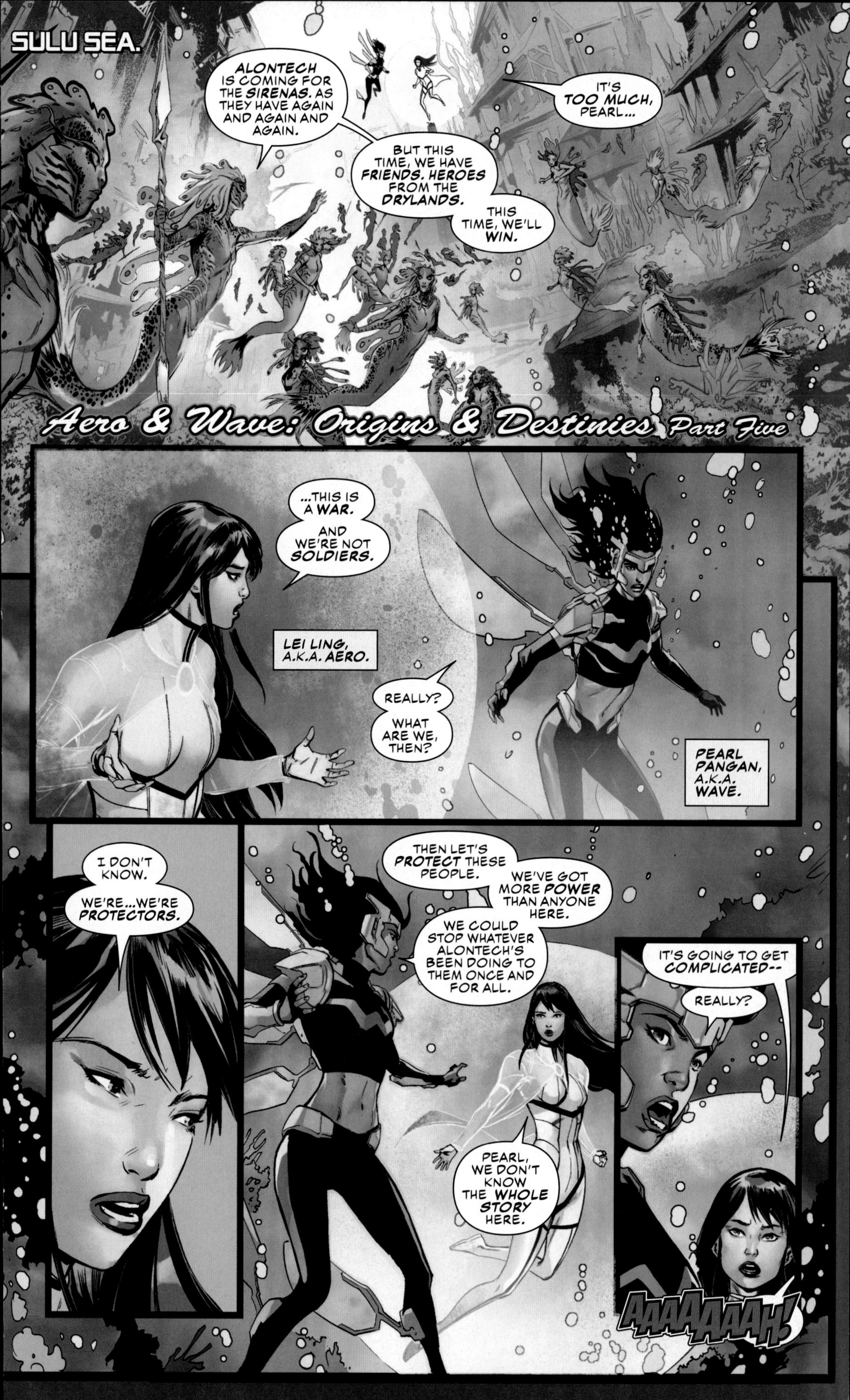
SULU SEA.
ALONTECH IS COMING FOR THE SIRENAS. AS THEY HAVE AGAIN AND AGAIN AND AGAIN.
IT'S TOO MUCH, PEARL...
BUT THIS TIME, WE HAVE FRIENDS. HEROES FROM THE DRYLANDS.
THIS TIME, WE'LL WIN.
Aero & Wave: Origins & Destinies Part Five
...THIS IS A WAR.
AND WE'RE NOT SOLDIERS.
LEI LING, A.K.A. AERO.
REALLY?
WHAT ARE WE, THEN?
PEARL PANGAN, A.K.A. WAVE.
I DON'T KNOW.
WE'RE...WE'RE PROTECTORS.
THEN LET'S PROTECT THESE PEOPLE.
WE'VE GOT MORE POWER THAN ANYONE HERE.
WE COULD STOP WHATEVER ALONTECH'S BEEN DOING TO THEM ONCE AND FOR ALL.
PEARL, WE DON'T KNOW THE WHOLE STORY HERE.
IT'S GOING TO GET COMPLICATED--
REALLY?
AAAAAAAH!

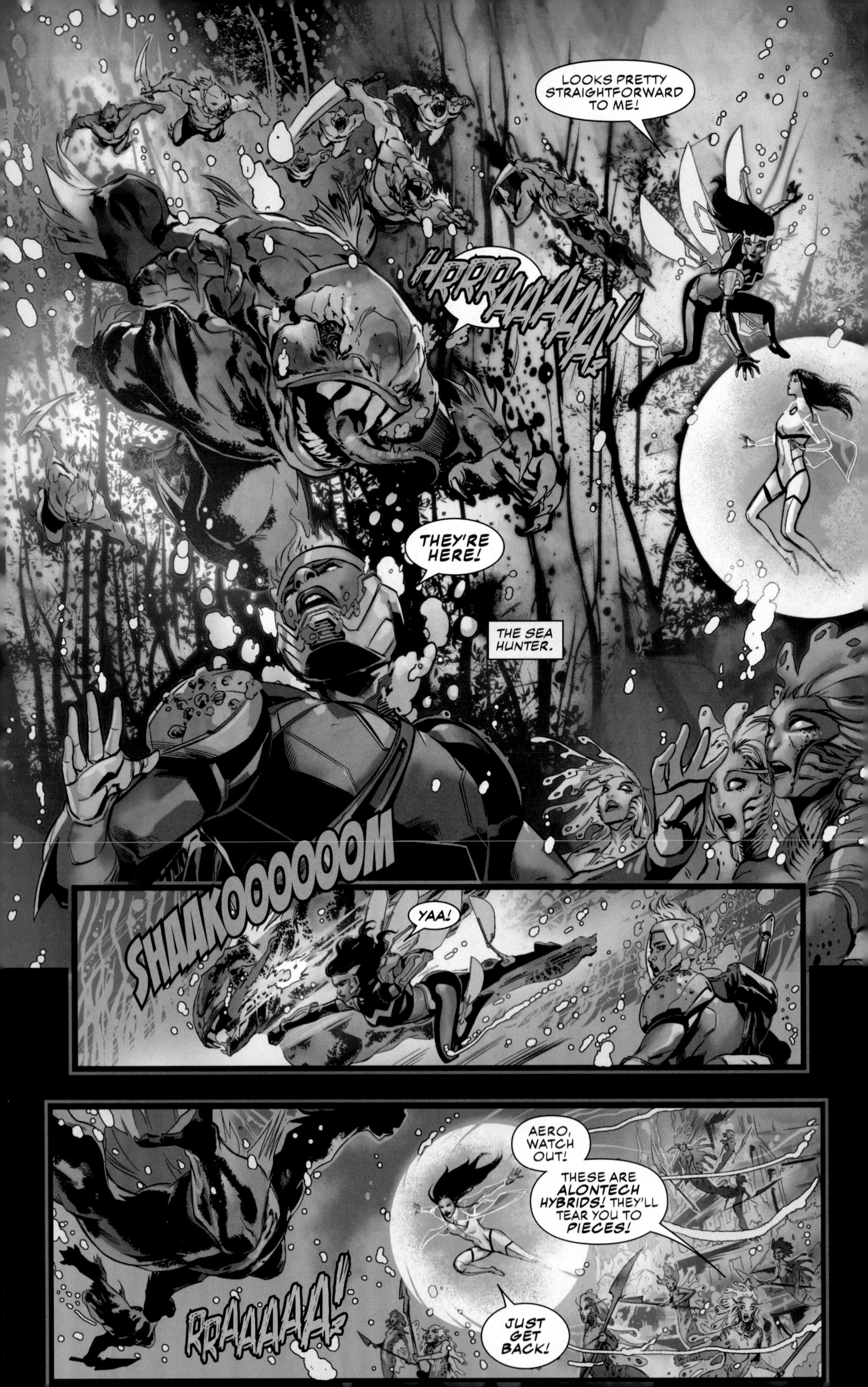
LOOKS PRETTY STRAIGHTFORWARD TO ME!
HRRRAAAAAA!
THEY'RE HERE!
THE SEA HUNTER.
SHAAKOOOOOOM
YAA!
AERO, WATCH OUT!
THESE ARE ALONTECH HYBRIDS! THEY'LL TEAR YOU TO PIECES!
RRAAAAAA!
JUST GET BACK!

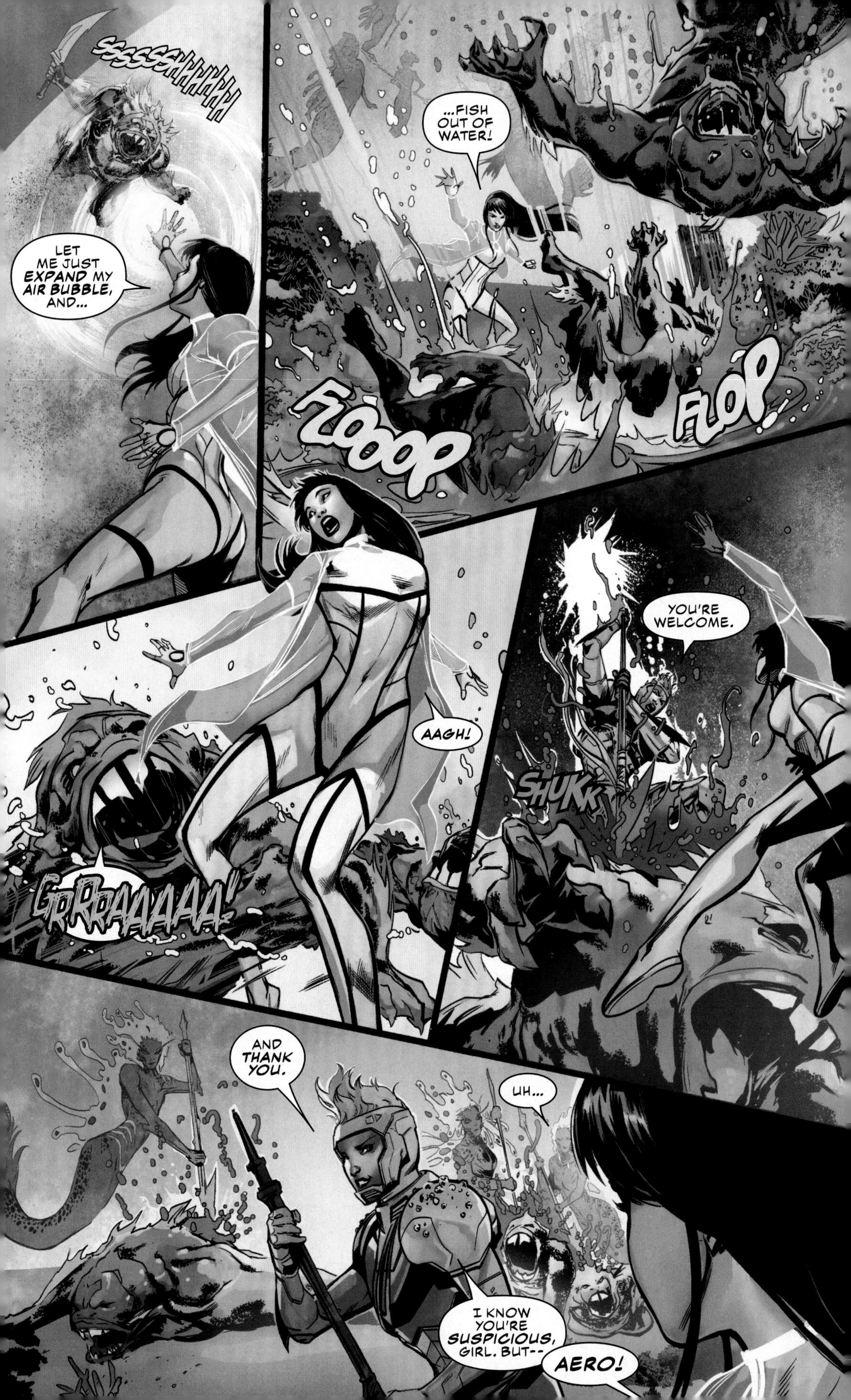
SSSSSSHHHHHH
LET ME JUST EXPAND MY AIR BUBBLE, AND...
...FISH OUT OF WATER!
FLOOOP
FLOP
AAGH!
GRRRAAAAAA!
YOU'RE WELCOME.
SHUKK
AND THANK YOU.
UH...
I KNOW YOU'RE SUSPICIOUS, GIRL. BUT--
AERO!

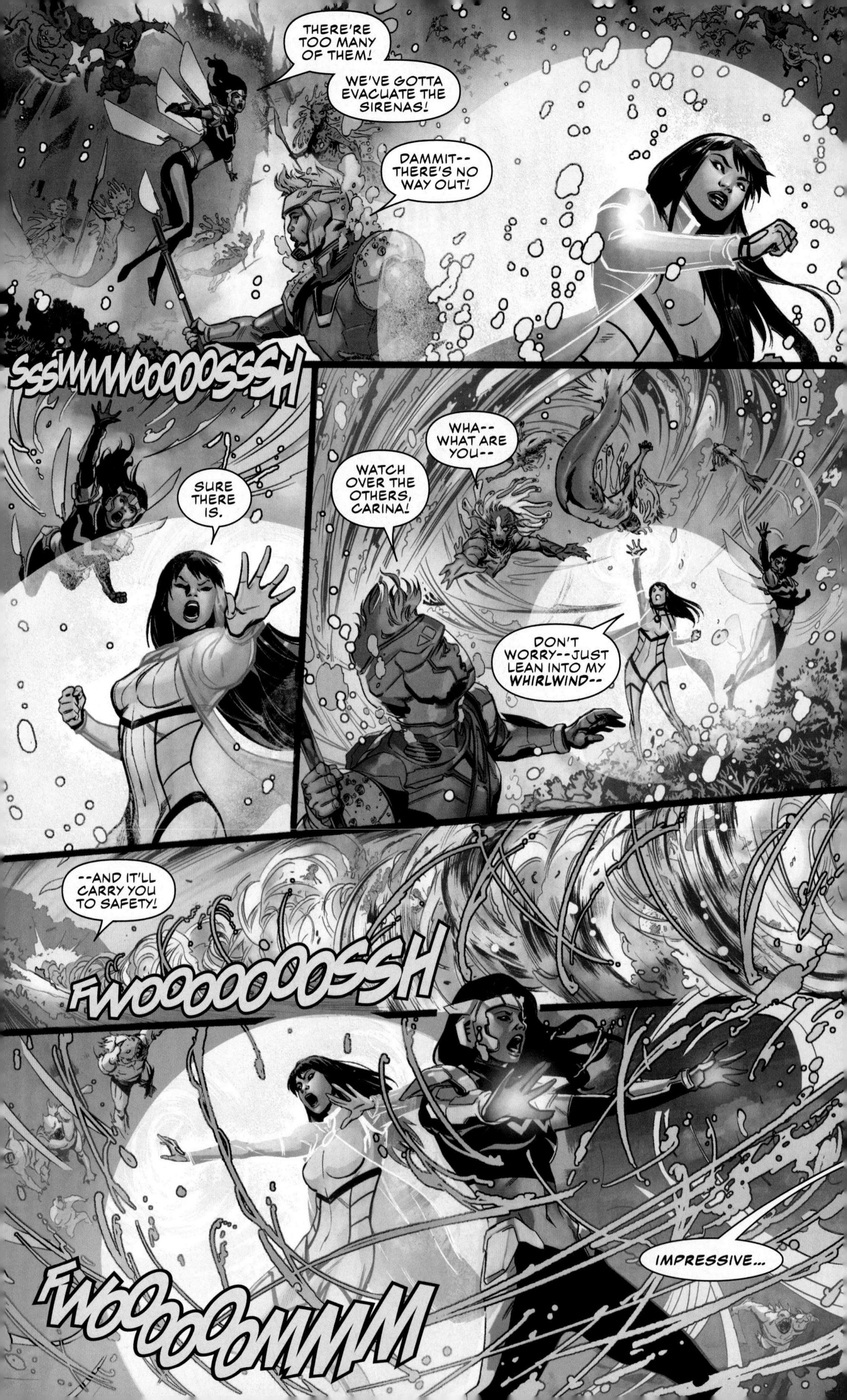
THERE'RE TOO MANY OF THEM!
WE'VE GOTTA EVACUATE THE SIRENAS!
DAMMIT-- THERE'S NO WAY OUT!
SSSWWWOOOOOSSSH
SURE THERE IS.
WATCH OVER THE OTHERS, CARINA!
WHA-- WHAT ARE YOU--
DON'T WORRY--JUST LEAN INTO MY WHIRLWIND--
--AND IT'LL CARRY YOU TO SAFETY!
FWOOOOOOOOSSH
IMPRESSIVE...
FWOOOOOOMMMM

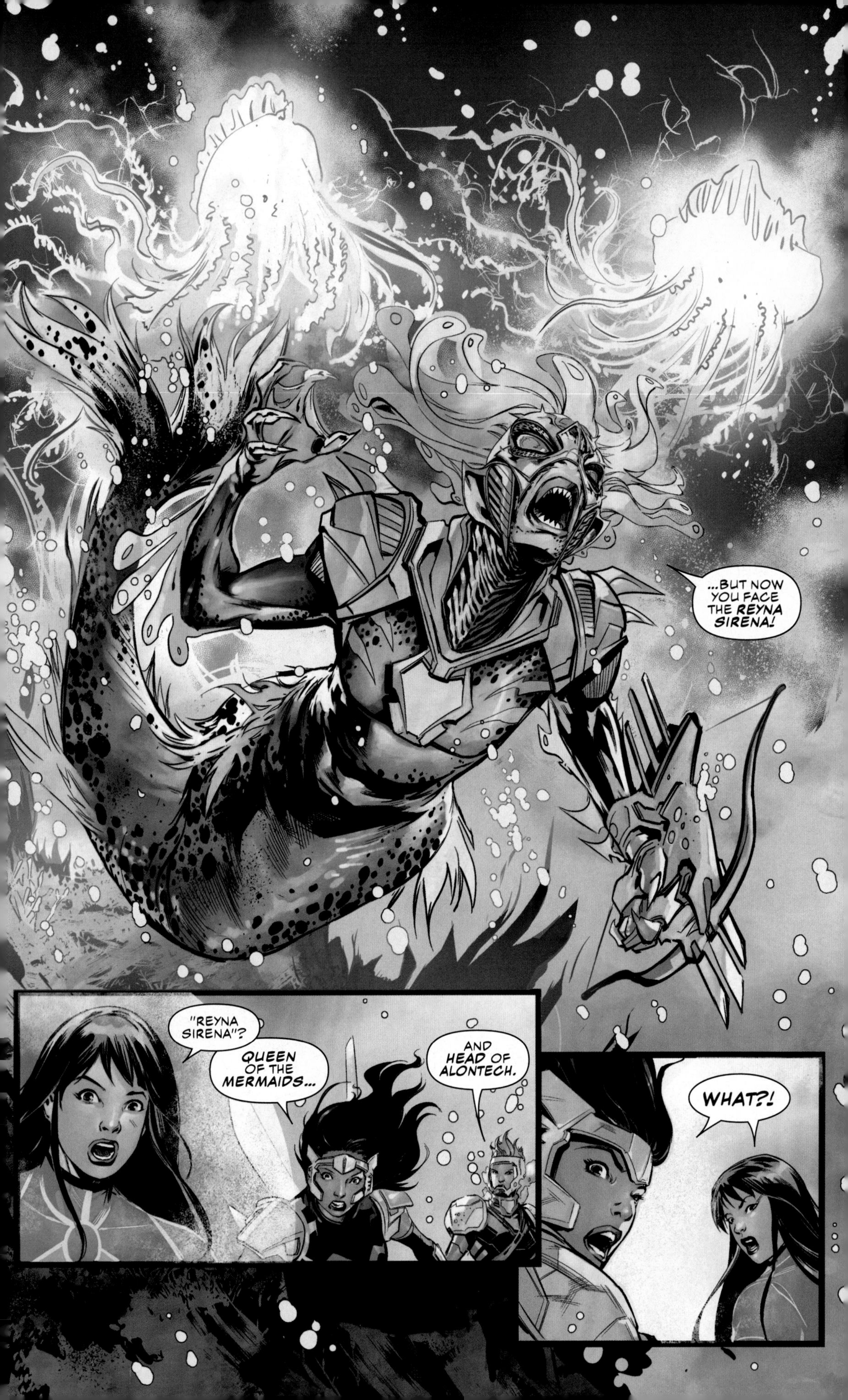
...BUT NOW YOU FACE THE REYNA SIRENA!
"REYNA SIRENA"?
QUEEN OF THE MERMAIDS...
AND HEAD OF ALONTECH.
WHAT?!

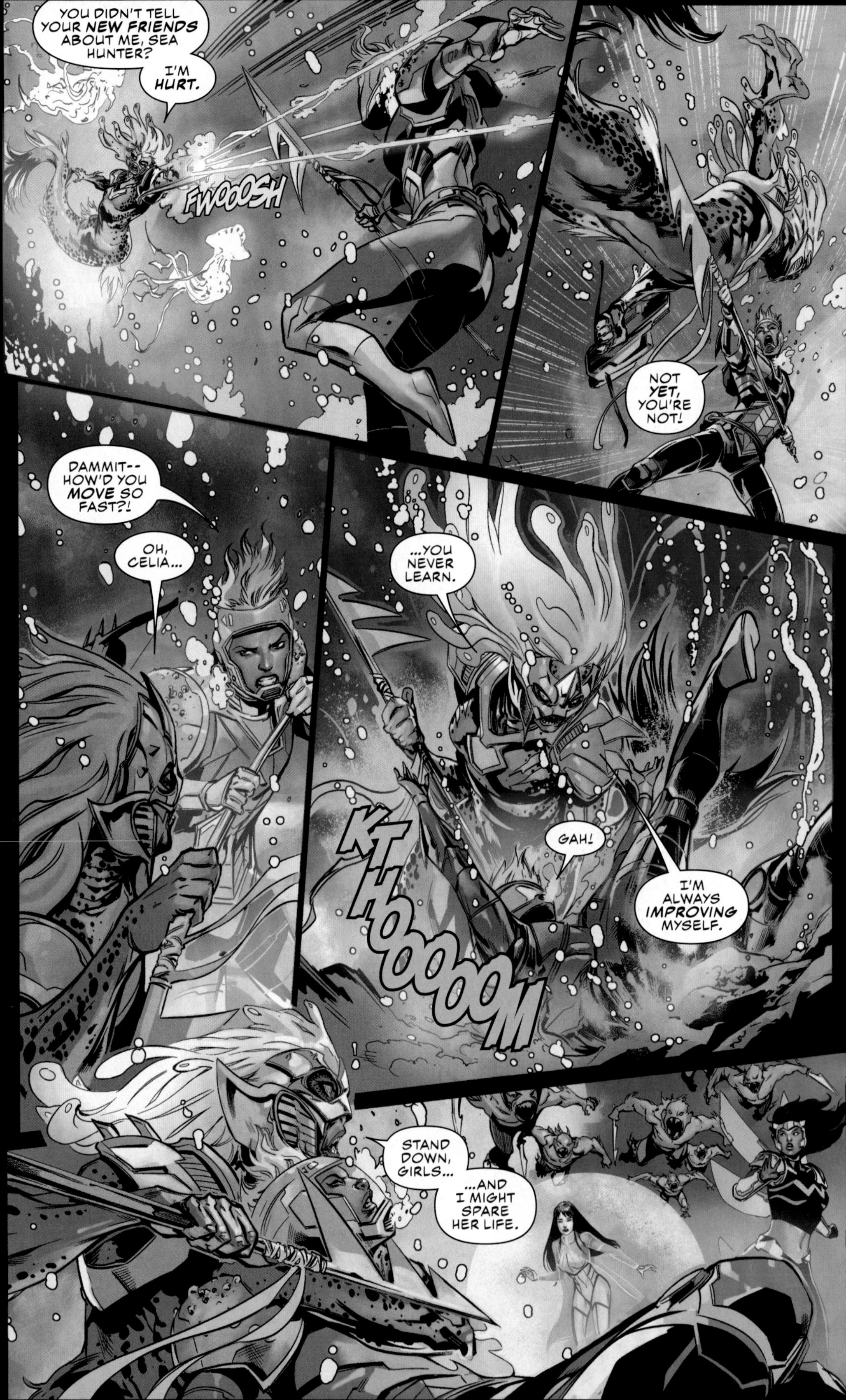
YOU DIDN'T TELL YOUR NEW FRIENDS ABOUT ME, SEA HUNTER?
I'M HURT.
FWOOOSH
NOT YET, YOU'RE NOT!
DAMMIT--HOW'D YOU MOVE SO FAST?!
OH, CELIA...
...YOU NEVER LEARN.
KTHOOOOOM
GAH!
I'M ALWAYS IMPROVING MYSELF.
STAND DOWN, GIRLS...
...AND I MIGHT SPARE HER LIFE.

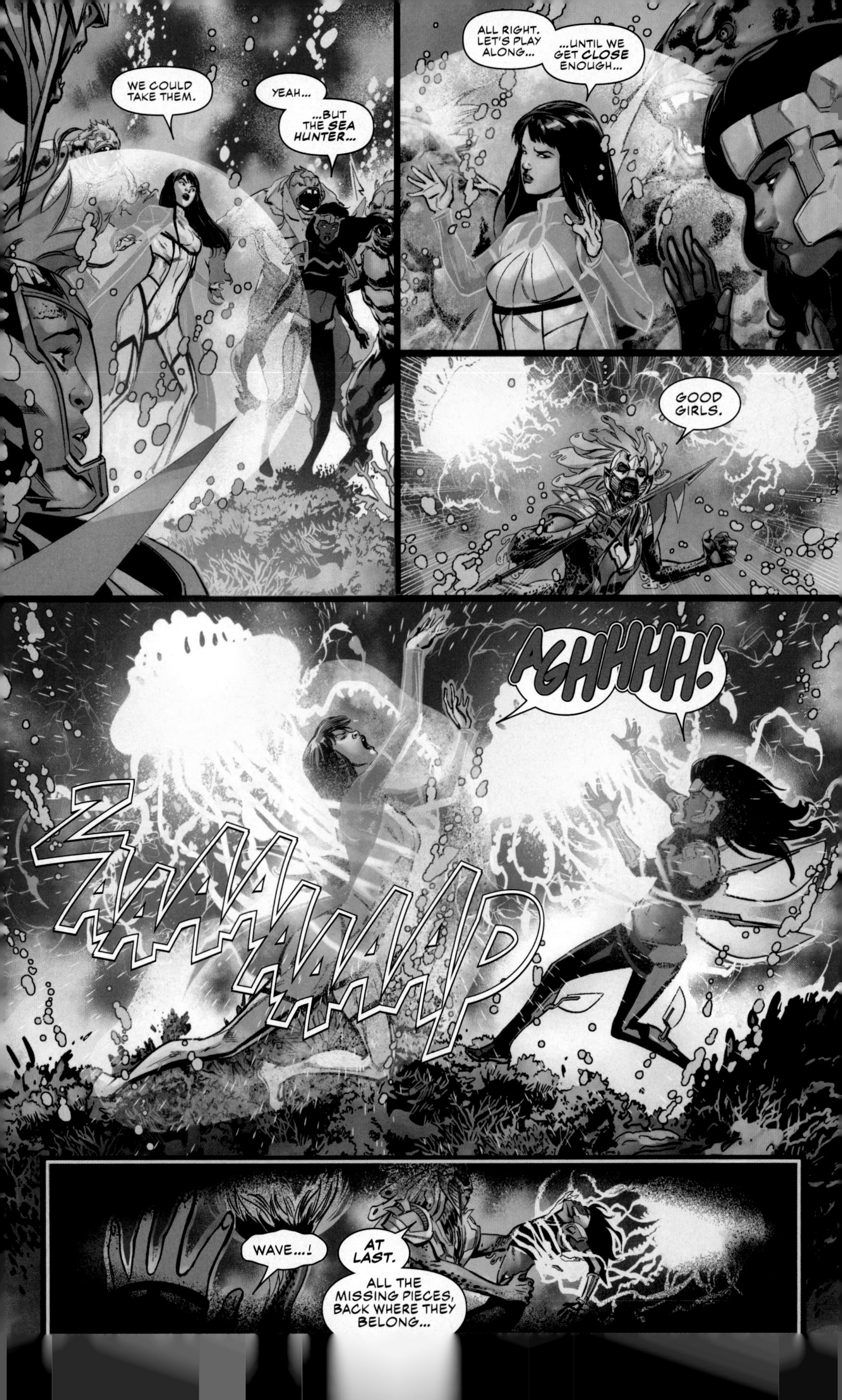
WE COULD TAKE THEM.
YEAH...
...BUT THE SEA HUNTER...
ALL RIGHT. LET'S PLAY ALONG...
...UNTIL WE GET CLOSE ENOUGH...
GOOD GIRLS.
AGHHHH!
ZWAAAAAAAP
WAVE...!
AT LAST.
ALL THE MISSING PIECES, BACK WHERE THEY BELONG...

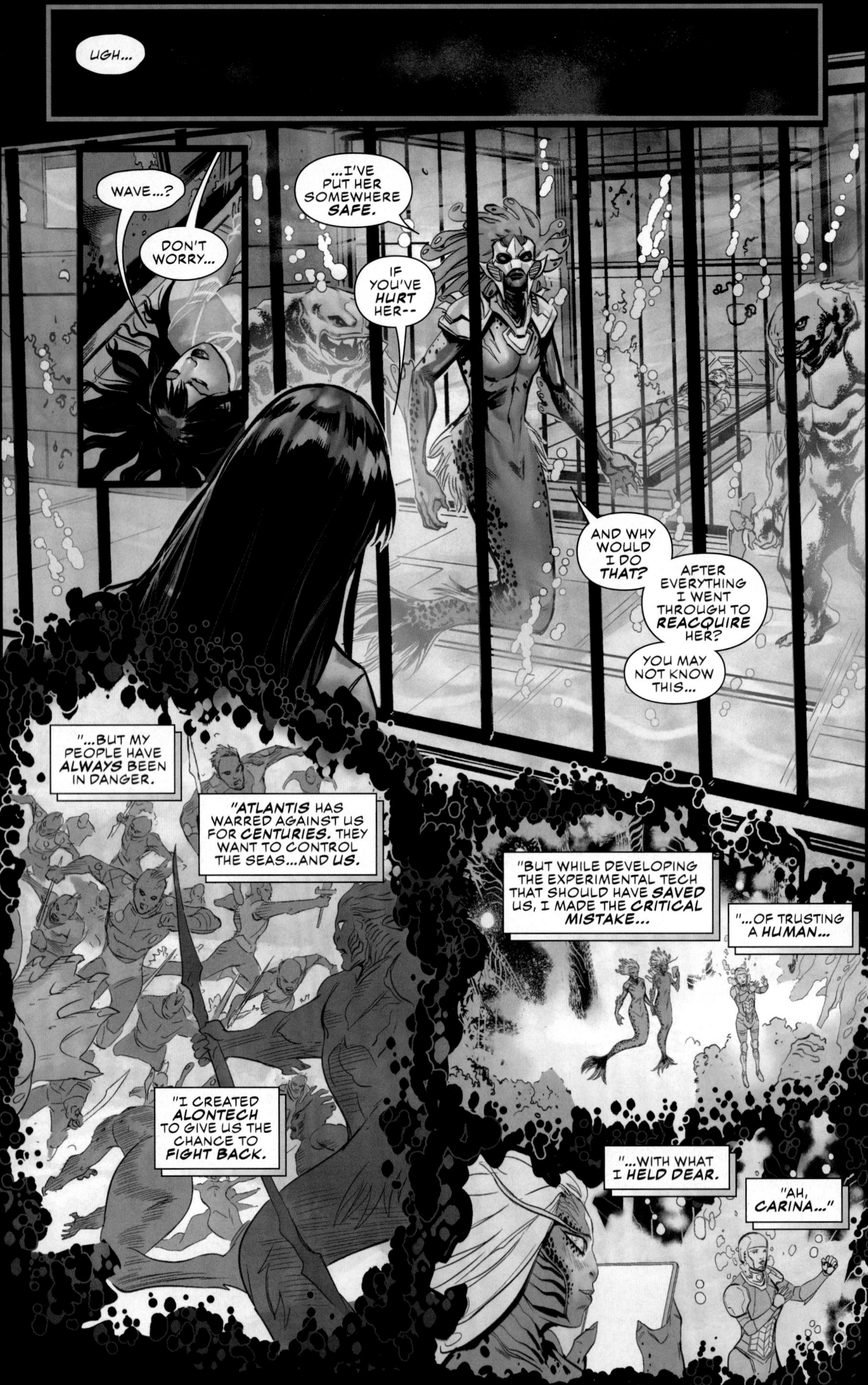
UGH...
WAVE...?
DON'T WORRY...
...I'VE PUT HER SOMEWHERE SAFE.
IF YOU'VE HURT HER--
AND WHY WOULD I DO THAT?
AFTER EVERYTHING I WENT THROUGH TO REACQUIRE HER?
YOU MAY NOT KNOW THIS...
"...BUT MY PEOPLE HAVE ALWAYS BEEN IN DANGER.
"ATLANTIS HAS WARRED AGAINST US FOR CENTURIES. THEY WANT TO CONTROL THE SEAS...AND US.
"I CREATED ALONTECH TO GIVE US THE CHANCE TO FIGHT BACK.
"BUT WHILE DEVELOPING THE EXPERIMENTAL TECH THAT SHOULD HAVE SAVED US, I MADE THE CRITICAL MISTAKE...
"...OF TRUSTING A HUMAN...
"...WITH WHAT I HELD DEAR.
"AH, CARINA..."

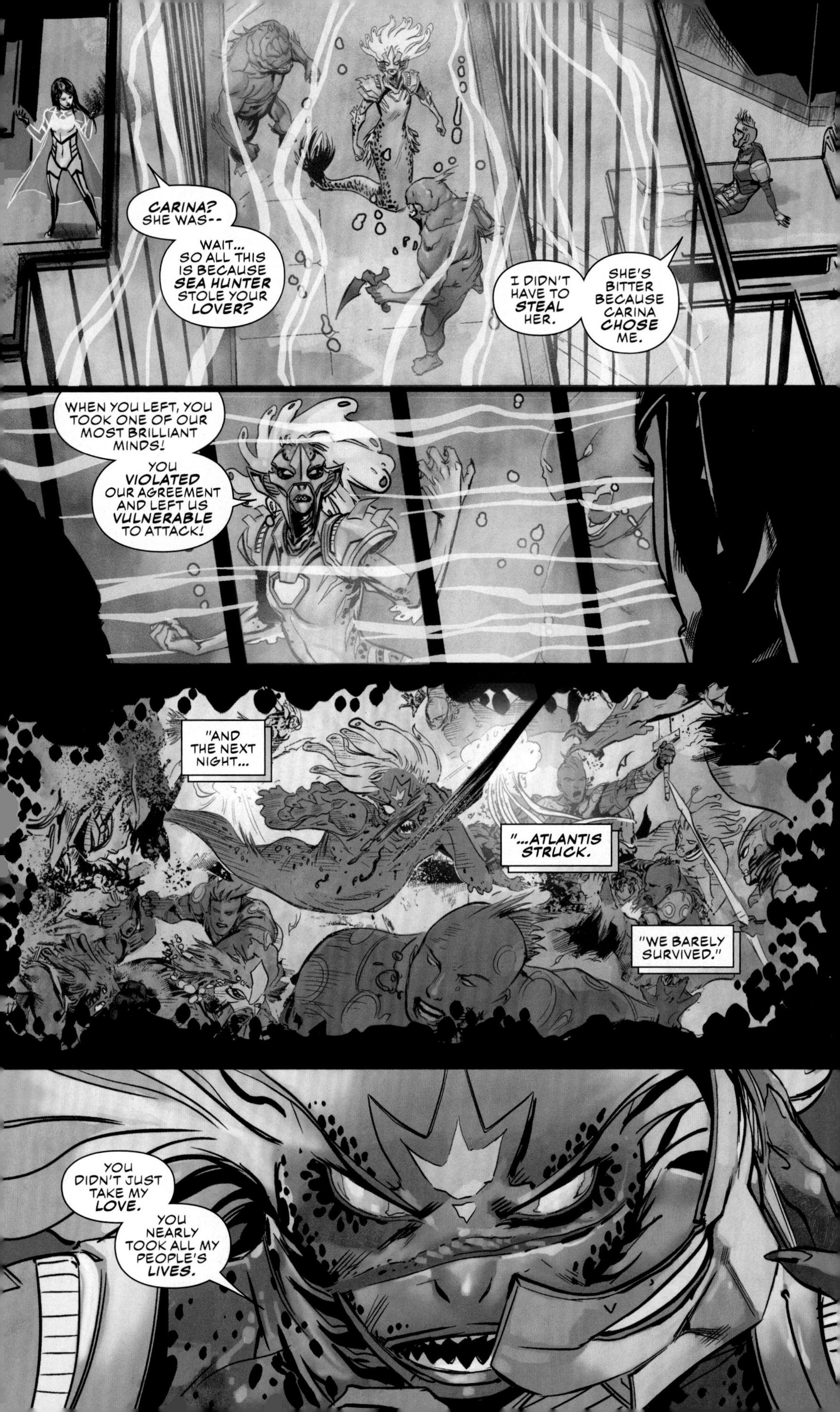
CARINA? SHE WAS--
WAIT... SO ALL THIS IS BECAUSE SEA HUNTER STOLE YOUR LOVER?
I DIDN'T HAVE TO STEAL HER.
SHE'S BITTER BECAUSE CARINA CHOSE ME.
WHEN YOU LEFT, YOU TOOK ONE OF OUR MOST BRILLIANT MINDS!
YOU VIOLATED OUR AGREEMENT AND LEFT US VULNERABLE TO ATTACK!
"AND THE NEXT NIGHT...
"...ATLANTIS STRUCK.
"WE BARELY SURVIVED."
YOU DIDN'T JUST TAKE MY LOVE.
YOU NEARLY TOOK ALL MY PEOPLE'S LIVES.

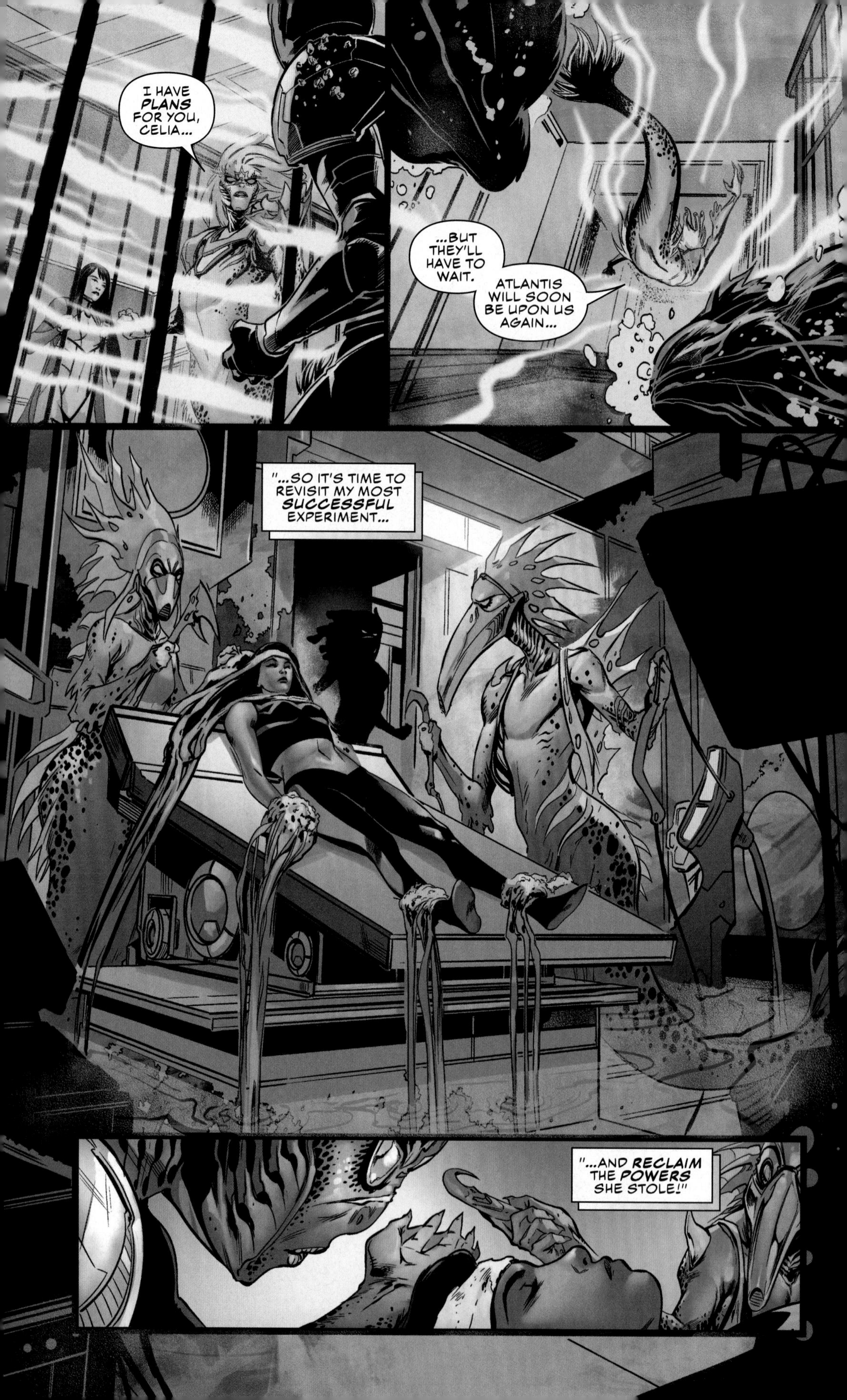
I HAVE PLANS FOR YOU, CELIA...
...BUT THEY'LL HAVE TO WAIT.
ATLANTIS WILL SOON BE UPON US AGAIN...
"...SO IT'S TIME TO REVISIT MY MOST SUCCESSFUL EXPERIMENT...
"...AND RECLAIM THE POWERS SHE STOLE!"

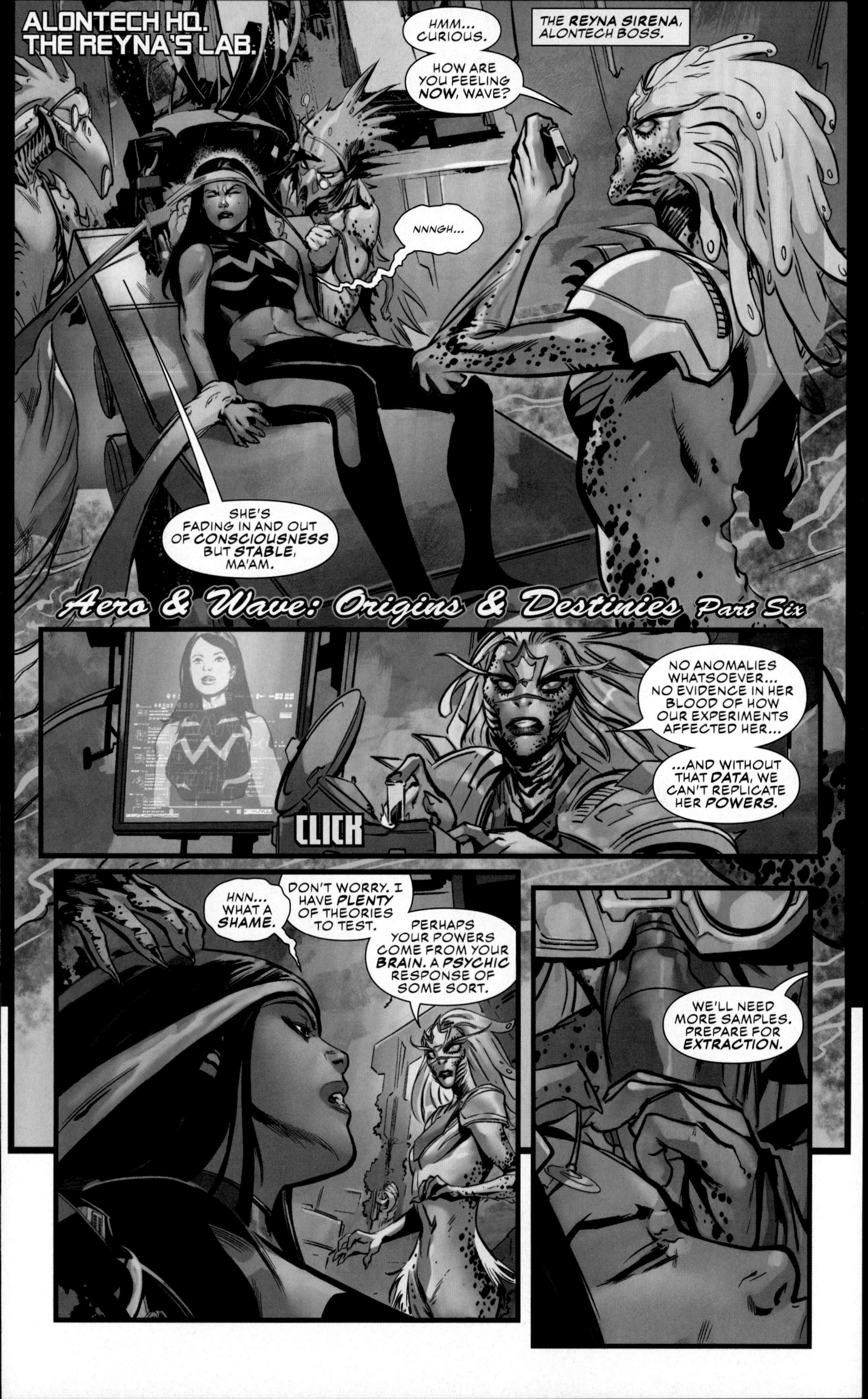
ALONTECH HQ. THE REYNA'S LAB.
HMM... CURIOUS.
HOW ARE YOU FEELING NOW, WAVE?
THE REYNA SIRENA, ALONTECH BOSS.
NNNGH...
SHE'S FADING IN AND OUT OF CONSCIOUSNESS BUT STABLE, MA'AM.
Aero & Wave: Origins & Destinies Part Six
NO ANOMALIES WHATSOEVER... NO EVIDENCE IN HER BLOOD OF HOW OUR EXPERIMENTS AFFECTED HER...
...AND WITHOUT THAT DATA, WE CAN'T REPLICATE HER POWERS.
CLICK
HNN... WHAT A SHAME.
DON'T WORRY. I HAVE PLENTY OF THEORIES TO TEST.
PERHAPS YOUR POWERS COME FROM YOUR BRAIN. A PSYCHIC RESPONSE OF SOME SORT.
WE'LL NEED MORE SAMPLES. PREPARE FOR EXTRACTION.

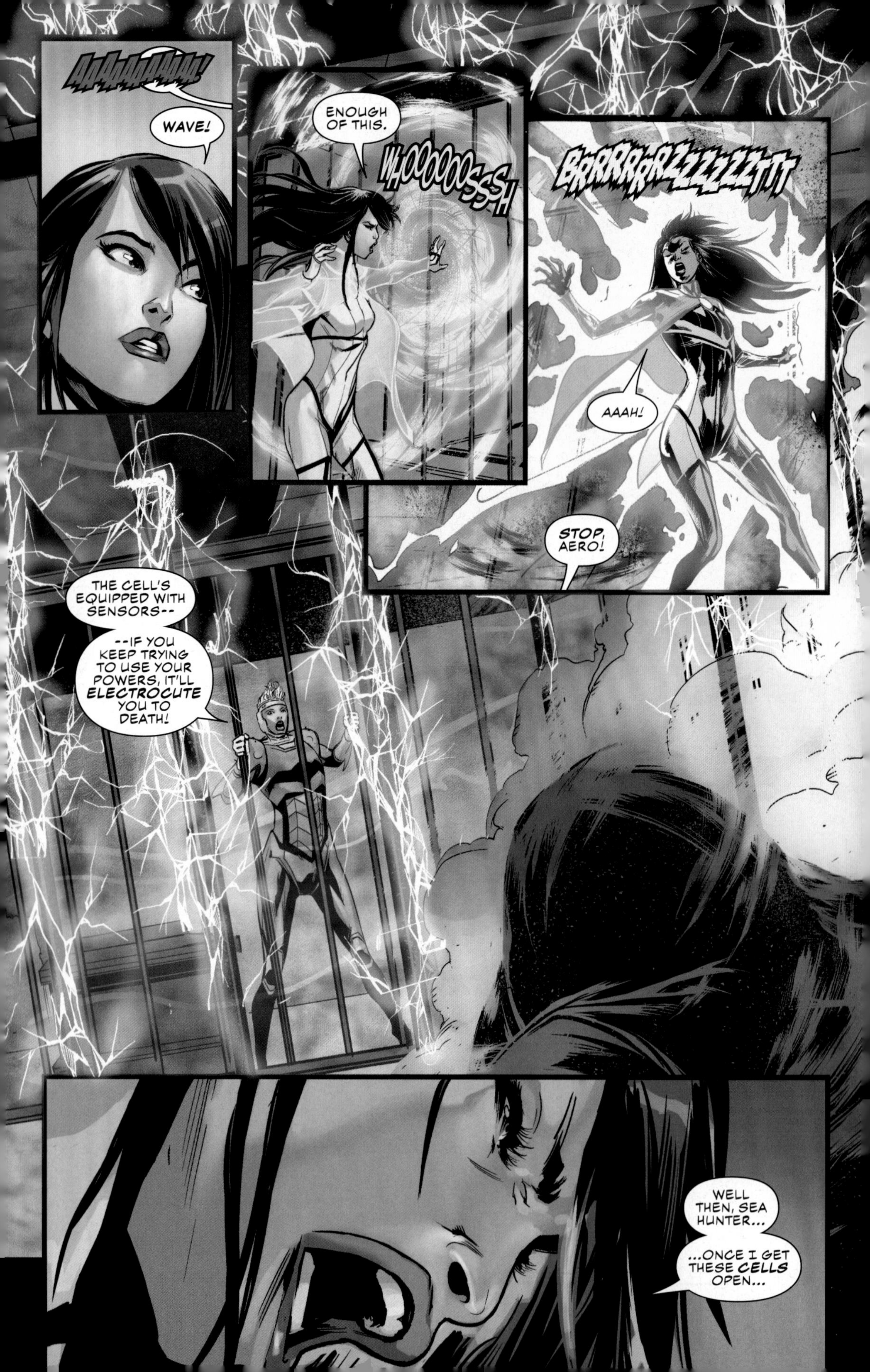

AAAAAAAAAA!
WAVE!
ENOUGH OF THIS.
WHOOOOOOSSSH
BRRRRRRZZZZZZZTTT
AAAH!
STOP, AERO!
THE CELL'S EQUIPPED WITH SENSORS--
--IF YOU KEEP TRYING TO USE YOUR POWERS, IT'LL ELECTROCUTE YOU TO DEATH!
WELL THEN, SEA HUNTER...
...ONCE I GET THESE CELLS OPEN...

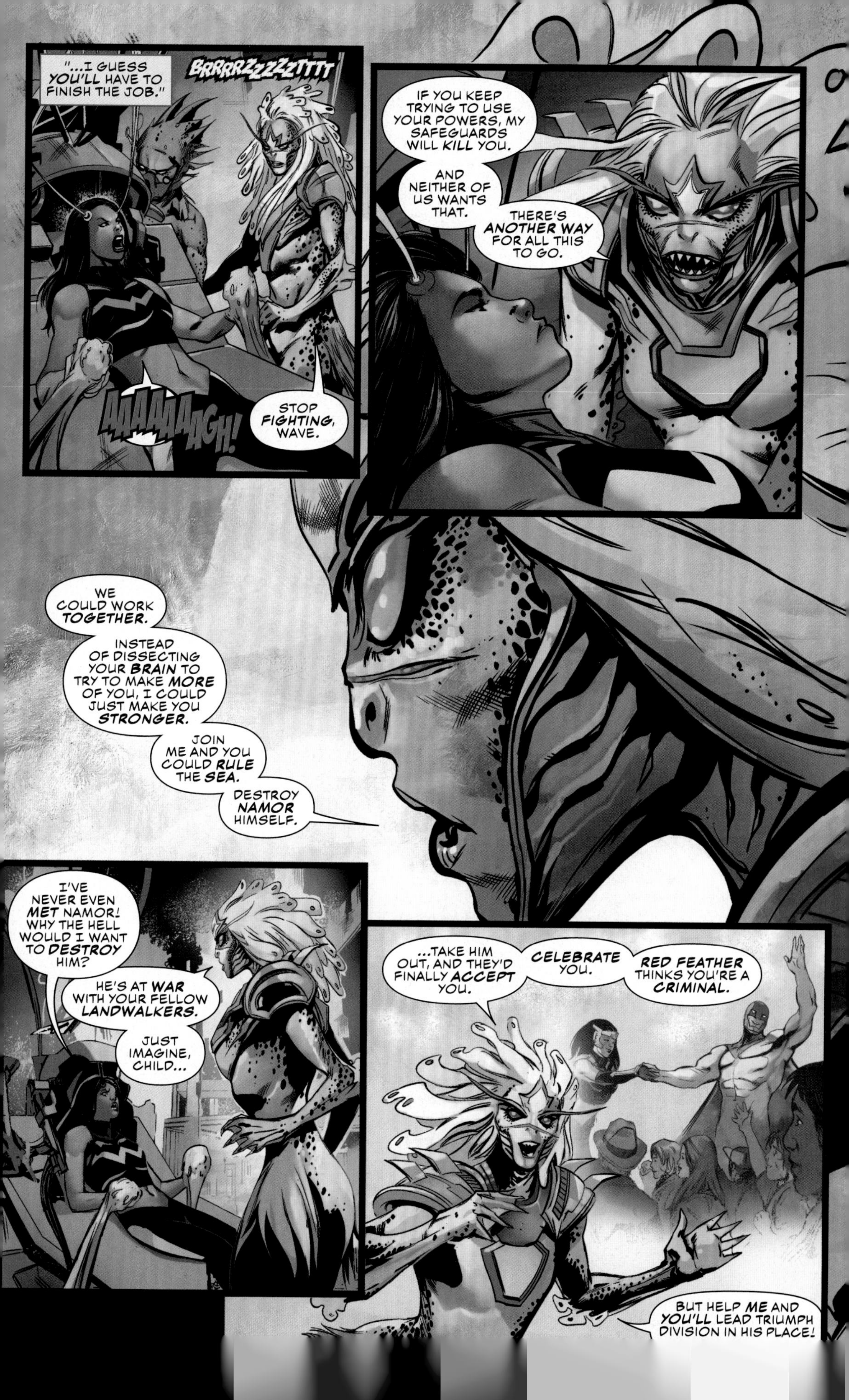

"...I GUESS YOU'LL HAVE TO FINISH THE JOB."
BRRRRZZZZZZTTTT
AAAAAAAGH!
STOP FIGHTING, WAVE.
IF YOU KEEP TRYING TO USE YOUR POWERS, MY SAFEGUARDS WILL KILL YOU.
AND NEITHER OF US WANTS THAT.
THERE'S ANOTHER WAY FOR ALL THIS TO GO.
WE COULD WORK TOGETHER.
INSTEAD OF DISSECTING YOUR BRAIN TO TRY TO MAKE MORE OF YOU, I COULD JUST MAKE YOU STRONGER.
JOIN ME AND YOU COULD RULE THE SEA.
DESTROY NAMOR HIMSELF.
I'VE NEVER EVEN MET NAMOR! WHY THE HELL WOULD I WANT TO DESTROY HIM?
HE'S AT WAR WITH YOUR FELLOW LANDWALKERS.
JUST IMAGINE, CHILD...
RED FEATHER THINKS YOU'RE A CRIMINAL.
...TAKE HIM OUT, AND THEY'D FINALLY ACCEPT YOU.
CELEBRATE YOU.
BUT HELP ME AND YOU'LL LEAD TRIUMPH DIVISION IN HIS PLACE!

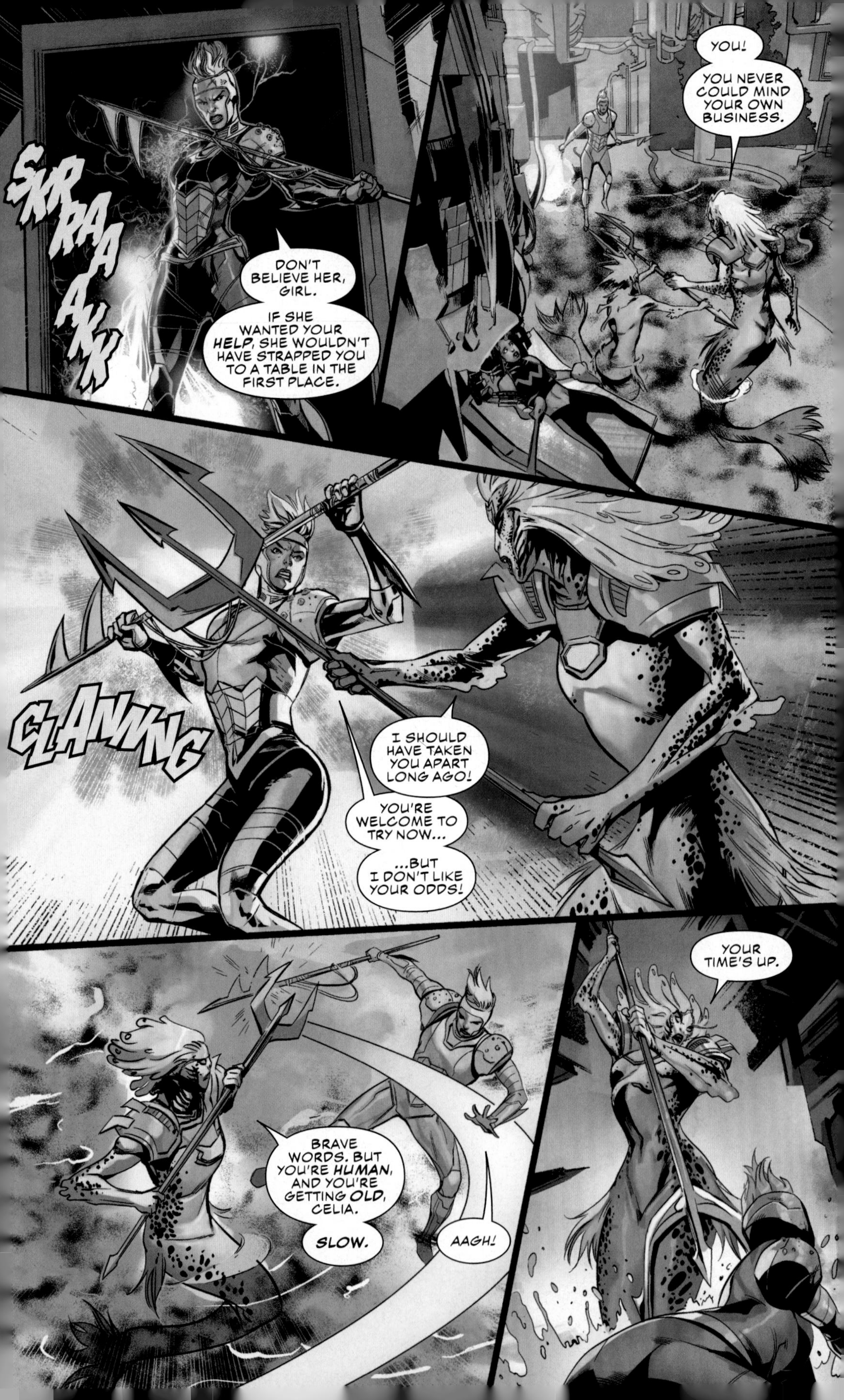
SKRRAAAKK
DON'T BELIEVE HER, GIRL.
IF SHE WANTED YOUR HELP, SHE WOULDN'T HAVE STRAPPED YOU TO A TABLE IN THE FIRST PLACE.
YOU!
YOU NEVER COULD MIND YOUR OWN BUSINESS.
CLANNNG
I SHOULD HAVE TAKEN YOU APART LONG AGO!
YOU'RE WELCOME TO TRY NOW...
...BUT I DON'T LIKE YOUR ODDS!
BRAVE WORDS. BUT YOU'RE HUMAN, AND YOU'RE GETTING OLD, CELIA.
SLOW.
AAGH!
YOUR TIME'S UP.

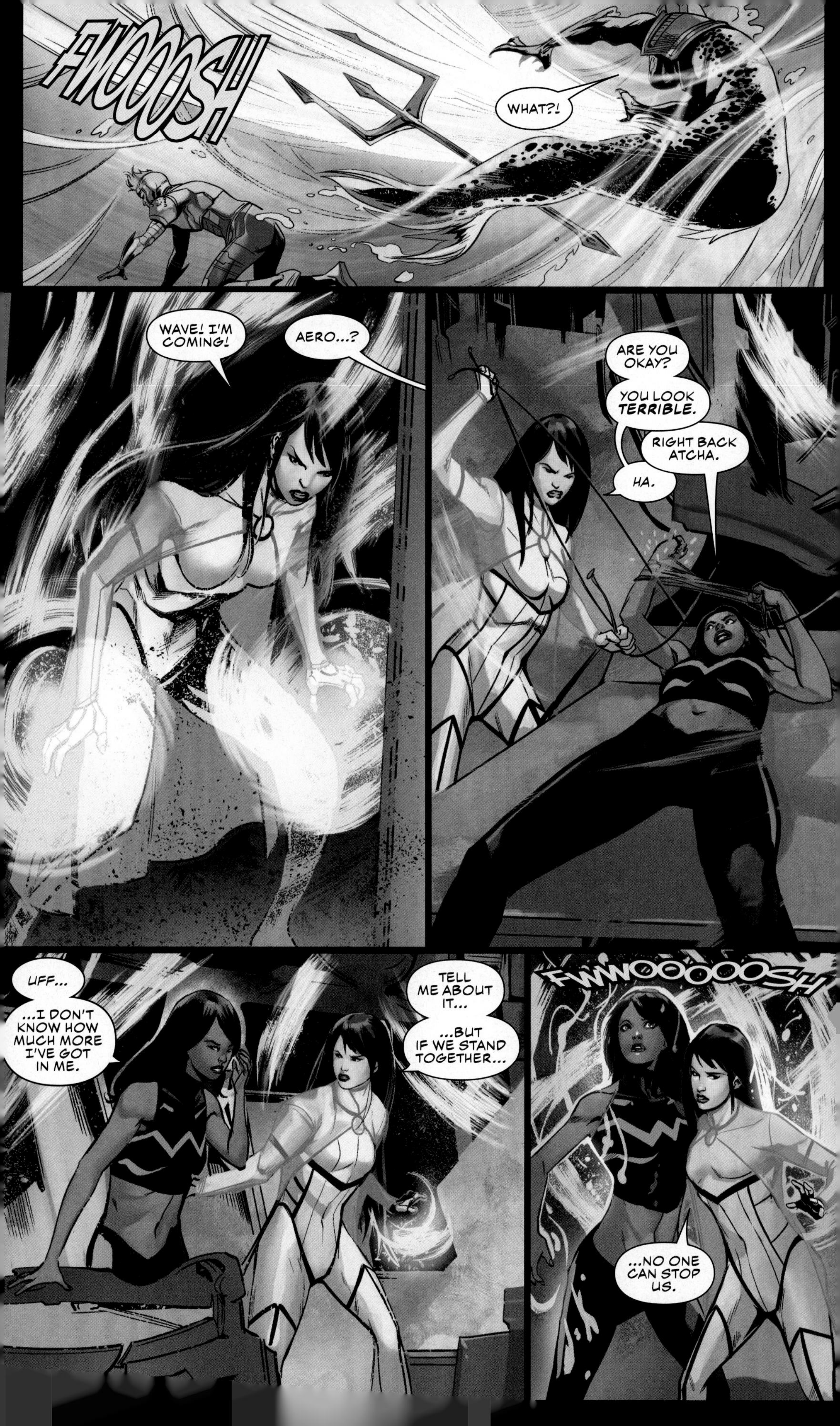
FWOOOSH
WHAT?!
WAVE! I'M COMING!
AERO...?
ARE YOU OKAY?
YOU LOOK TERRIBLE.
RIGHT BACK ATCHA.
HA.
UFF...
...I DON'T KNOW HOW MUCH MORE I'VE GOT IN ME.
TELL ME ABOUT IT...
...BUT IF WE STAND TOGETHER...
FWWOOOOOOSH
...NO ONE CAN STOP US.

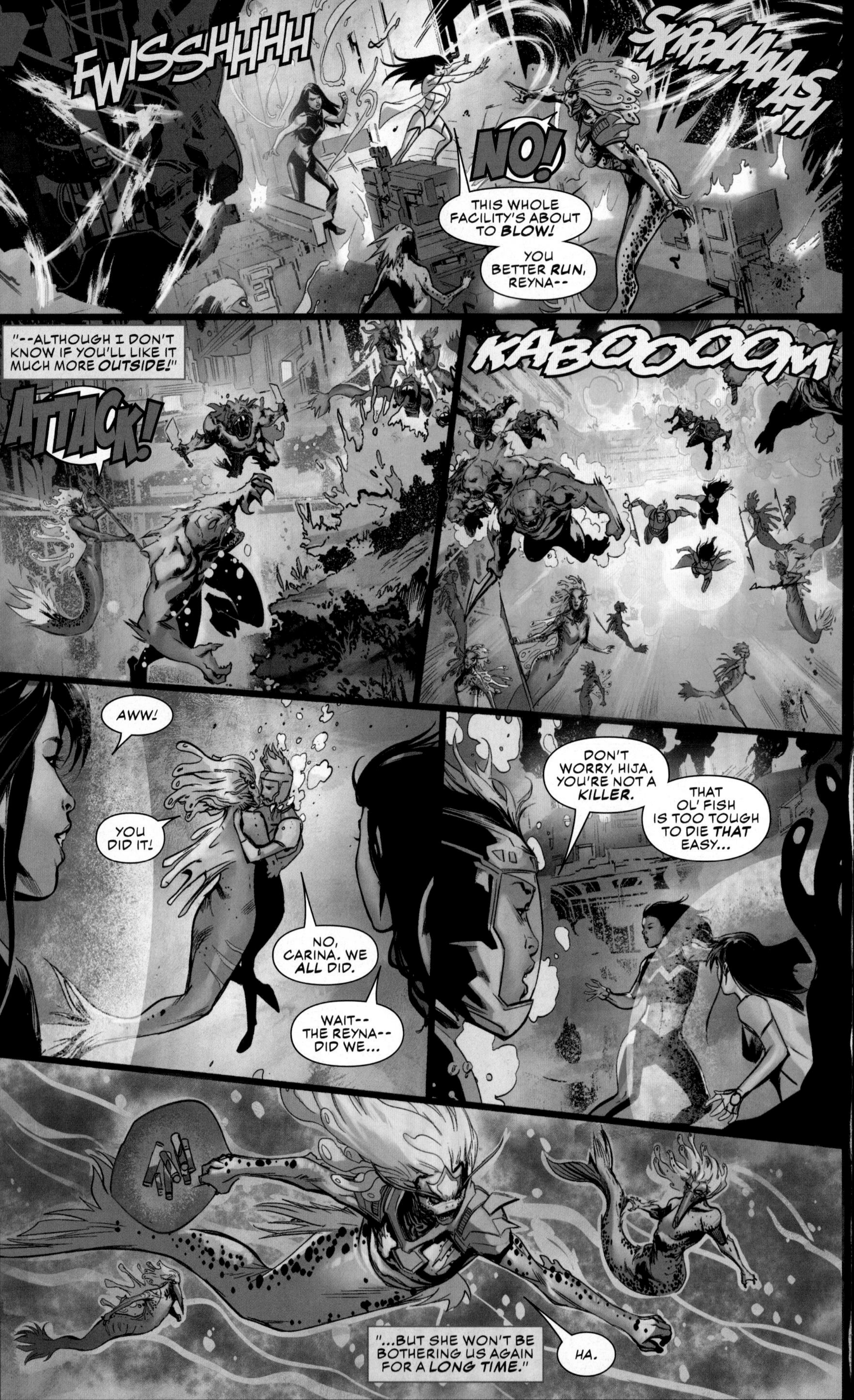
FWISSHHHH
SKRAAAASHH
NO!
THIS WHOLE FACILITY'S ABOUT TO BLOW!
YOU BETTER RUN, REYNA--
"--ALTHOUGH I DON'T KNOW IF YOU'LL LIKE IT MUCH MORE OUTSIDE!"
ATTACK!
KABOOOOOM
AWW!
YOU DID IT!
NO, CARINA. WE ALL DID.
WAIT-- THE REYNA-- DID WE...
DON'T WORRY, HIJA. YOU'RE NOT A KILLER.
THAT OL' FISH IS TOO TOUGH TO DIE THAT EASY...
"...BUT SHE WON'T BE BOTHERING US AGAIN FOR A LONG TIME."
HA.

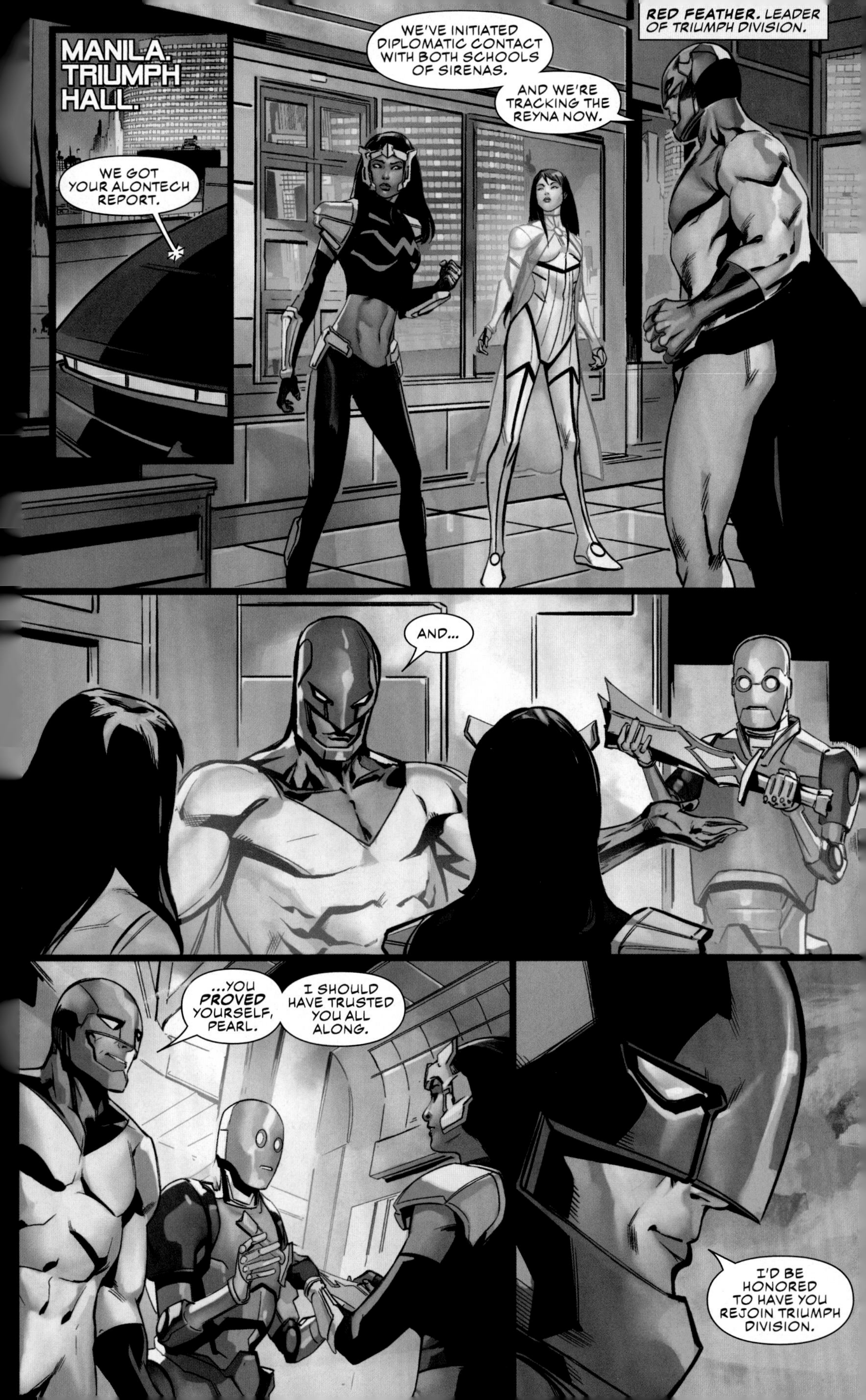
RED FEATHER. LEADER OF TRIUMPH DIVISION.
MANILA. TRIUMPH HALL.
WE'VE INITIATED DIPLOMATIC CONTACT WITH BOTH SCHOOLS OF SIRENAS.
AND WE'RE TRACKING THE REYNA NOW.
WE GOT YOUR ALONTECH REPORT.
AND...
...YOU PROVED YOURSELF, PEARL.
I SHOULD HAVE TRUSTED YOU ALL ALONG.
I'D BE HONORED TO HAVE YOU REJOIN TRIUMPH DIVISION.

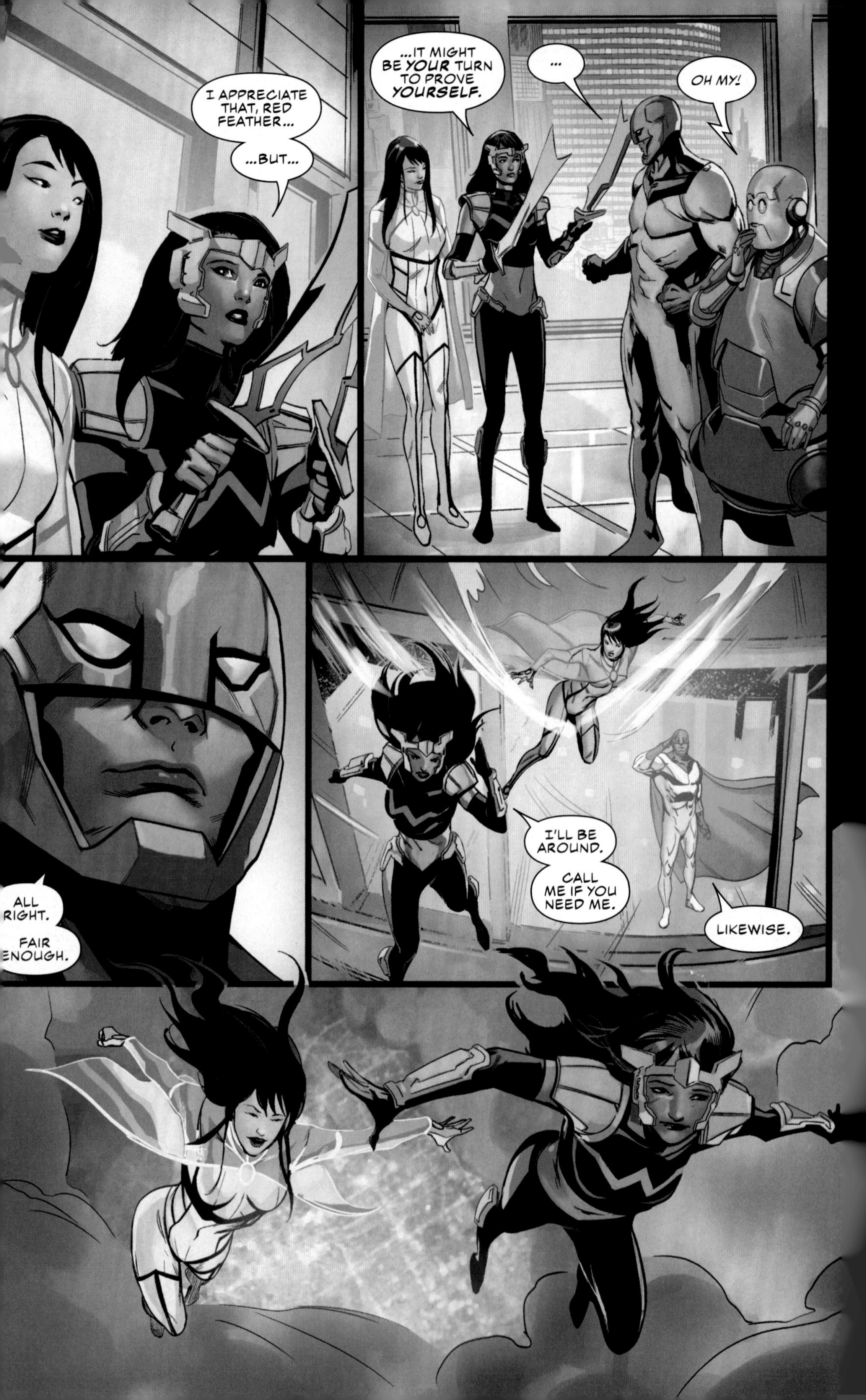
I APPRECIATE THAT, RED FEATHER...
...BUT...
...IT MIGHT BE YOUR TURN TO PROVE YOURSELF.
...
OH MY!
ALL RIGHT.
FAIR ENOUGH.
I'LL BE AROUND.
CALL ME IF YOU NEED ME.
LIKEWISE.

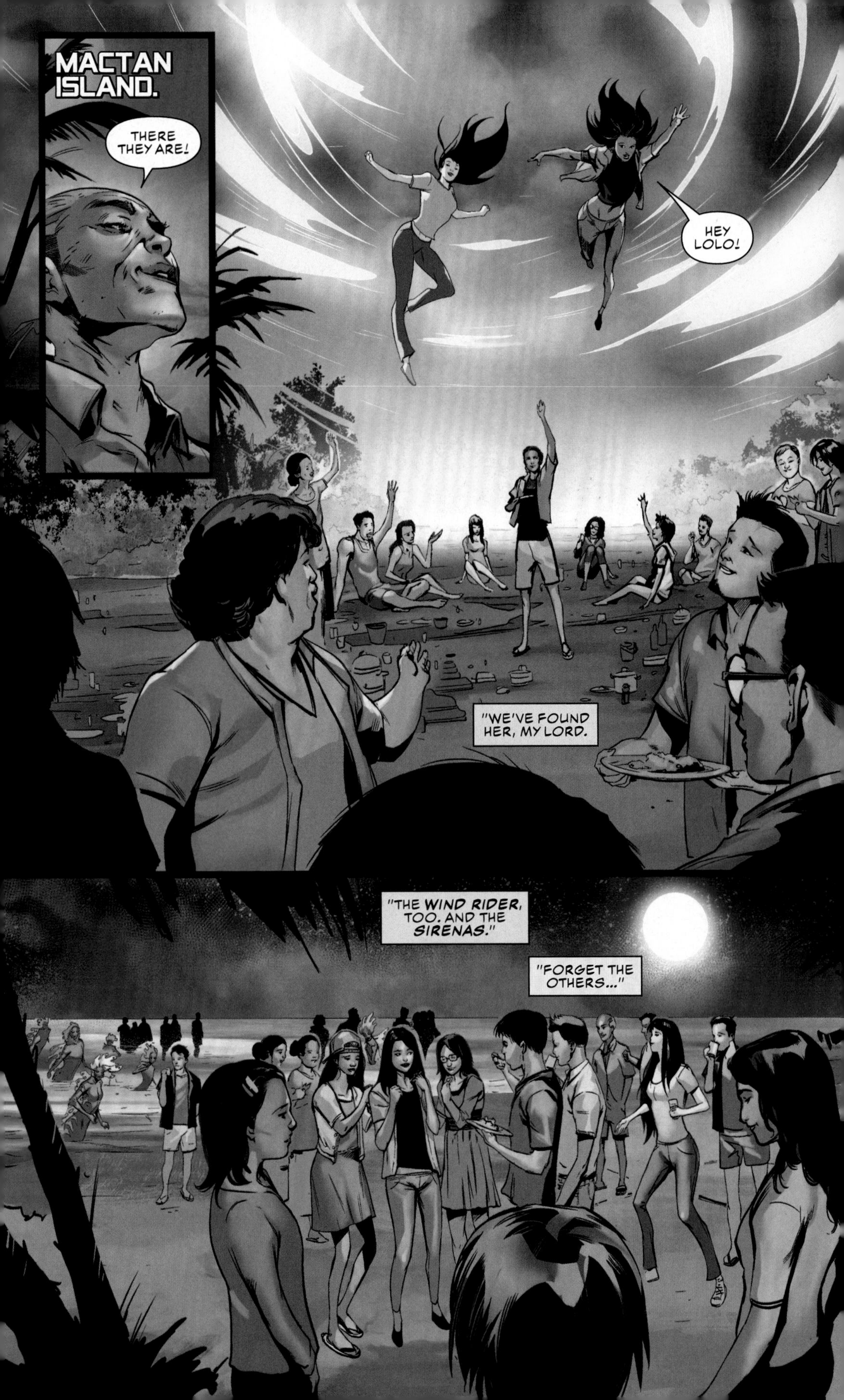
MACTAN ISLAND.
THERE THEY ARE!
HEY LOLO!
"WE'VE FOUND HER, MY LORD.
"THE WIND RIDER, TOO. AND THE SIRENAS."
"FORGET THE OTHERS..."

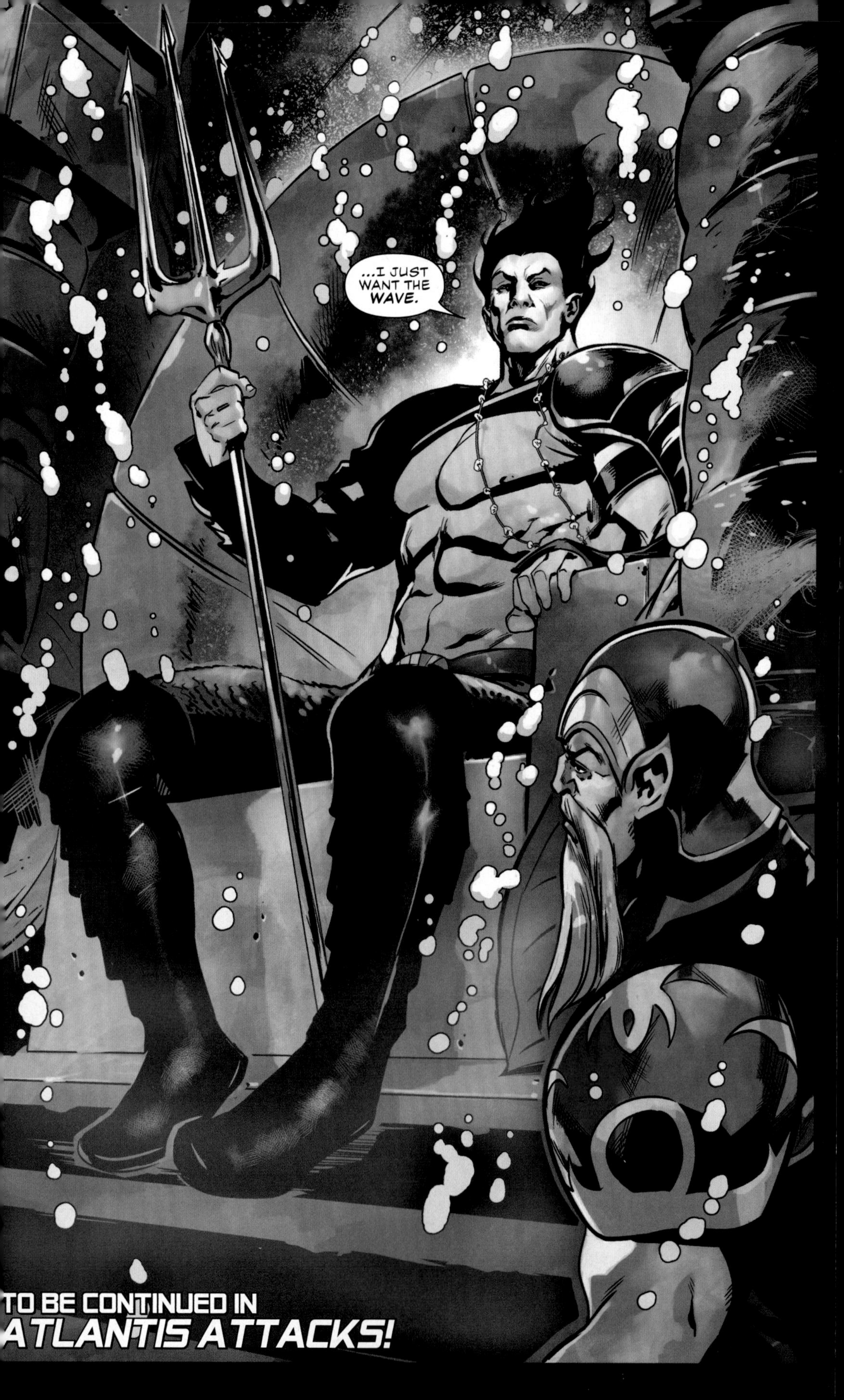
...I JUST WANT THE WAVE.
TO BE CONTINUED IN ATLANTIS ATTACKS!

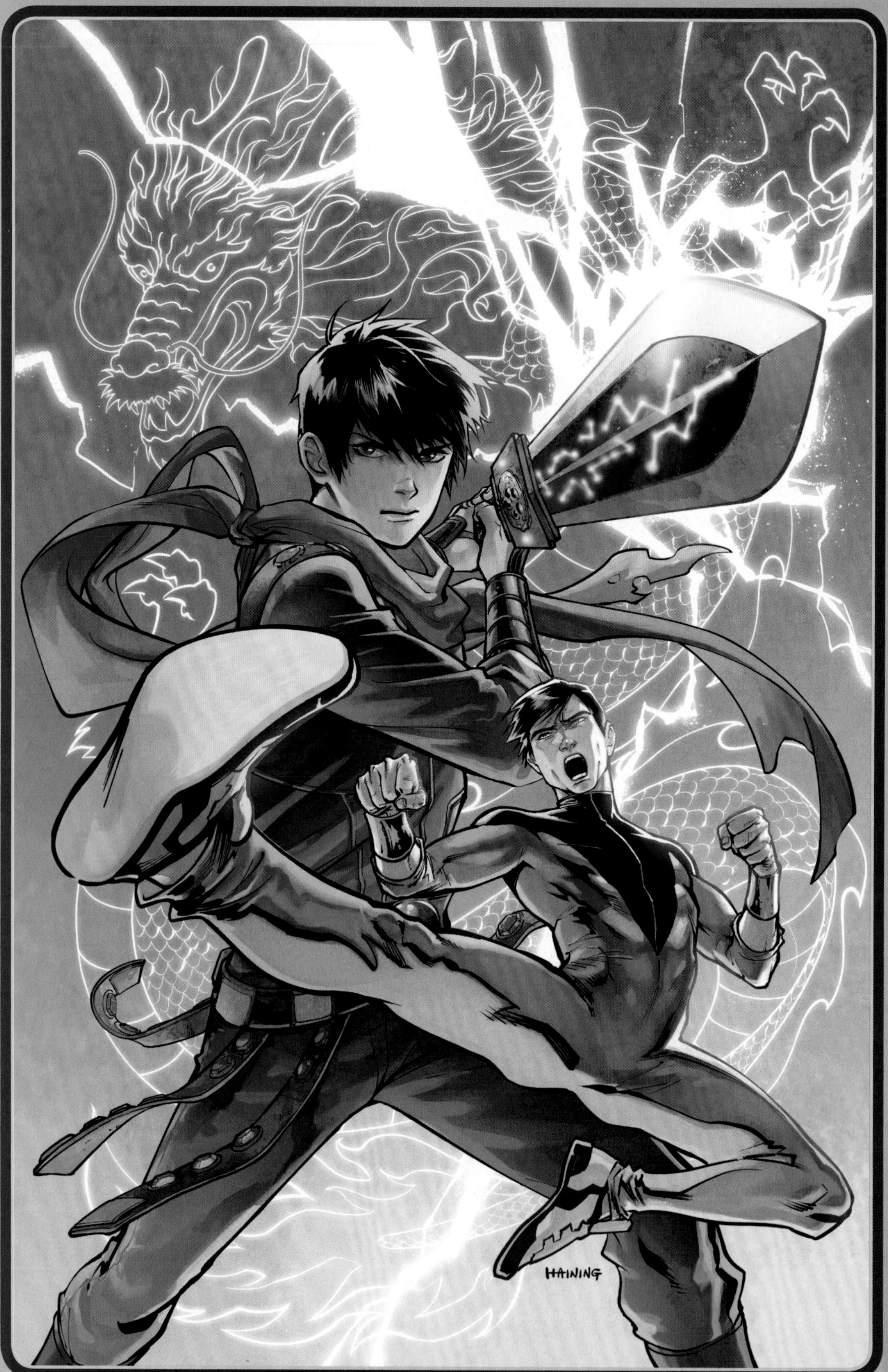
HAINING

SWORD MASTER & SHANG-CHI: MASTER CLASS

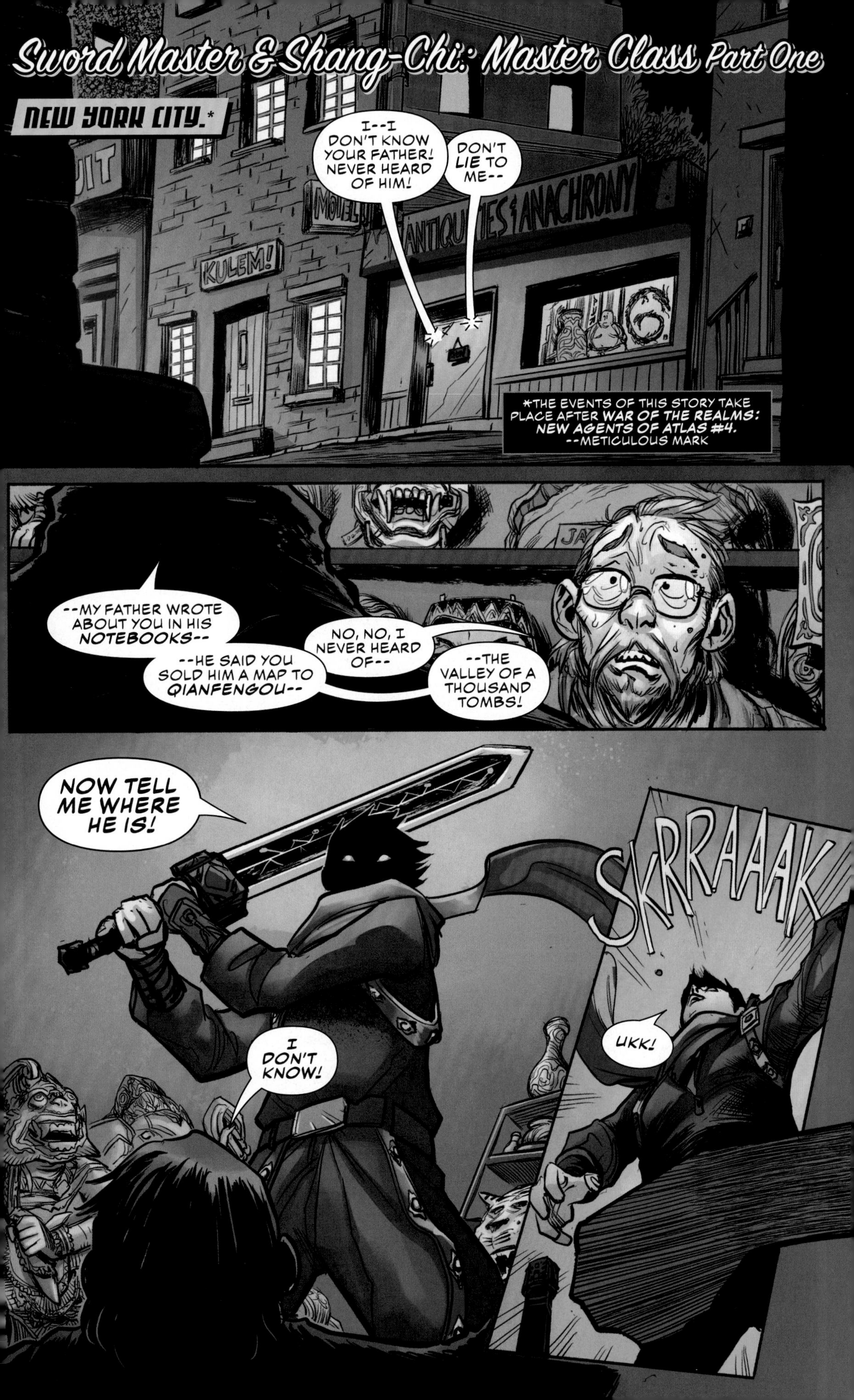
Sword Master & Shang-Chi: Master Class Part One
NEW YORK CITY.*
I--I DON'T KNOW YOUR FATHER! NEVER HEARD OF HIM!
DON'T LIE TO ME--
MOTEL
ANTIQUITIES & ANACHRONY
KULEM!
*THE EVENTS OF THIS STORY TAKE PLACE AFTER WAR OF THE REALMS: NEW AGENTS OF ATLAS #4. --METICULOUS MARK
--MY FATHER WROTE ABOUT YOU IN HIS NOTEBOOKS--
NO, NO, I NEVER HEARD OF--
--HE SAID YOU SOLD HIM A MAP TO QIANFENGOU--
--THE VALLEY OF A THOUSAND TOMBS!
NOW TELL ME WHERE HE IS!
SKRRAAAK
I DON'T KNOW!
UKK!

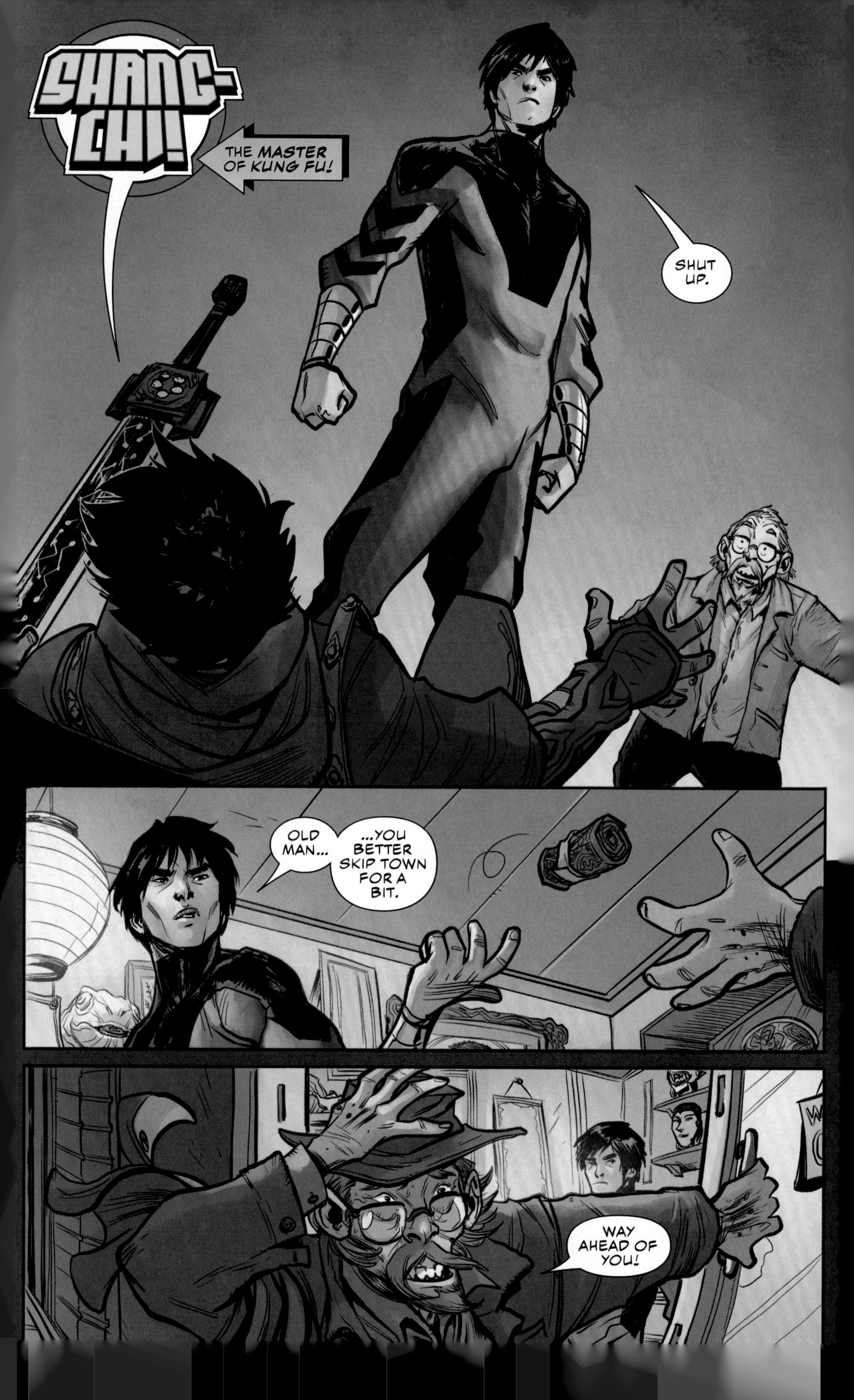
SHANG-CHI!
THE MASTER OF KUNG FU!
SHUT UP.
OLD MAN...
...YOU BETTER SKIP TOWN FOR A BIT.
WAY AHEAD OF YOU!

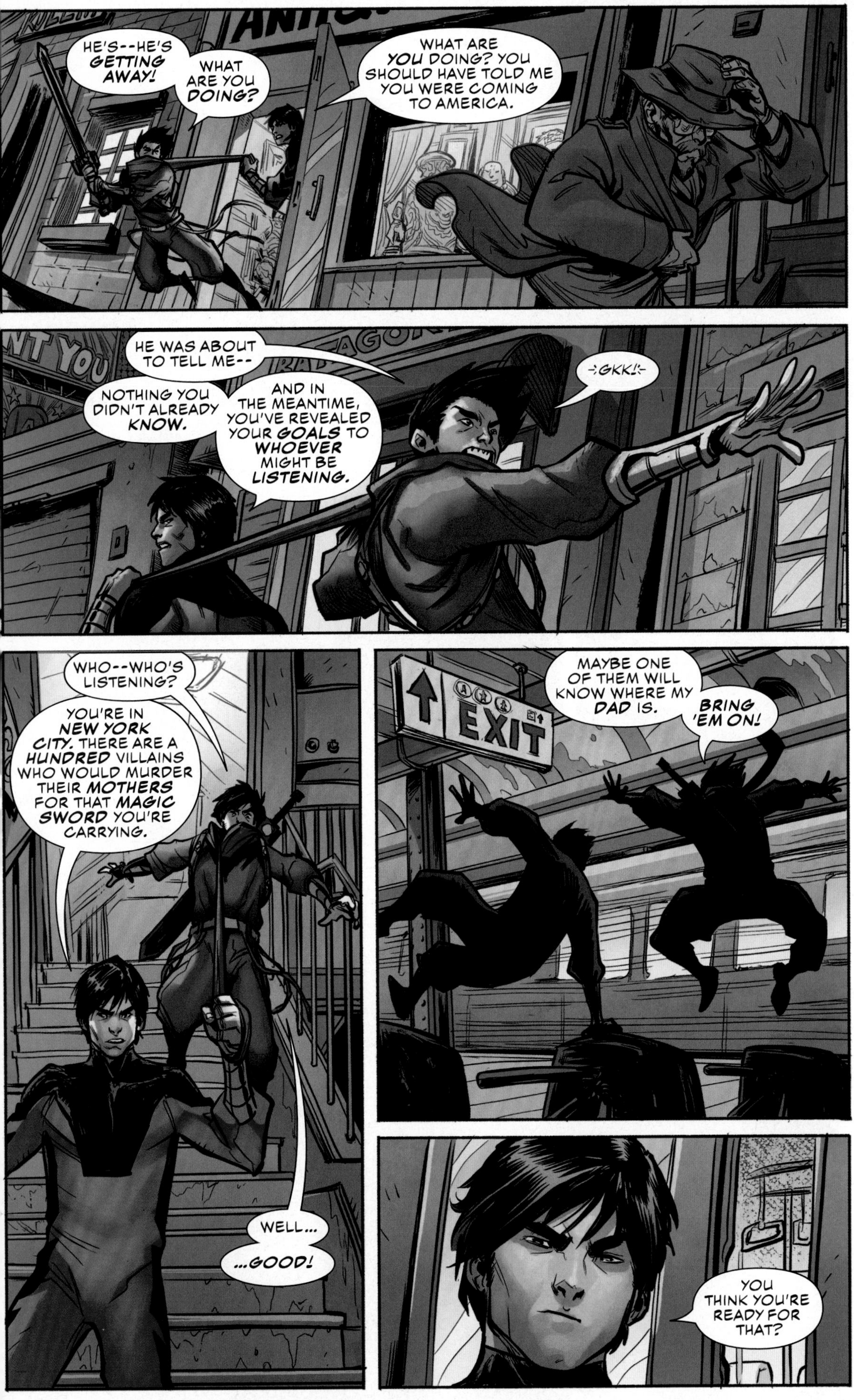
HE'S--HE'S GETTING AWAY!
WHAT ARE YOU DOING?
WHAT ARE YOU DOING? YOU SHOULD HAVE TOLD ME YOU WERE COMING TO AMERICA.
HE WAS ABOUT TO TELL ME--
NOTHING YOU DIDN'T ALREADY KNOW.
AND IN THE MEANTIME, YOU'VE REVEALED YOUR GOALS TO WHOEVER MIGHT BE LISTENING.
GKK!
WHO--WHO'S LISTENING?
YOU'RE IN NEW YORK CITY. THERE ARE A HUNDRED VILLAINS WHO WOULD MURDER THEIR MOTHERS FOR THAT MAGIC SWORD YOU'RE CARRYING.
WELL...
...GOOD!
EXIT
MAYBE ONE OF THEM WILL KNOW WHERE MY DAD IS.
BRING 'EM ON!
YOU THINK YOU'RE READY FOR THAT?

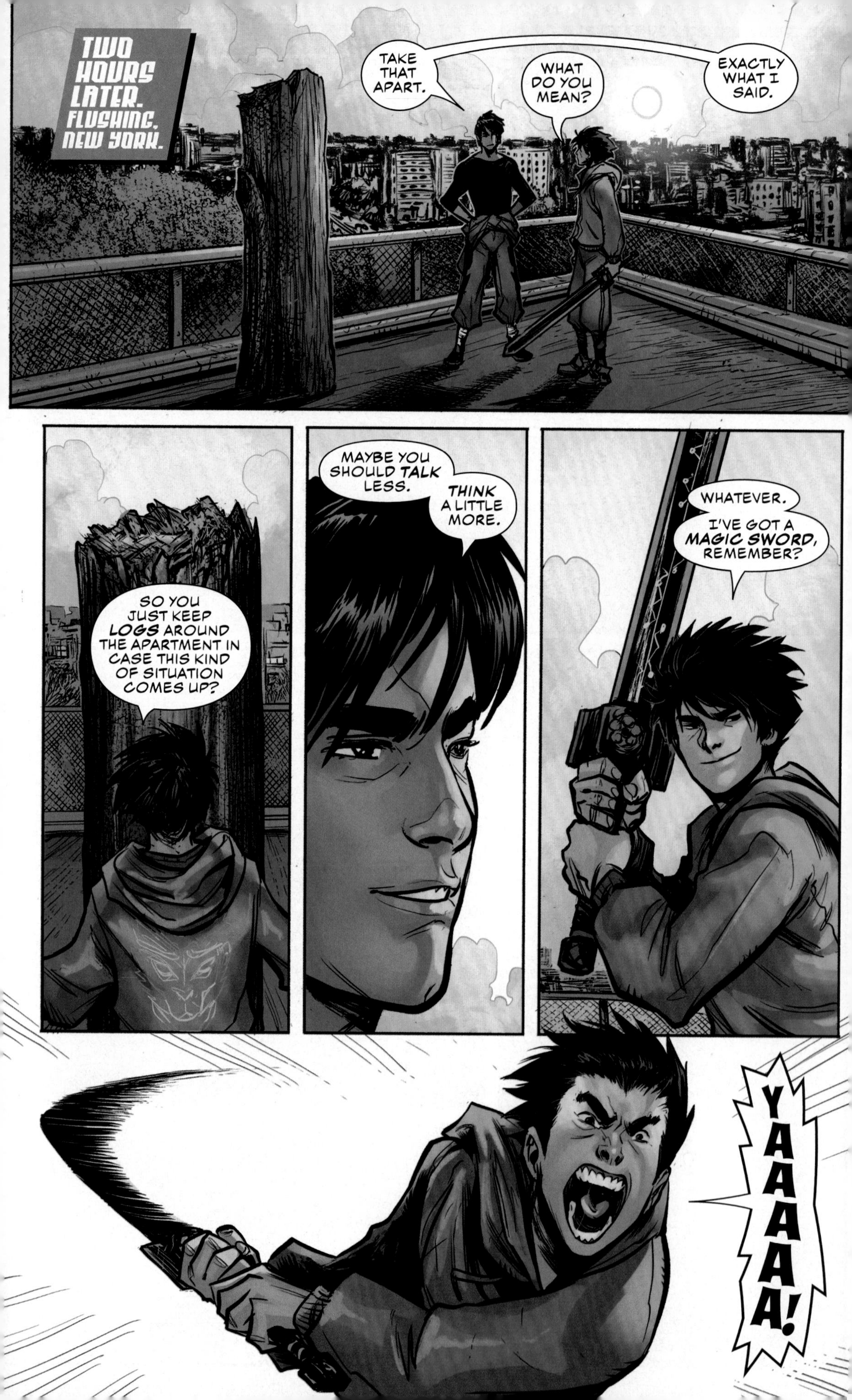
TWO HOURS LATER. FLUSHING, NEW YORK.
TAKE THAT APART.
WHAT DO YOU MEAN?
EXACTLY WHAT I SAID.
SO YOU JUST KEEP LOGS AROUND THE APARTMENT IN CASE THIS KIND OF SITUATION COMES UP?
MAYBE YOU SHOULD TALK LESS.
THINK A LITTLE MORE.
WHATEVER.
I'VE GOT A MAGIC SWORD, REMEMBER?
YAAAAA!

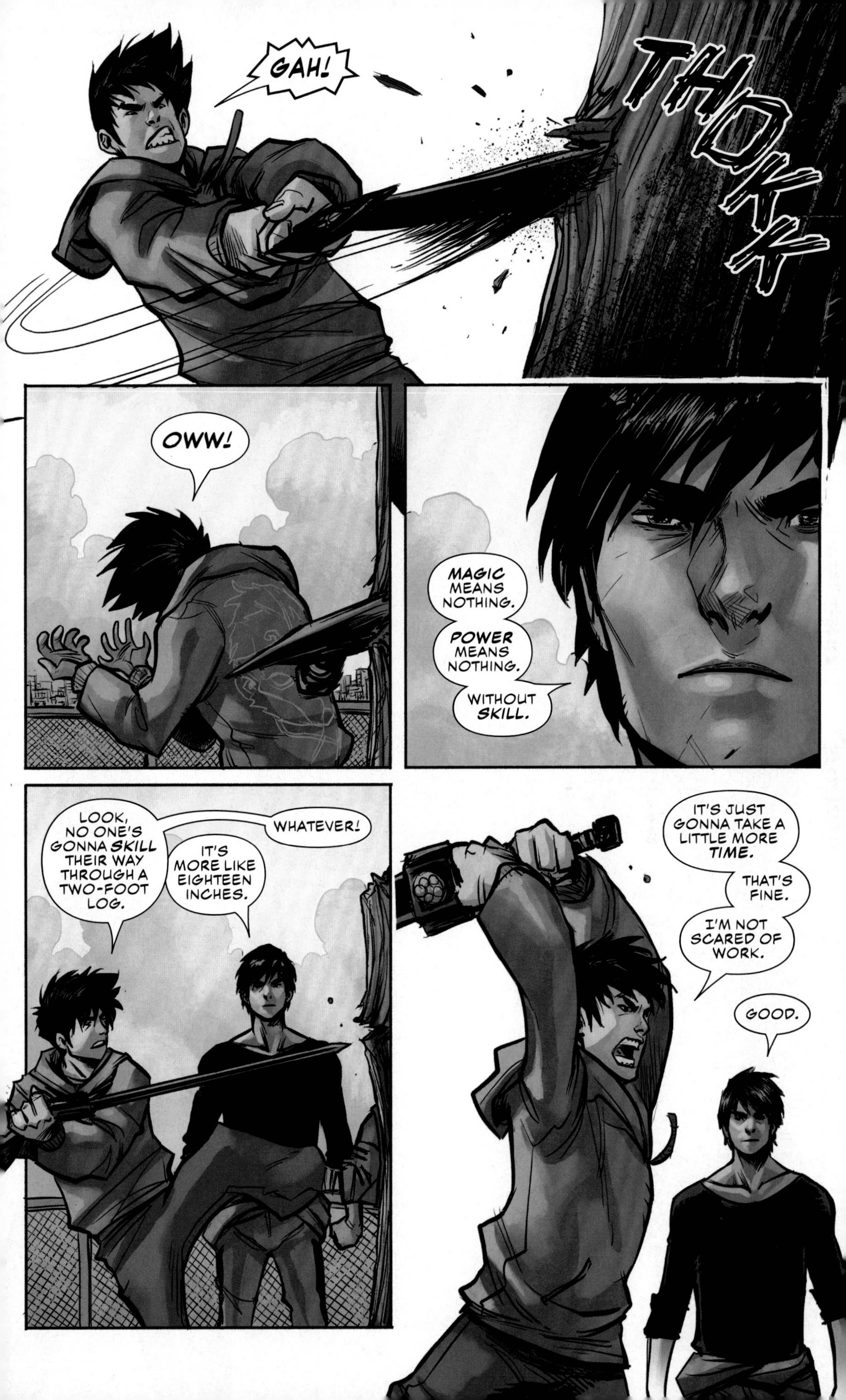
GAH!
THOKK
OWW!
MAGIC MEANS NOTHING.
POWER MEANS NOTHING.
WITHOUT SKILL.
LOOK, NO ONE'S GONNA SKILL THEIR WAY THROUGH A TWO-FOOT LOG.
WHATEVER!
IT'S MORE LIKE EIGHTEEN INCHES.
IT'S JUST GONNA TAKE A LITTLE MORE TIME.
THAT'S FINE.
I'M NOT SCARED OF WORK.
GOOD.

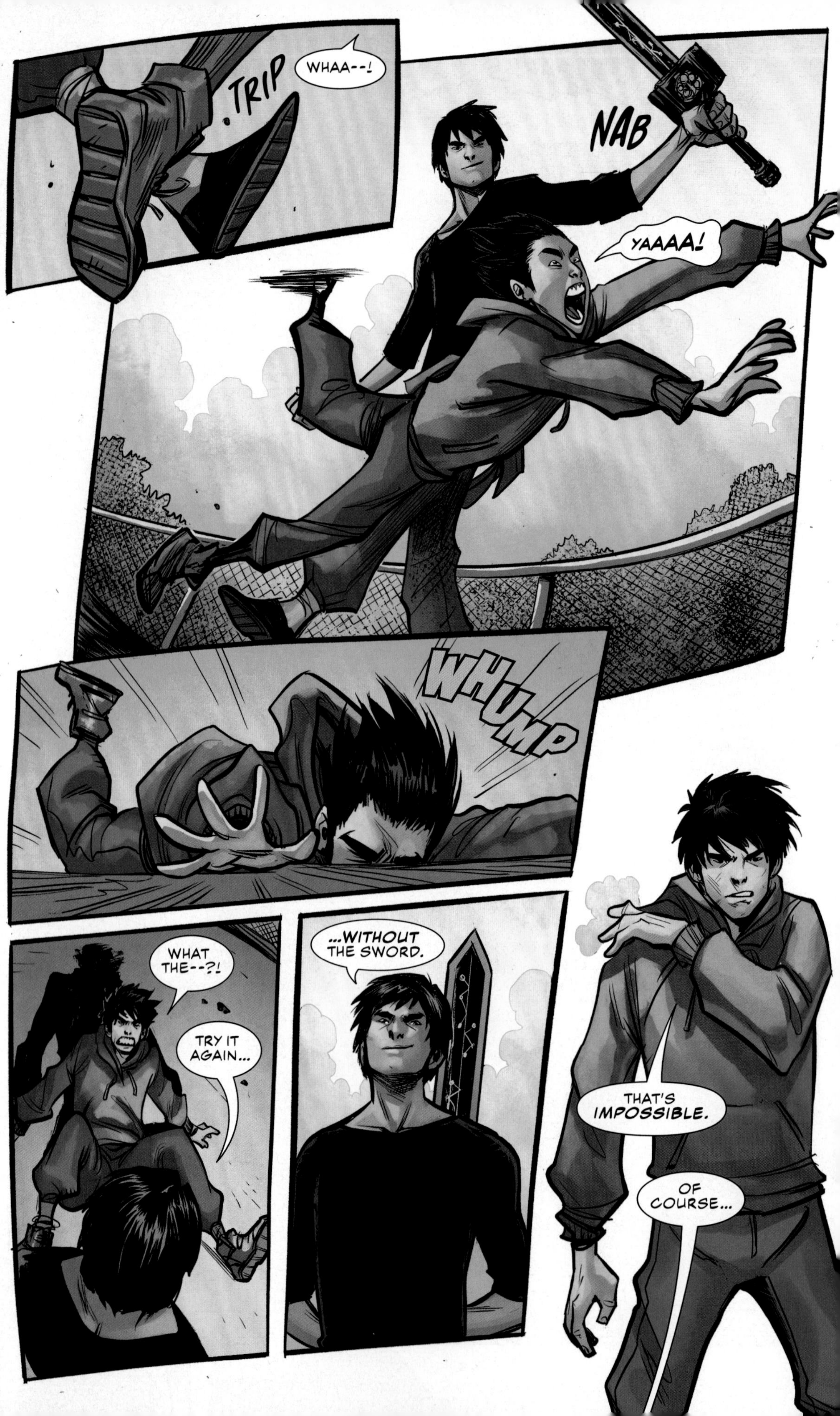
TRIP
WHAA--!
NAB
YAAAA!
WHUMP
WHAT THE--?!
TRY IT AGAIN...
...WITHOUT THE SWORD.
THAT'S IMPOSSIBLE.
OF COURSE...

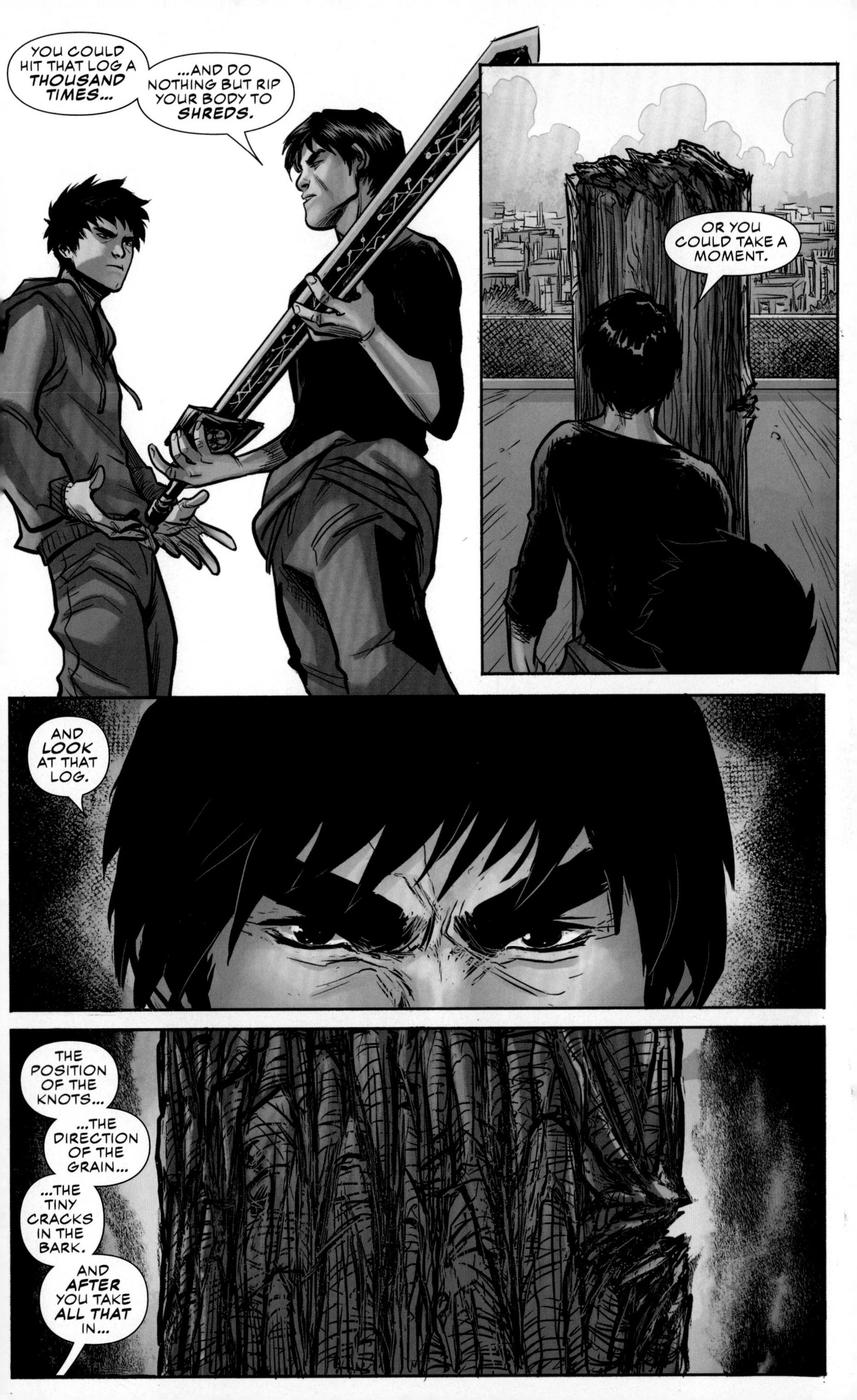
YOU COULD HIT THAT LOG A THOUSAND TIMES...
...AND DO NOTHING BUT RIP YOUR BODY TO SHREDS.
OR YOU COULD TAKE A MOMENT.
AND LOOK AT THAT LOG.
THE POSITION OF THE KNOTS...
...THE DIRECTION OF THE GRAIN...
...THE TINY CRACKS IN THE BARK.
AND AFTER YOU TAKE ALL THAT IN...

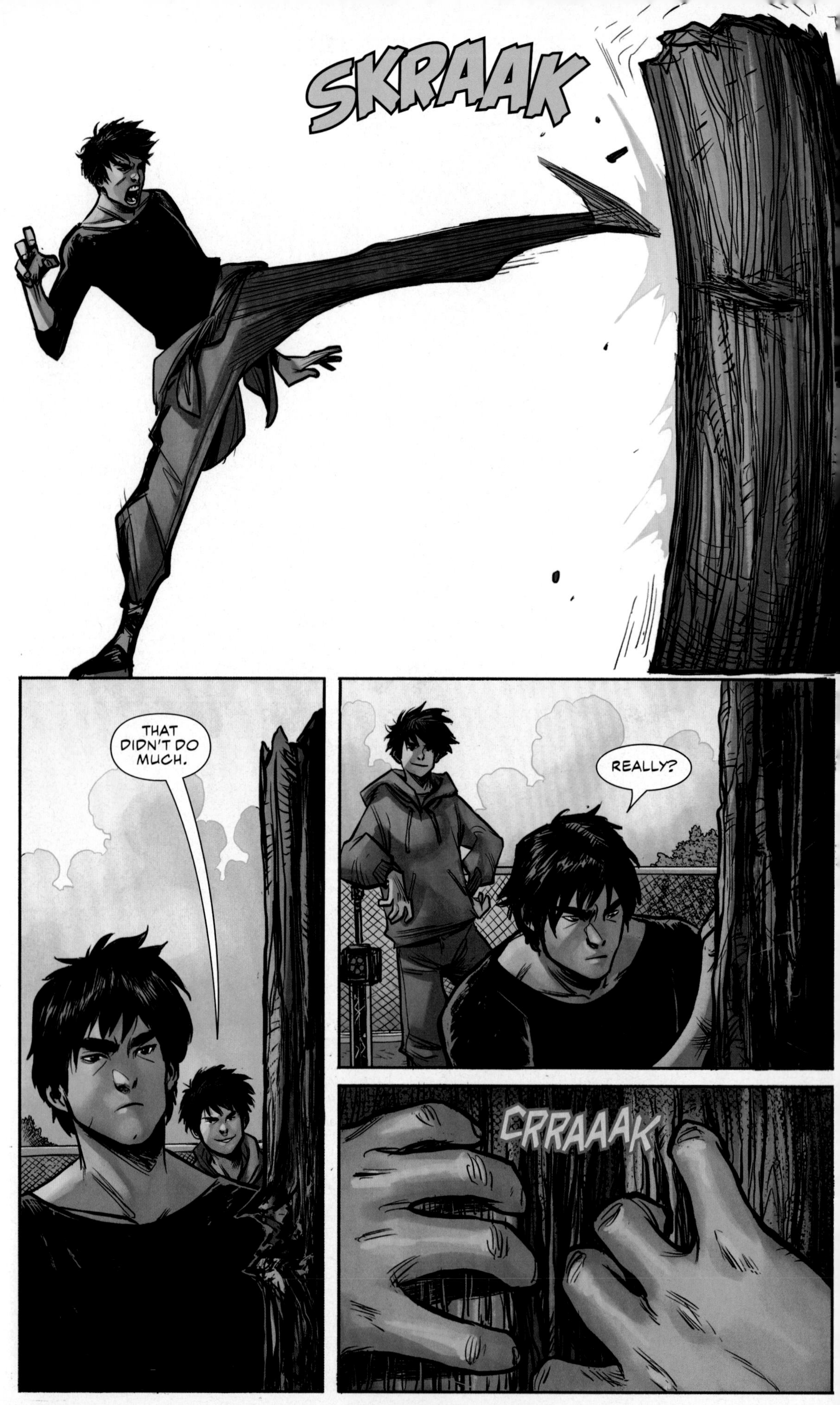
SKRAAK
THAT DIDN'T DO MUCH.
REALLY?
CRRAAK

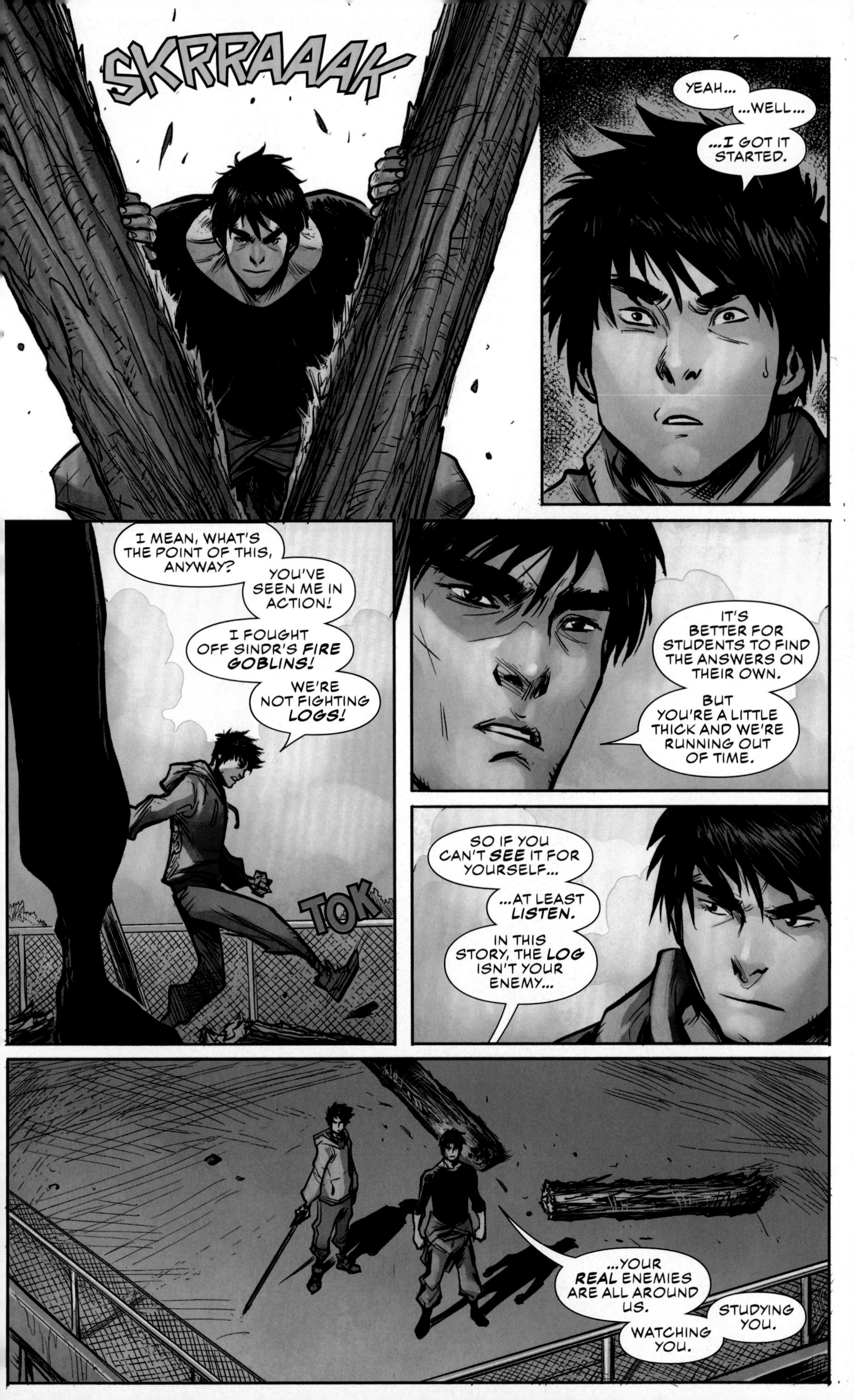
SKRRAAAK
YEAH...
...WELL...
...I GOT IT STARTED.
I MEAN, WHAT'S THE POINT OF THIS, ANYWAY?
YOU'VE SEEN ME IN ACTION!
I FOUGHT OFF SINDR'S FIRE GOBLINS!
WE'RE NOT FIGHTING LOGS!
TOK
IT'S BETTER FOR STUDENTS TO FIND THE ANSWERS ON THEIR OWN.
BUT YOU'RE A LITTLE THICK AND WE'RE RUNNING OUT OF TIME.
SO IF YOU CAN'T SEE IT FOR YOURSELF...
...AT LEAST LISTEN.
IN THIS STORY, THE LOG ISN'T YOUR ENEMY...
...YOUR REAL ENEMIES ARE ALL AROUND US.
WATCHING YOU.
STUDYING YOU.

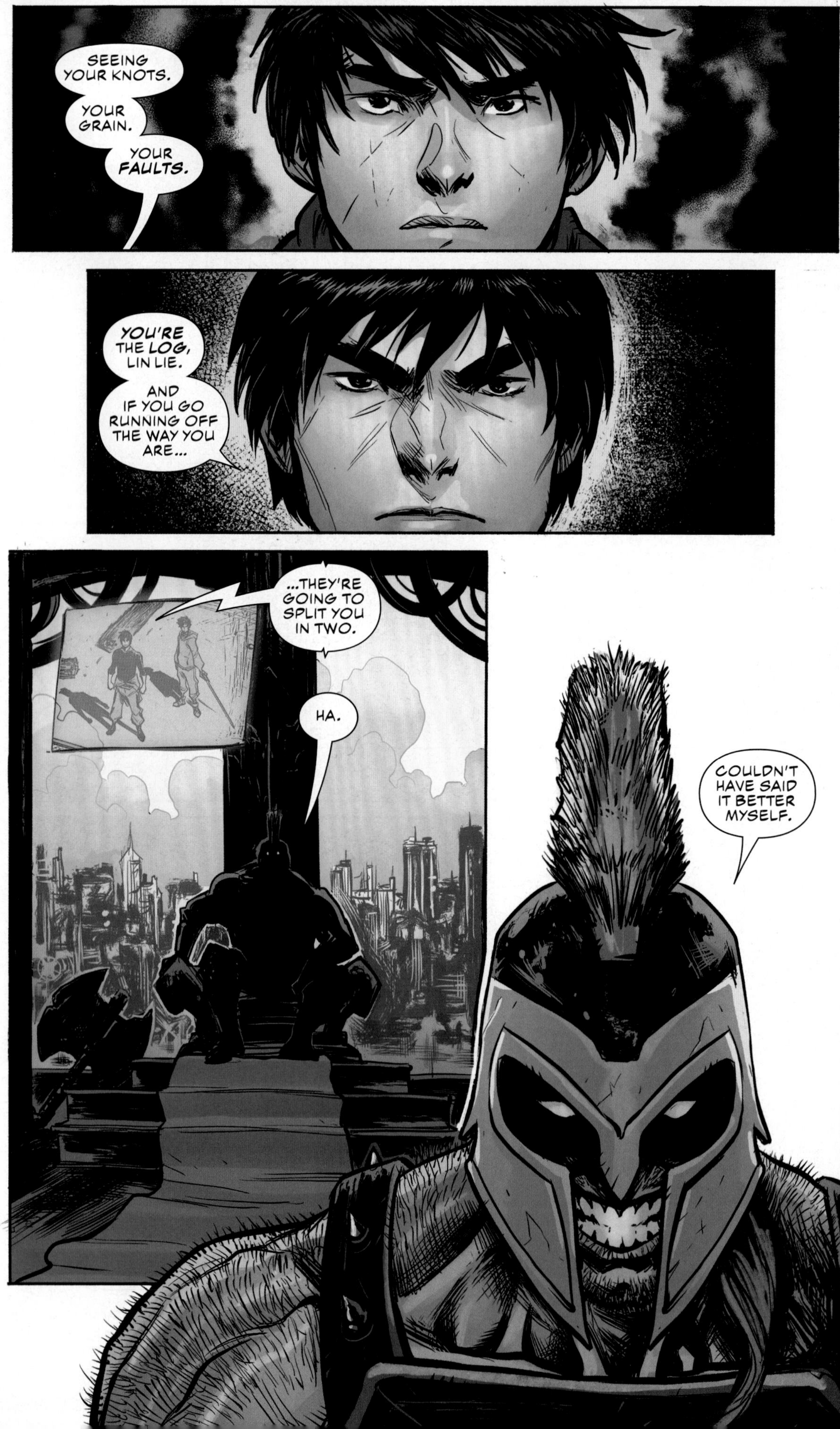
SEEING YOUR KNOTS.
YOUR GRAIN.
YOUR FAULTS.
YOU'RE THE LOG, LIN LIE.
AND IF YOU GO RUNNING OFF THE WAY YOU ARE...
...THEY'RE GOING TO SPLIT YOU IN TWO.
HA.
COULDN'T HAVE SAID IT BETTER MYSELF.

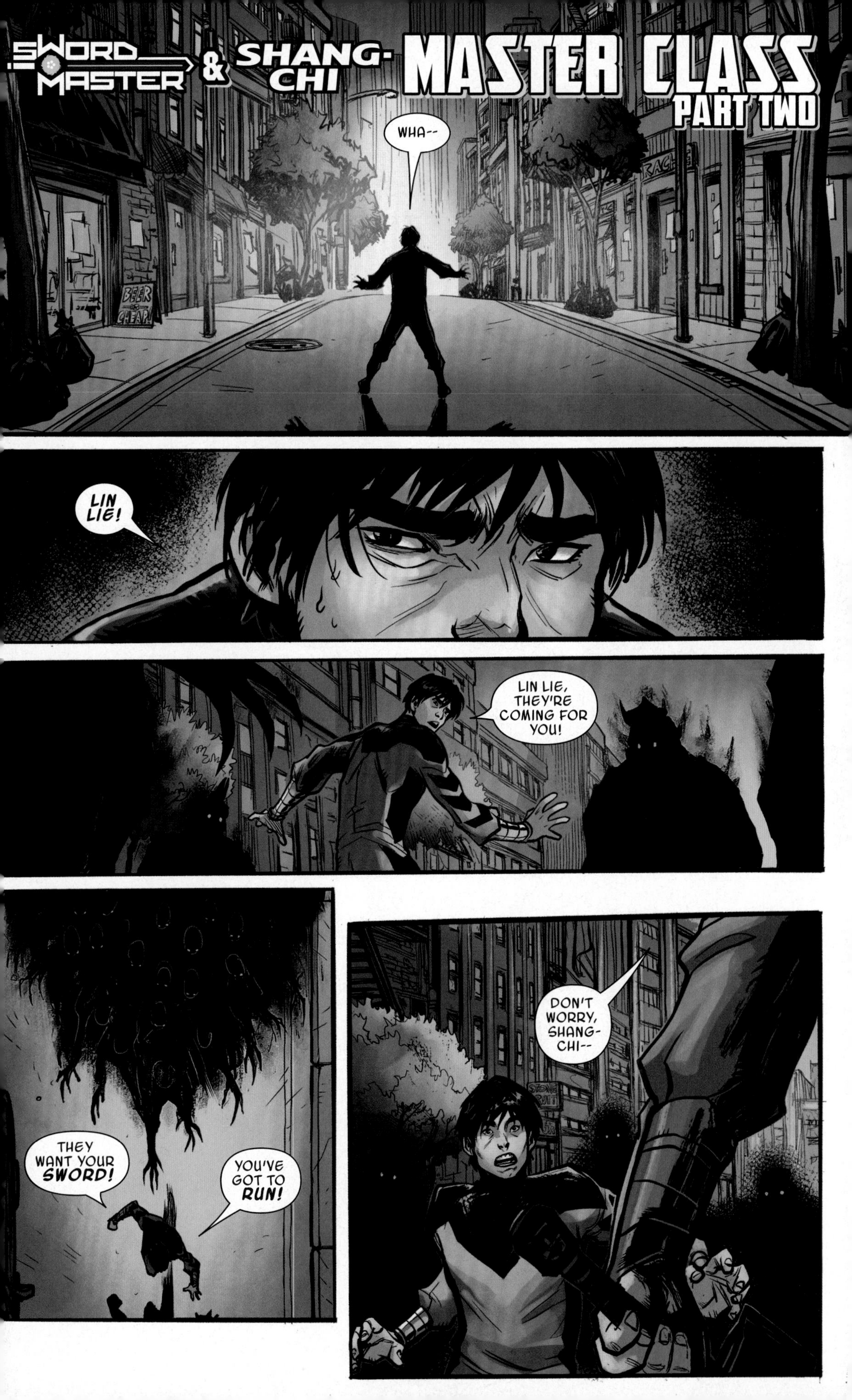
SWORD MASTER & SHANG-CHI
MASTER CLASS
PART TWO
WHA--
BEER IS CHEAP!
LIN LIE!
LIN LIE, THEY'RE COMING FOR YOU!
THEY WANT YOUR SWORD!
YOU'VE GOT TO RUN!
DON'T WORRY, SHANG-CHI--

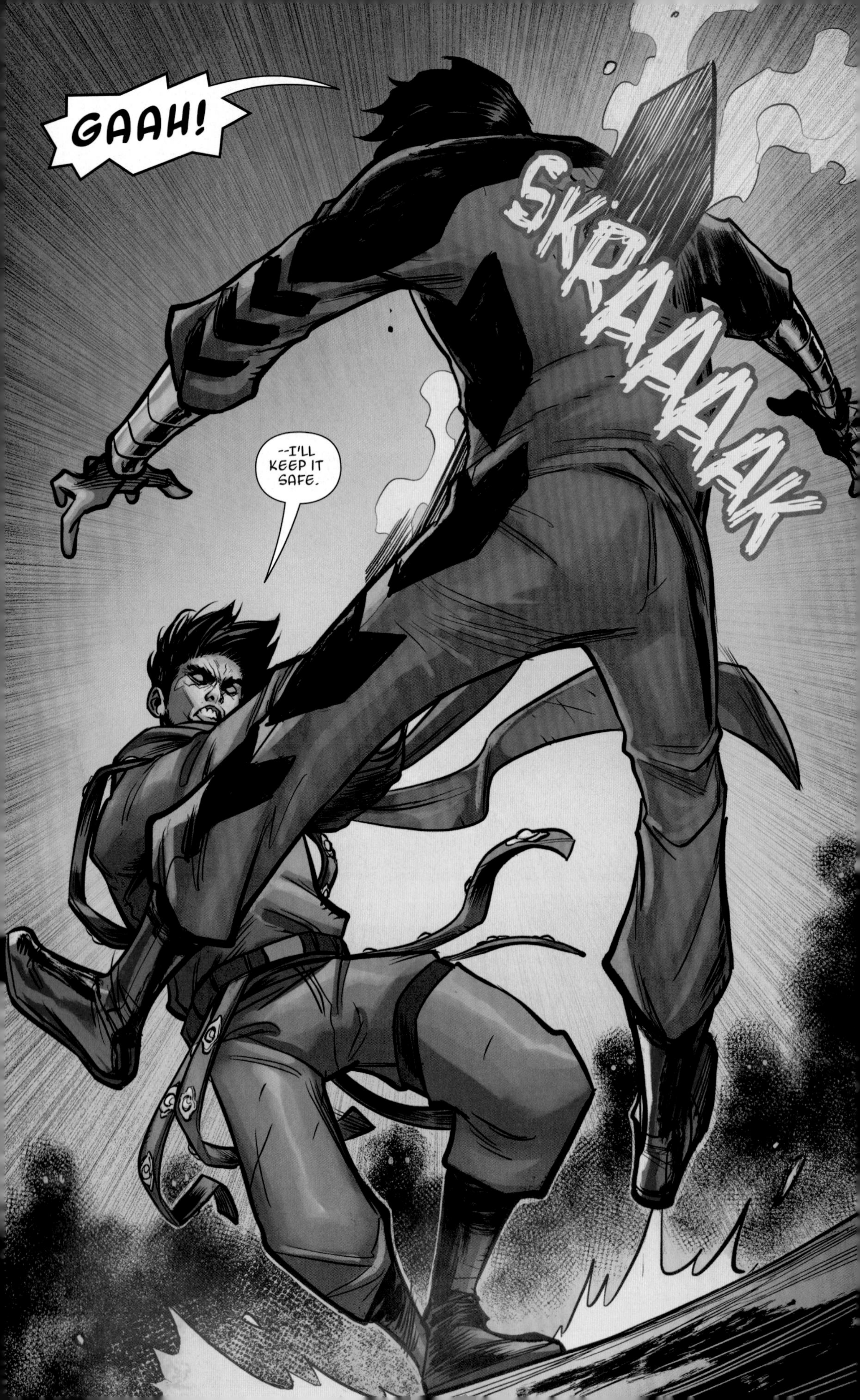
GAAH!
SKRAAAAAK
--I'LL KEEP IT SAFE.

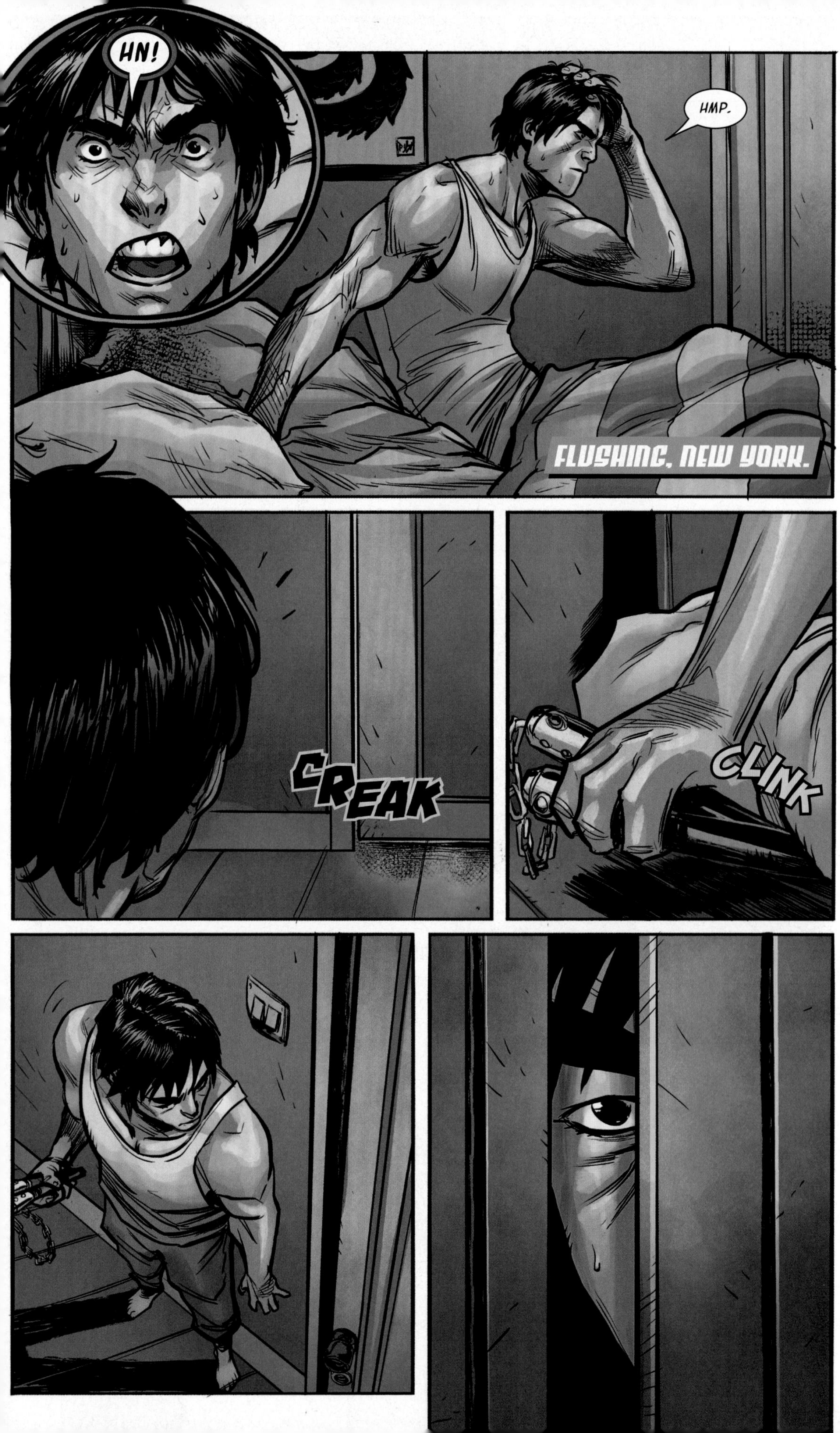
HN!
HMP.
FLUSHING, NEW YORK.
CREAK
CLINK

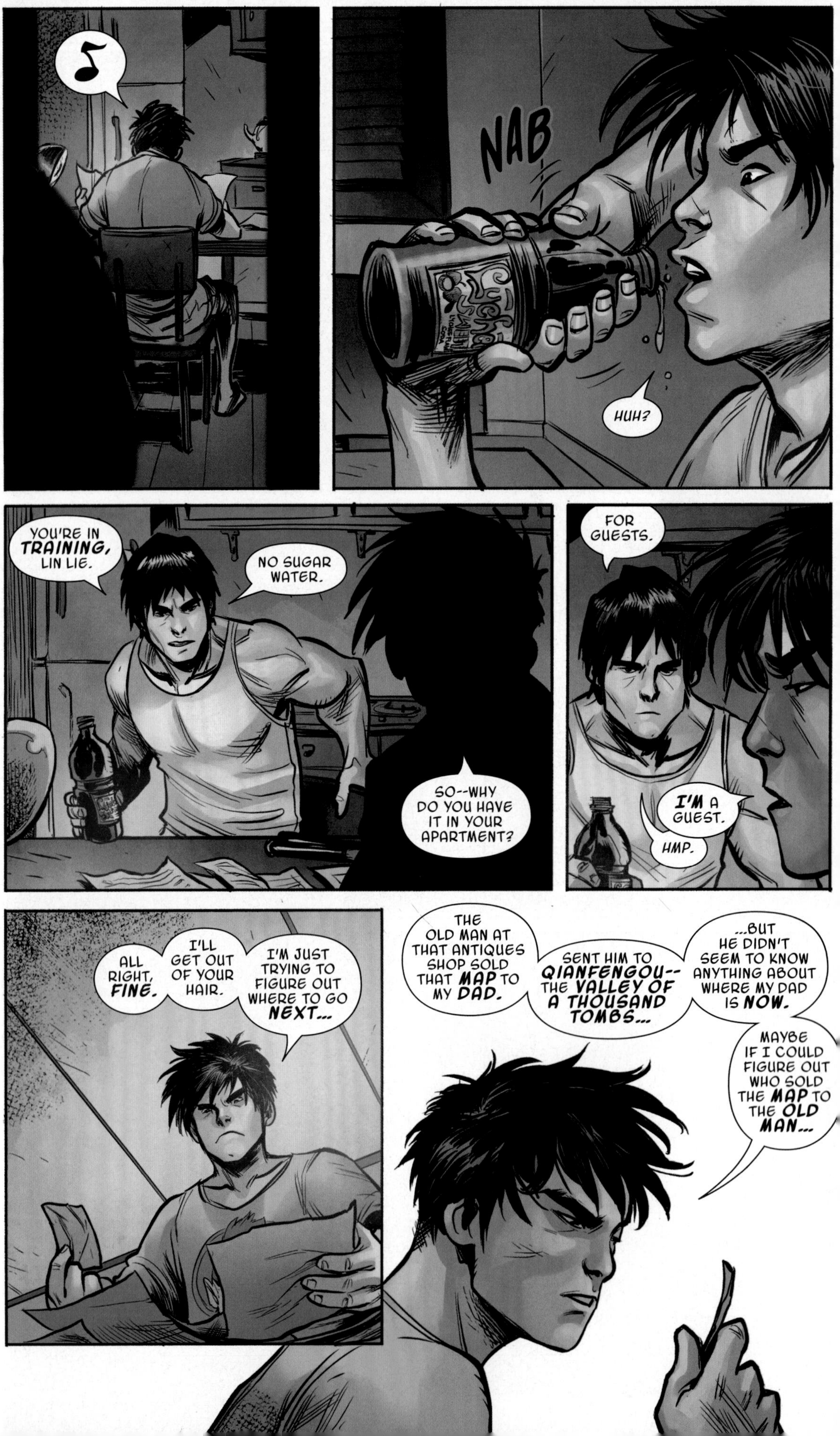
NAB
HUH?
YOU'RE IN TRAINING, LIN LIE.
NO SUGAR WATER.
SO--WHY DO YOU HAVE IT IN YOUR APARTMENT?
FOR GUESTS.
I'M A GUEST.
HMP.
ALL RIGHT, FINE.
I'LL GET OUT OF YOUR HAIR.
I'M JUST TRYING TO FIGURE OUT WHERE TO GO NEXT...
THE OLD MAN AT THAT ANTIQUES SHOP SOLD THAT MAP TO MY DAD.
SENT HIM TO QIANFENGOU--THE VALLEY OF A THOUSAND TOMBS...
...BUT HE DIDN'T SEEM TO KNOW ANYTHING ABOUT WHERE MY DAD IS NOW.
MAYBE IF I COULD FIGURE OUT WHO SOLD THE MAP TO THE OLD MAN...

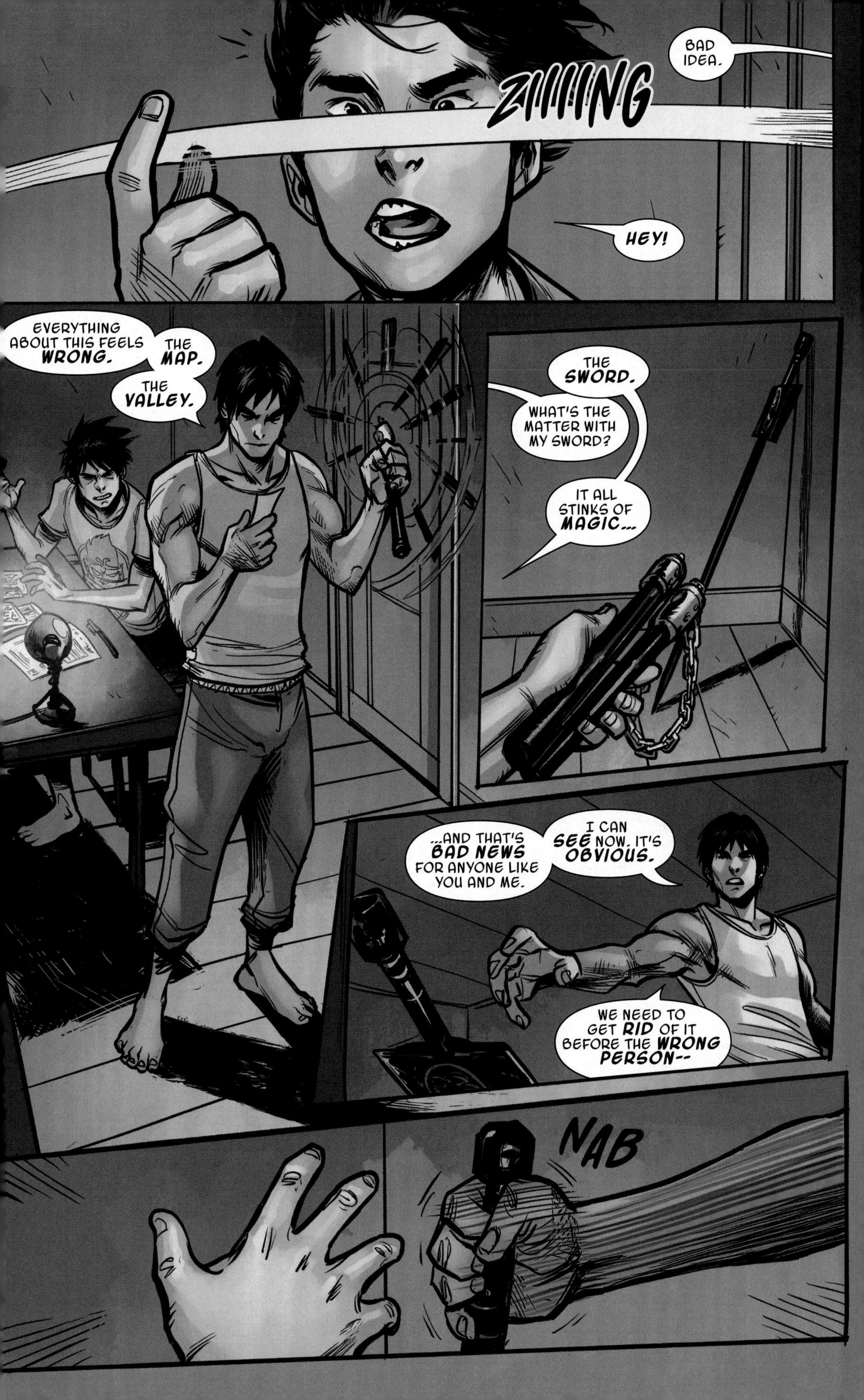
BAD IDEA.
ZIIIING
HEY!
EVERYTHING ABOUT THIS FEELS WRONG.
THE MAP.
THE VALLEY.
THE SWORD.
WHAT'S THE MATTER WITH MY SWORD?
IT ALL STINKS OF MAGIC...
I CAN SEE NOW. IT'S OBVIOUS.
...AND THAT'S BAD NEWS FOR ANYONE LIKE YOU AND ME.
WE NEED TO GET RID OF IT BEFORE THE WRONG PERSON--
NAB

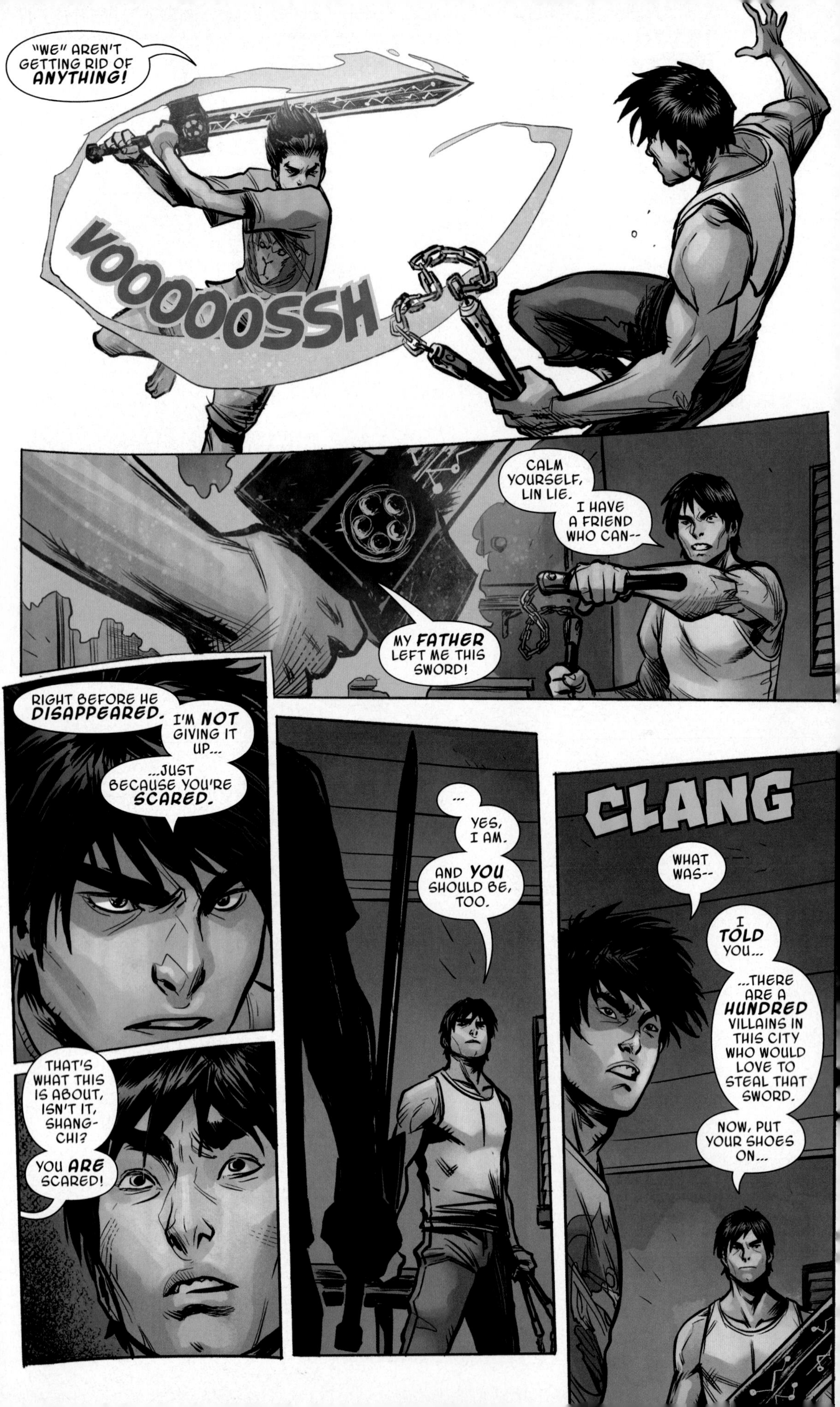
"WE" AREN'T GETTING RID OF ANYTHING!
VOOOOOOSSH
CALM YOURSELF, LIN LIE.
I HAVE A FRIEND WHO CAN--
MY FATHER LEFT ME THIS SWORD!
RIGHT BEFORE HE DISAPPEARED.
I'M NOT GIVING IT UP...
...JUST BECAUSE YOU'RE SCARED.
THAT'S WHAT THIS IS ABOUT, ISN'T IT, SHANG-CHI?
YOU ARE SCARED!
...
YES, I AM.
AND YOU SHOULD BE, TOO.
CLANG
WHAT WAS--
I TOLD YOU...
...THERE ARE A HUNDRED VILLAINS IN THIS CITY WHO WOULD LOVE TO STEAL THAT SWORD.
NOW, PUT YOUR SHOES ON...

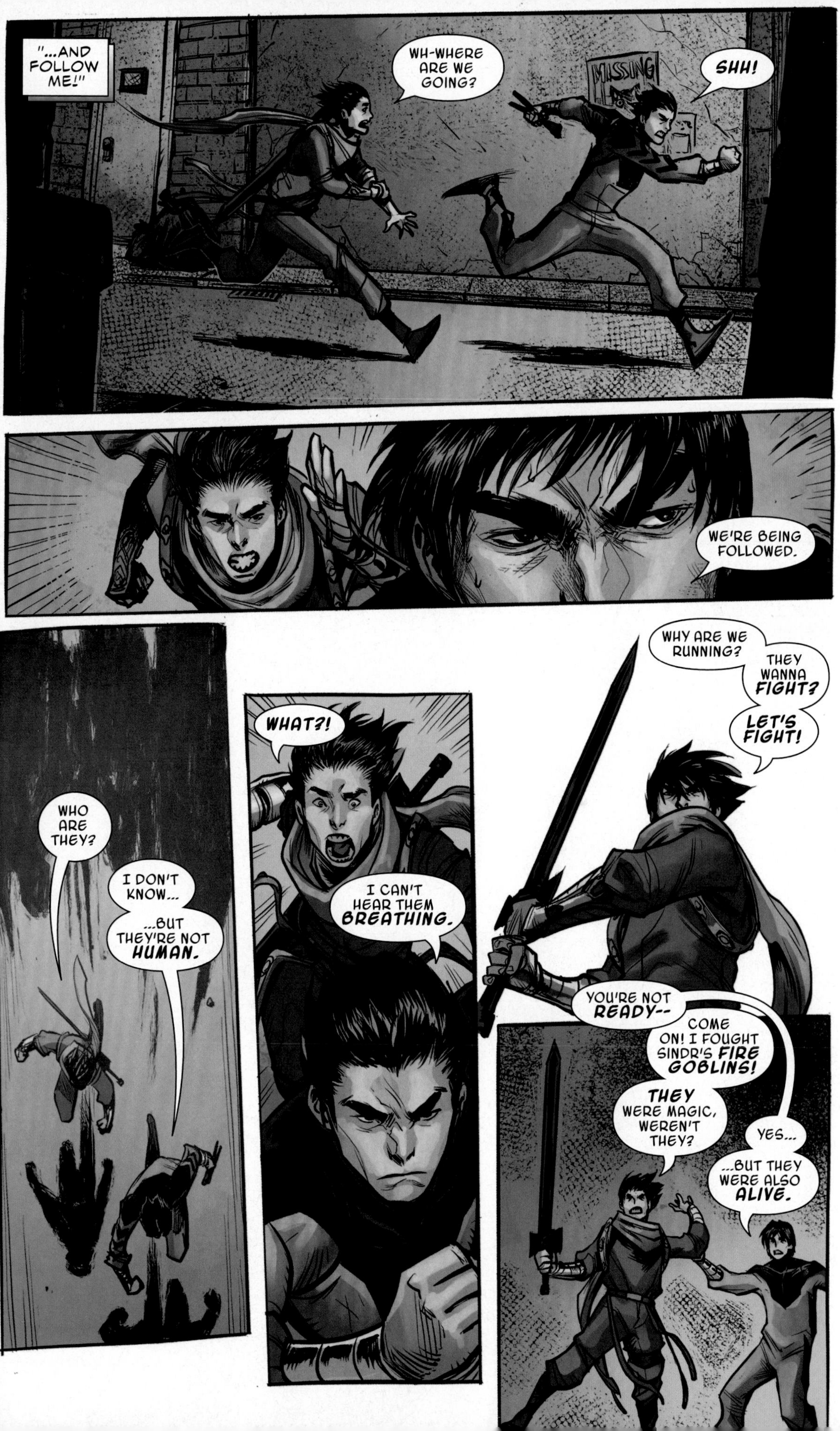
"...AND FOLLOW ME!"
WH-WHERE ARE WE GOING?
SHH!
WE'RE BEING FOLLOWED.
WHO ARE THEY?
I DON'T KNOW...
...BUT THEY'RE NOT HUMAN.
WHAT?!
I CAN'T HEAR THEM BREATHING.
WHY ARE WE RUNNING?
THEY WANNA FIGHT?
LET'S FIGHT!
YOU'RE NOT READY--
COME ON! I FOUGHT SINDR'S FIRE GOBLINS!
THEY WERE MAGIC, WEREN'T THEY?
YES...
...BUT THEY WERE ALSO ALIVE.

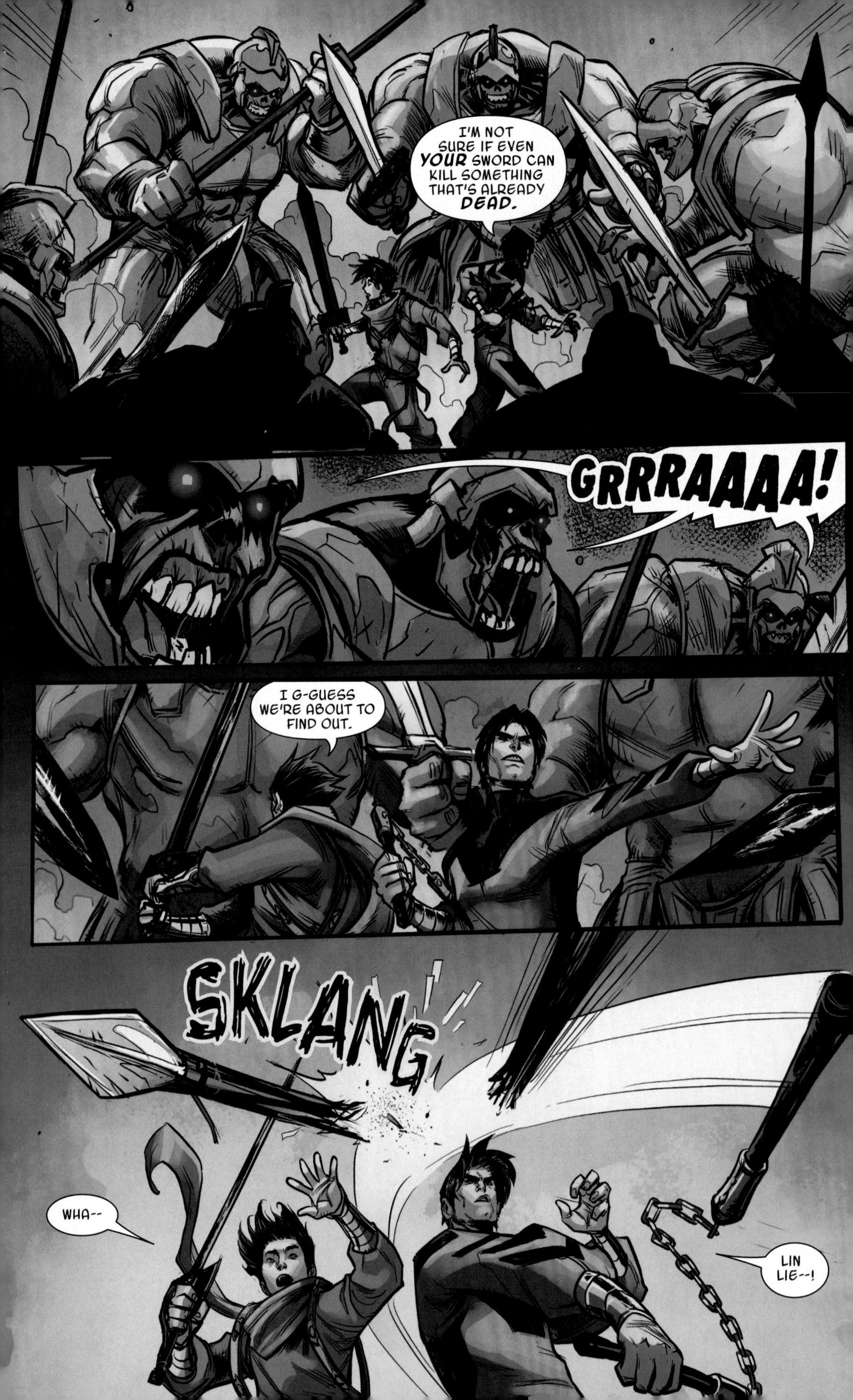
I'M NOT SURE IF EVEN YOUR SWORD CAN KILL SOMETHING THAT'S ALREADY DEAD.
GRRRAAAA!
I G-GUESS WE'RE ABOUT TO FIND OUT.
SKLANG
WHA--
LIN LIE--!

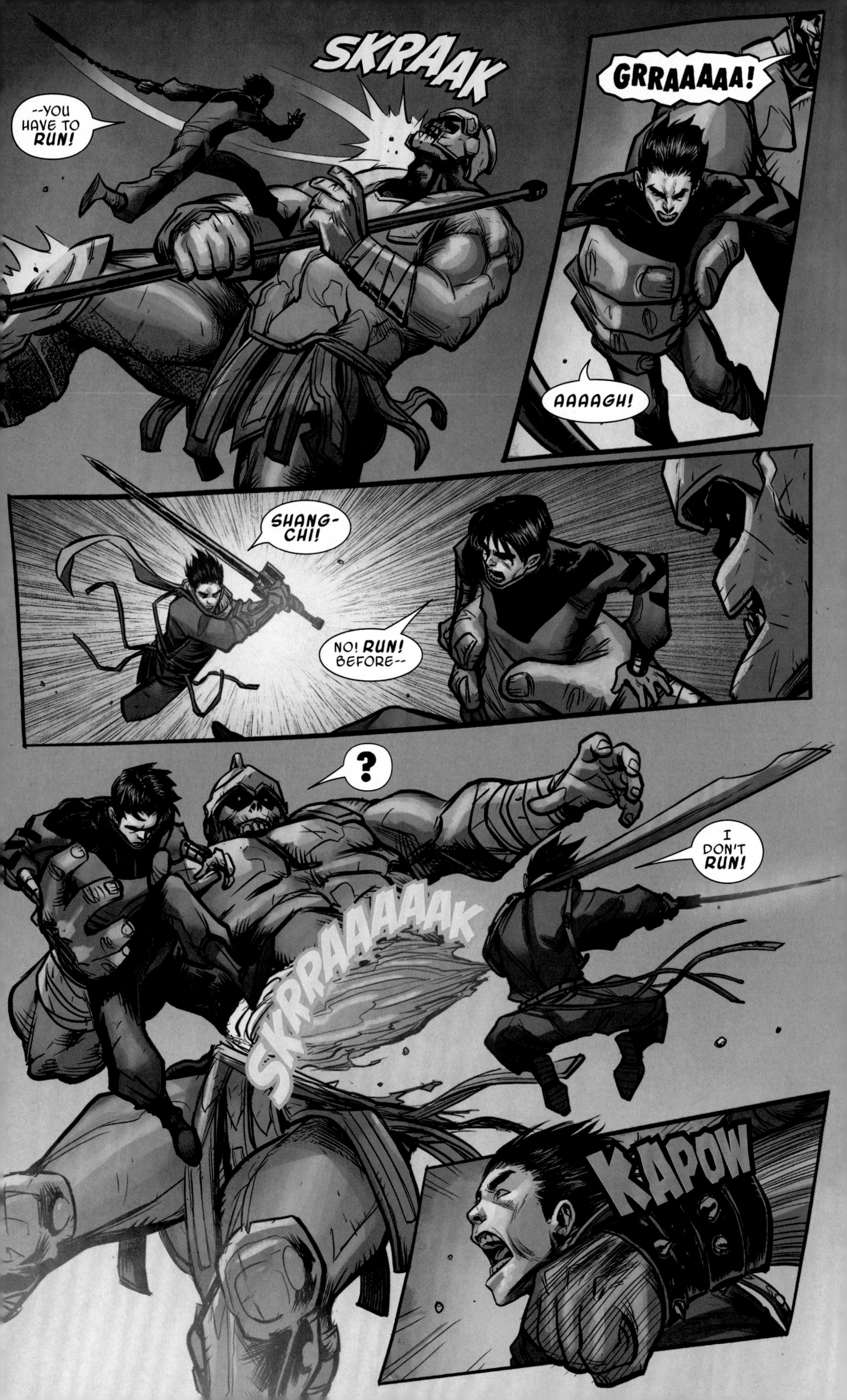
SKRAAK
--YOU HAVE TO RUN!
GRRAAAAA!
AAAAGH!
SHANG-CHI!
NO! RUN! BEFORE--
?
I DON'T RUN!
SKRRAAAAAK
KAPOW

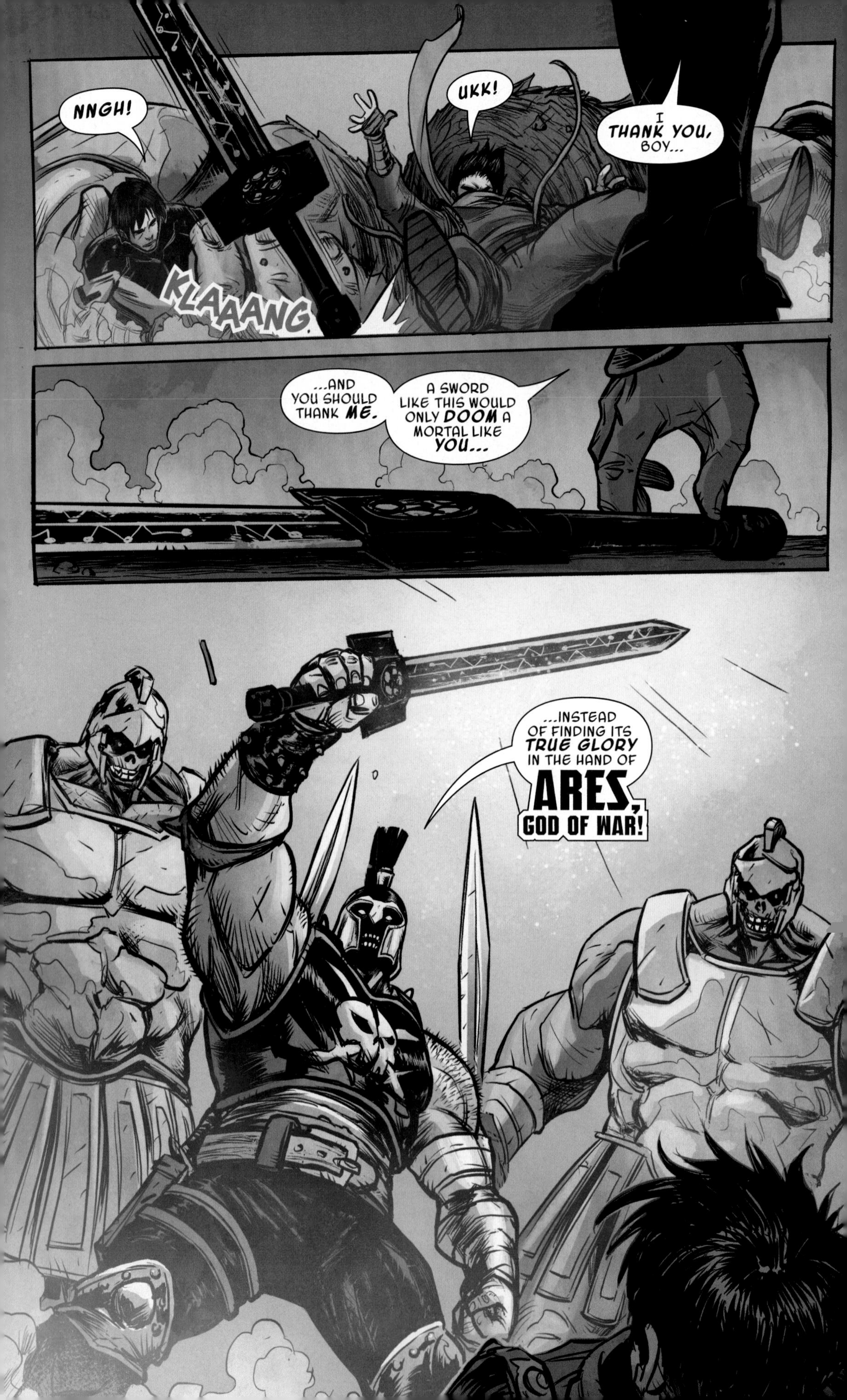

NNGH!
UKK!
I THANK YOU, BOY...
KLAAANG
...AND YOU SHOULD THANK ME.
A SWORD LIKE THIS WOULD ONLY DOOM A MORTAL LIKE YOU...
...INSTEAD OF FINDING ITS TRUE GLORY IN THE HAND OF
ARES, GOD OF WAR!

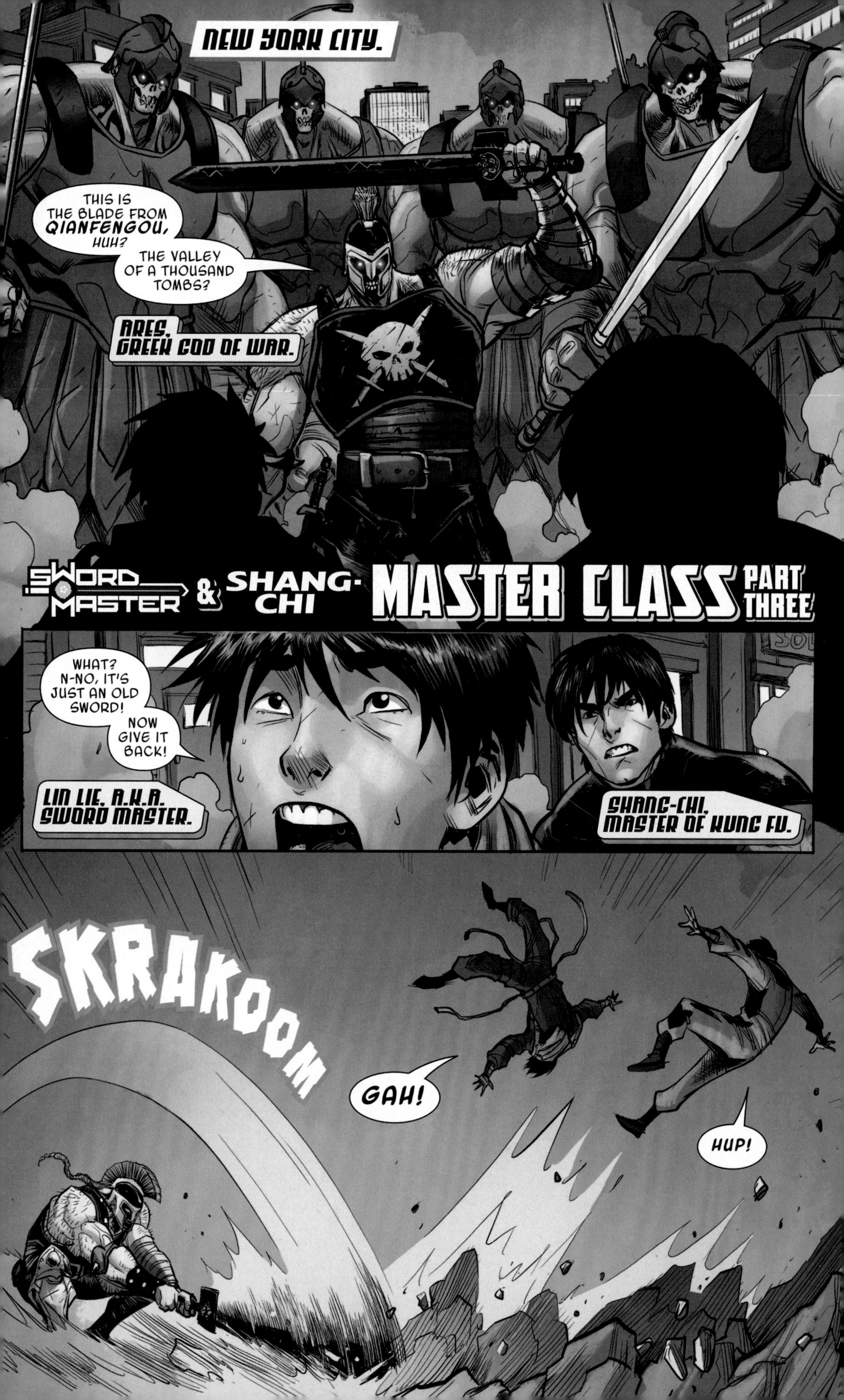
NEW YORK CITY.
THIS IS THE BLADE FROM QIANFENGOU, HUH?
THE VALLEY OF A THOUSAND TOMBS?
ARES, GREEK GOD OF WAR.
SWORD MASTER & SHANG-CHI
MASTER CLASS PART THREE
WHAT? N-NO, IT'S JUST AN OLD SWORD!
NOW GIVE IT BACK!
LIN LIE, A.K.A. SWORD MASTER.
SHANG-CHI, MASTER OF KUNG FU.
SKRAKOOM
GAH!
HUP!

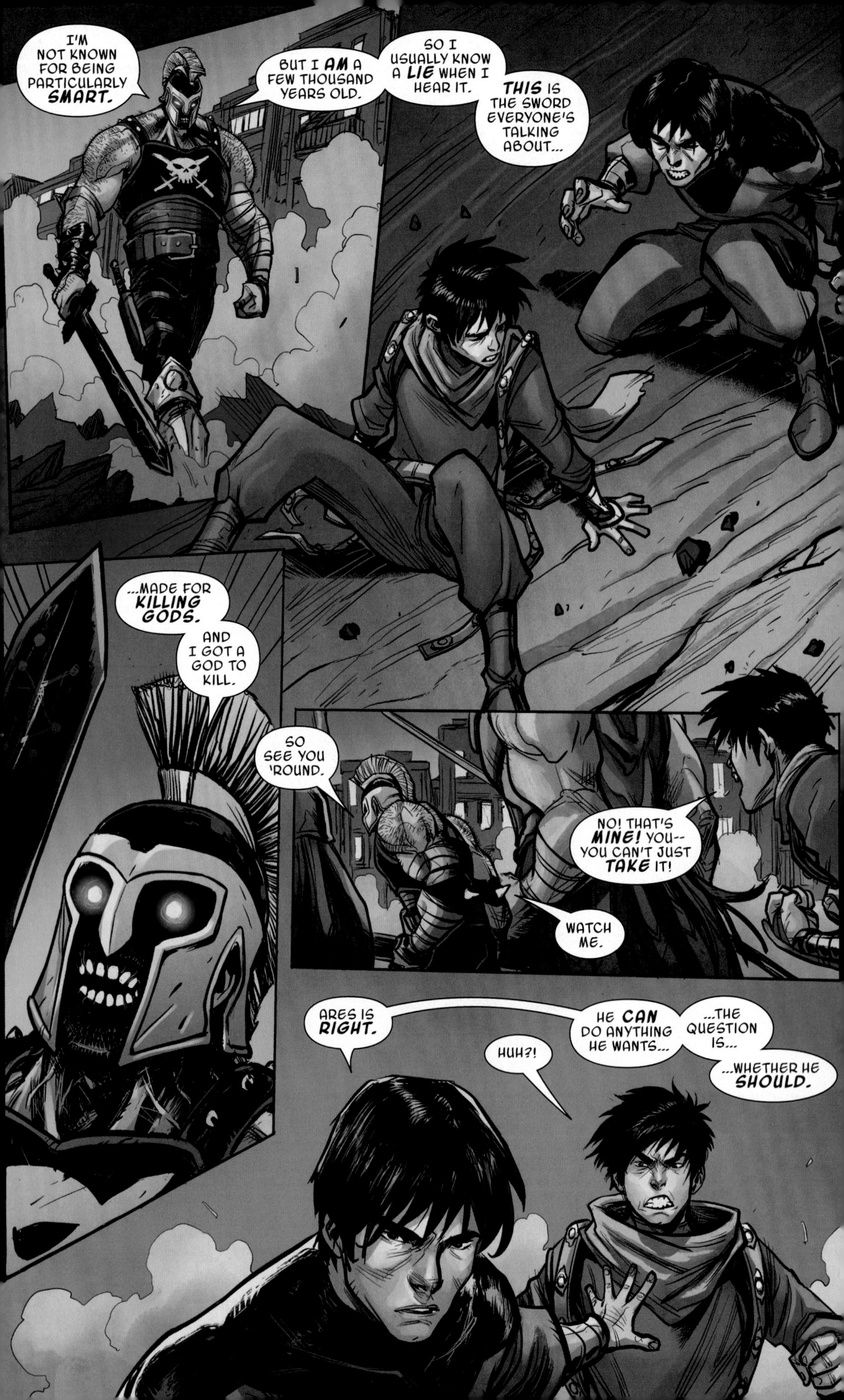
I'M NOT KNOWN FOR BEING PARTICULARLY SMART.
BUT I AM A FEW THOUSAND YEARS OLD.
SO I USUALLY KNOW A LIE WHEN I HEAR IT.
THIS IS THE SWORD EVERYONE'S TALKING ABOUT...
...MADE FOR KILLING GODS.
AND I GOT A GOD TO KILL.
SO SEE YOU 'ROUND.
NO! THAT'S MINE! YOU-- YOU CAN'T JUST TAKE IT!
WATCH ME.
ARES IS RIGHT.
HE CAN DO ANYTHING HE WANTS...
HUH?!
...THE QUESTION IS...
...WHETHER HE SHOULD.

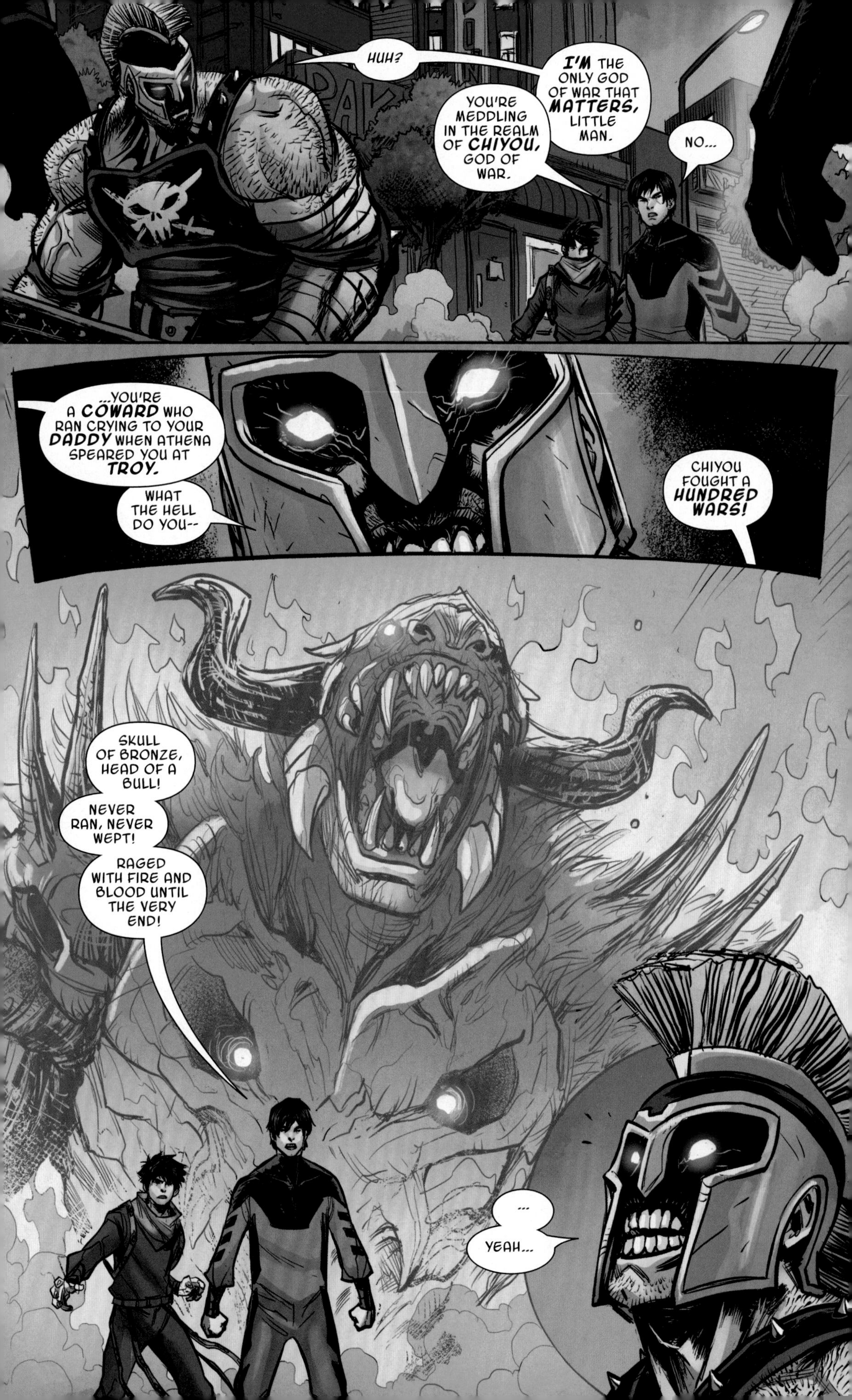
HUH?
YOU'RE MEDDLING IN THE REALM OF CHIYOU, GOD OF WAR.
I'M THE ONLY GOD OF WAR THAT MATTERS, LITTLE MAN.
NO...
...YOU'RE A COWARD WHO RAN CRYING TO YOUR DADDY WHEN ATHENA SPEARED YOU AT TROY.
WHAT THE HELL DO YOU--
CHIYOU FOUGHT A HUNDRED WARS!
SKULL OF BRONZE, HEAD OF A BULL!
NEVER RAN, NEVER WEPT!
RAGED WITH FIRE AND BLOOD UNTIL THE VERY END!
...
YEAH...

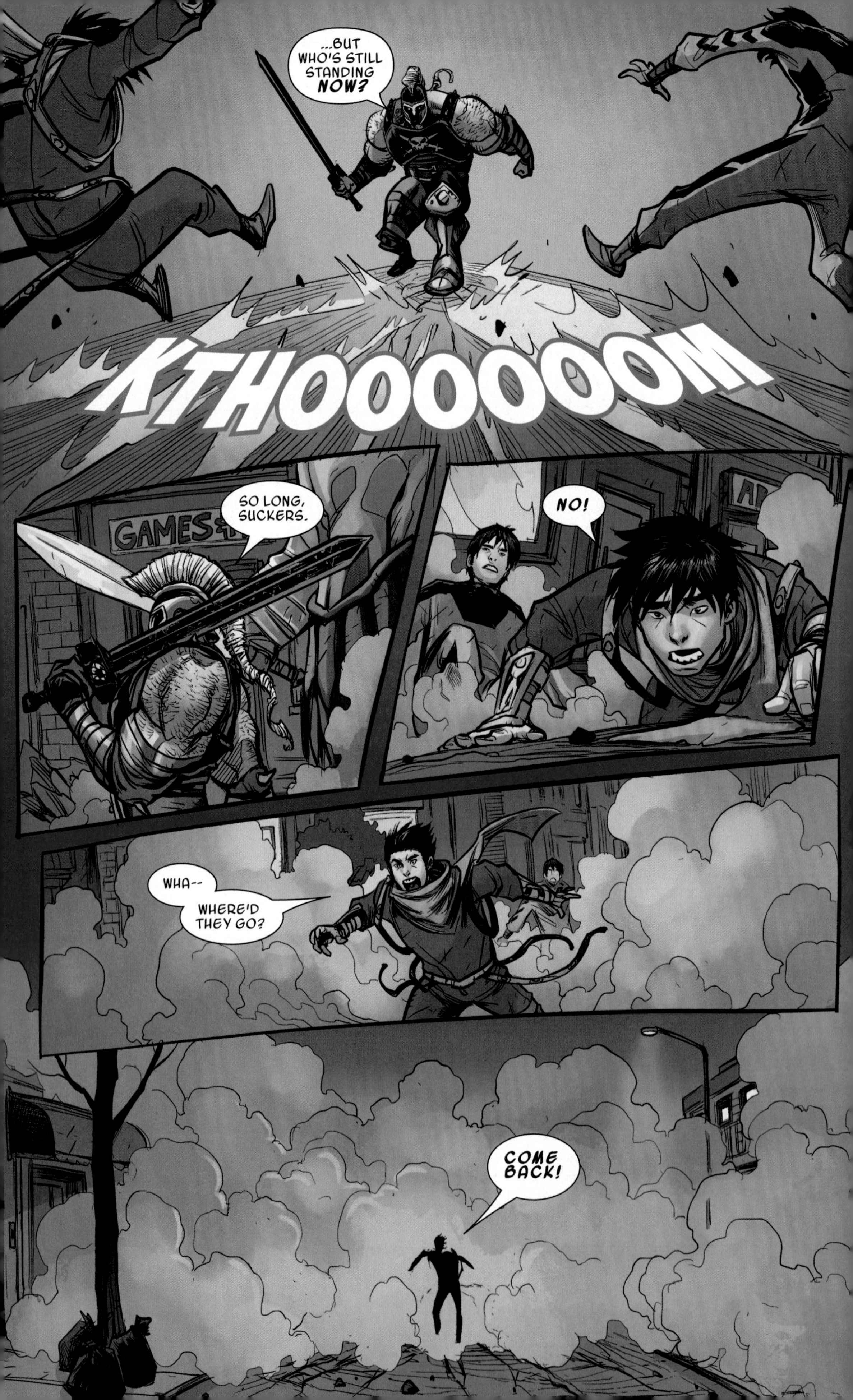
...BUT WHO'S STILL STANDING NOW?
KTHOOOOOOOM
SO LONG, SUCKERS.
NO!
WHA--
WHERE'D THEY GO?
COME BACK!

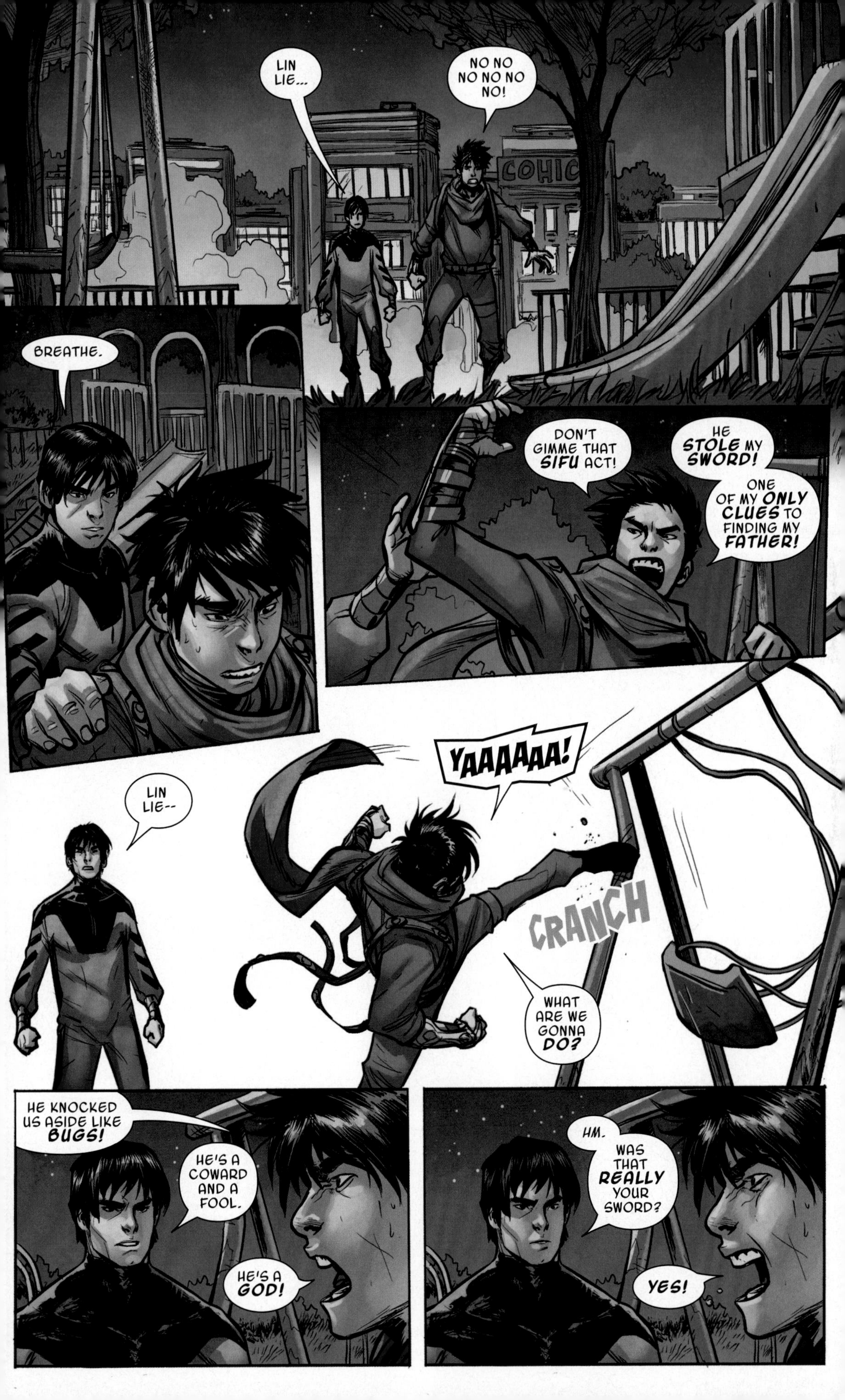
LIN LIE...
NO NO NO NO NO NO NO!
COMIC
BREATHE.
DON'T GIMME THAT SIFU ACT!
HE STOLE MY SWORD!
ONE OF MY ONLY CLUES TO FINDING MY FATHER!
LIN LIE--
YAAAAAA!
CRANCH
WHAT ARE WE GONNA DO?
HE KNOCKED US ASIDE LIKE BUGS!
HE'S A COWARD AND A FOOL.
HE'S A GOD!
HM.
WAS THAT REALLY YOUR SWORD?
YES!

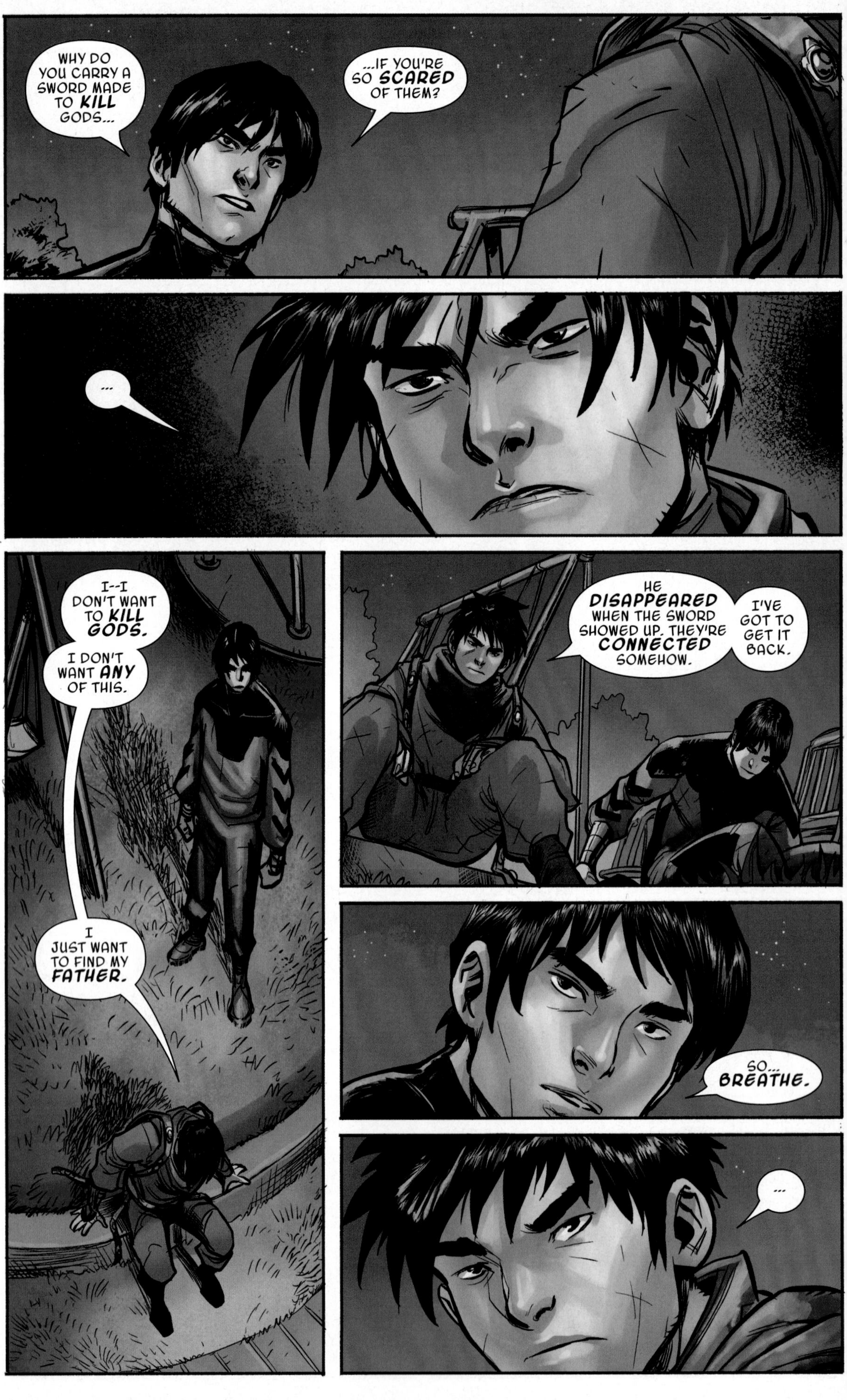
WHY DO YOU CARRY A SWORD MADE TO KILL GODS...
...IF YOU'RE SO SCARED OF THEM?
...
I--I DON'T WANT TO KILL GODS.
I DON'T WANT ANY OF THIS.
I JUST WANT TO FIND MY FATHER.
HE DISAPPEARED WHEN THE SWORD SHOWED UP. THEY'RE CONNECTED SOMEHOW.
I'VE GOT TO GET IT BACK.
SO... BREATHE.
...

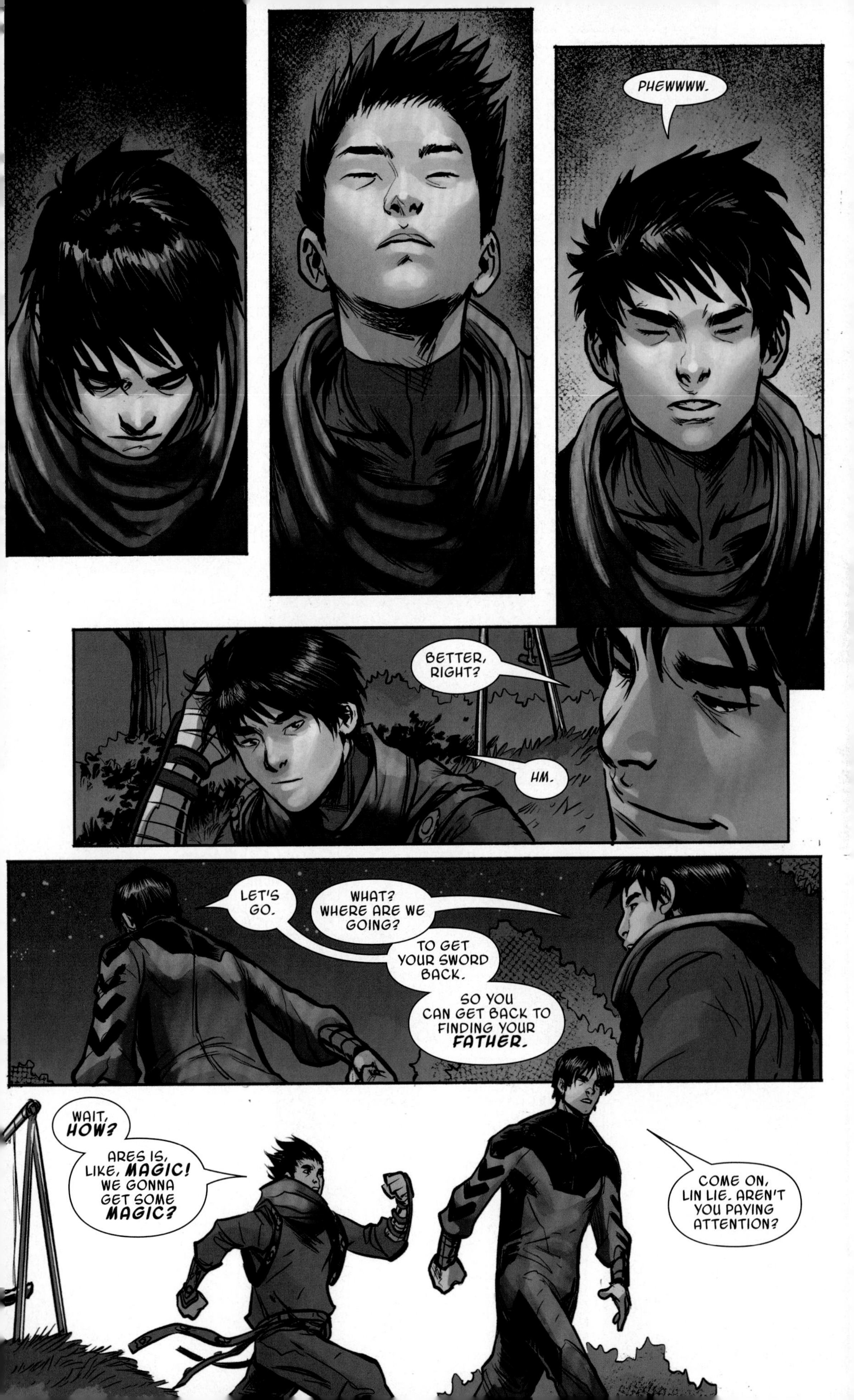
PHEWWWW.
BETTER, RIGHT?
HM.
LET'S GO.
WHAT? WHERE ARE WE GOING?
TO GET YOUR SWORD BACK.
SO YOU CAN GET BACK TO FINDING YOUR FATHER.
WAIT, HOW?
ARES IS, LIKE, MAGIC! WE GONNA GET SOME MAGIC?
COME ON, LIN LIE. AREN'T YOU PAYING ATTENTION?

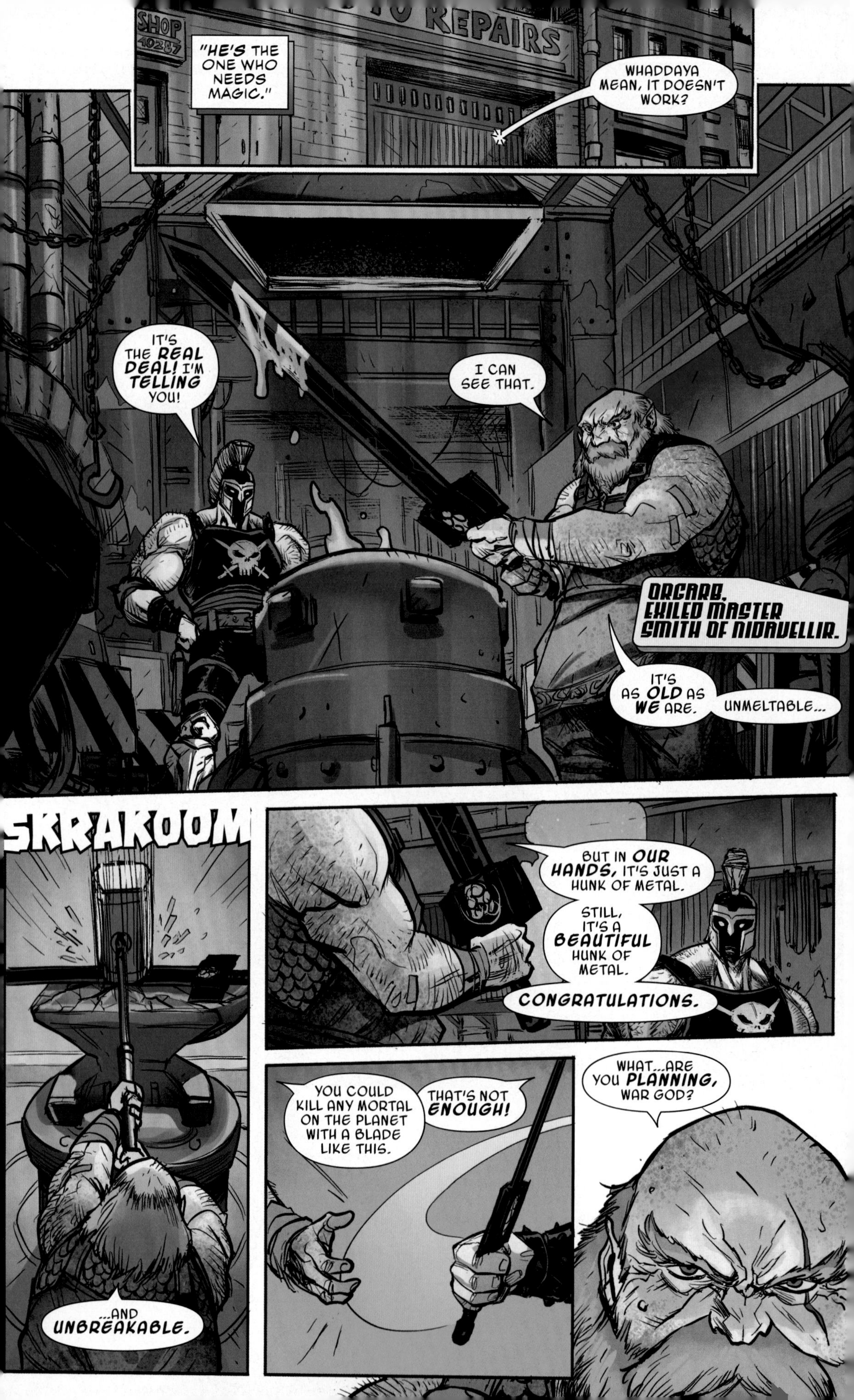

SHOP
10287
REPAIRS
"HE'S THE ONE WHO NEEDS MAGIC."
WHADDAYA MEAN, IT DOESN'T WORK?
IT'S THE REAL DEAL! I'M TELLING YOU!
I CAN SEE THAT.
ORCARB, EXILED MASTER SMITH OF NIDAVELLIR.
IT'S AS OLD AS WE ARE.
UNMELTABLE...
SKRAKOOM
...AND UNBREAKABLE.
BUT IN OUR HANDS, IT'S JUST A HUNK OF METAL.
STILL, IT'S A BEAUTIFUL HUNK OF METAL.
CONGRATULATIONS.
YOU COULD KILL ANY MORTAL ON THE PLANET WITH A BLADE LIKE THIS.
THAT'S NOT ENOUGH!
WHAT...ARE YOU PLANNING, WAR GOD?

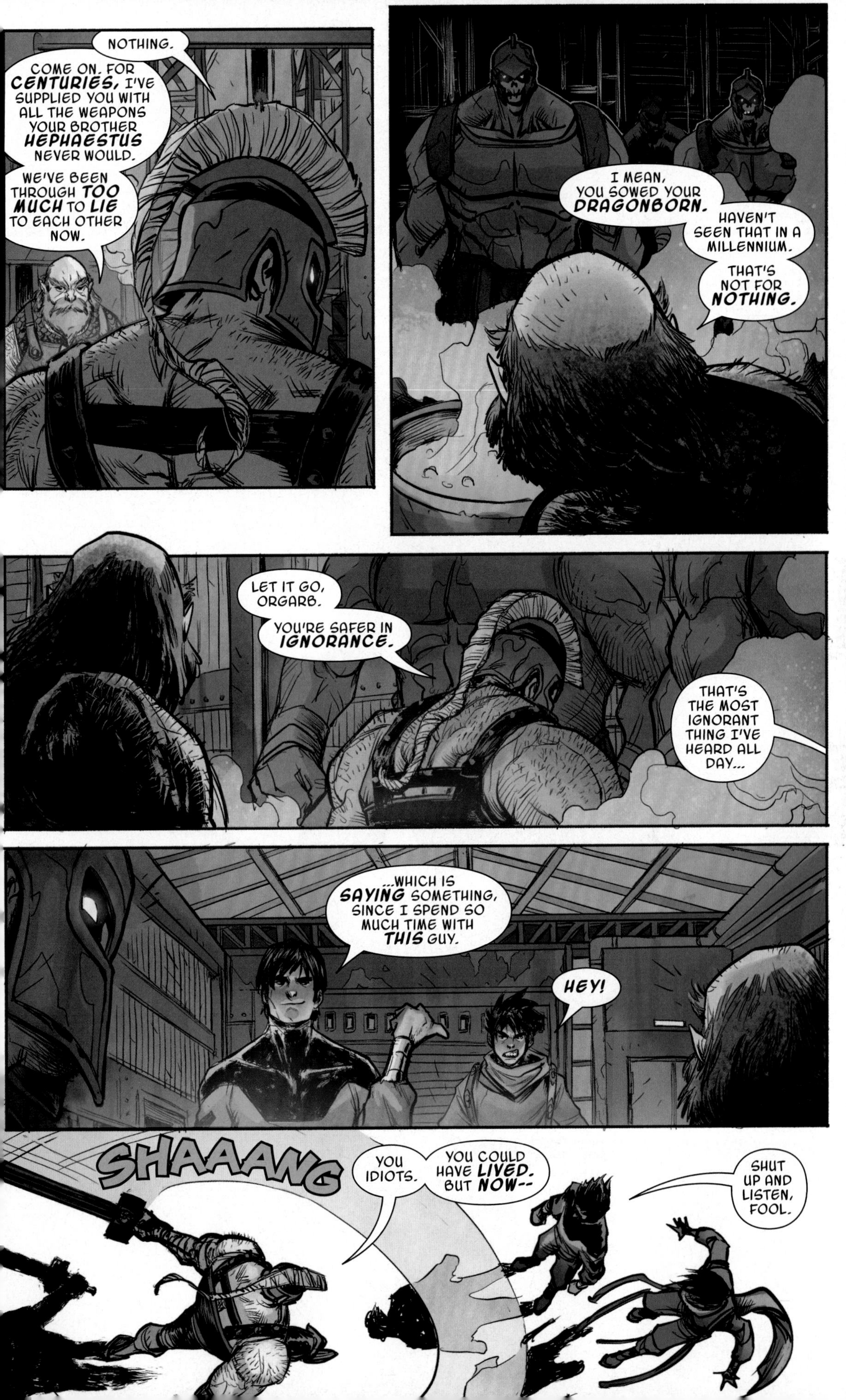
NOTHING.
COME ON. FOR CENTURIES, I'VE SUPPLIED YOU WITH ALL THE WEAPONS YOUR BROTHER HEPHAESTUS NEVER WOULD.
WE'VE BEEN THROUGH TOO MUCH TO LIE TO EACH OTHER NOW.
I MEAN, YOU SOWED YOUR DRAGONBORN.
HAVEN'T SEEN THAT IN A MILLENNIUM.
THAT'S NOT FOR NOTHING.
LET IT GO, ORGARB.
YOU'RE SAFER IN IGNORANCE.
THAT'S THE MOST IGNORANT THING I'VE HEARD ALL DAY...
...WHICH IS SAYING SOMETHING, SINCE I SPEND SO MUCH TIME WITH THIS GUY.
HEY!
SHAAANG
YOU IDIOTS.
YOU COULD HAVE LIVED. BUT NOW--
SHUT UP AND LISTEN, FOOL.

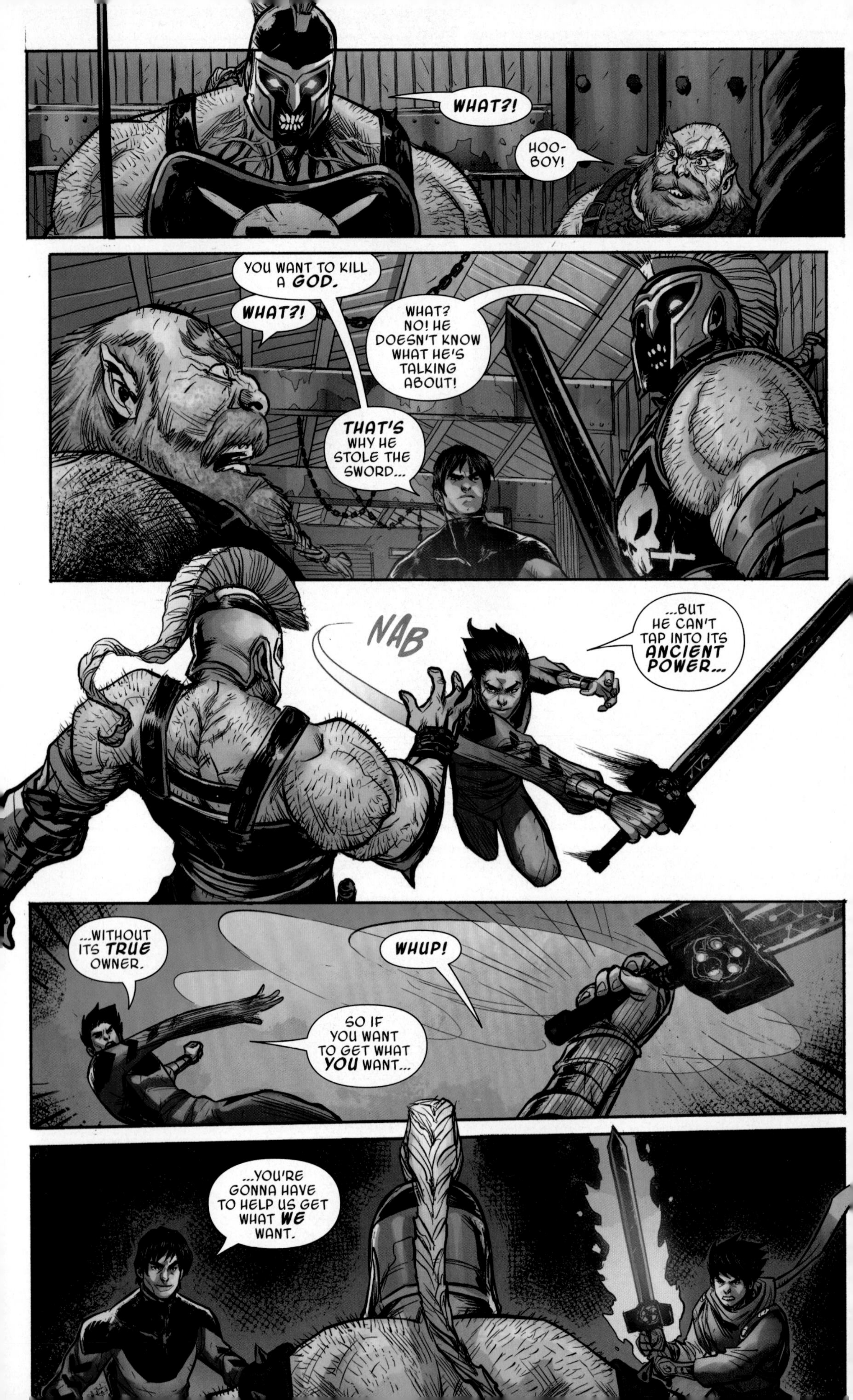
WHAT?!
HOO-BOY!
YOU WANT TO KILL A GOD.
WHAT?!
WHAT? NO! HE DOESN'T KNOW WHAT HE'S TALKING ABOUT!
THAT'S WHY HE STOLE THE SWORD...
NAB
...BUT HE CAN'T TAP INTO ITS ANCIENT POWER...
...WITHOUT ITS TRUE OWNER.
WHUP!
SO IF YOU WANT TO GET WHAT YOU WANT...
...YOU'RE GONNA HAVE TO HELP US GET WHAT WE WANT.

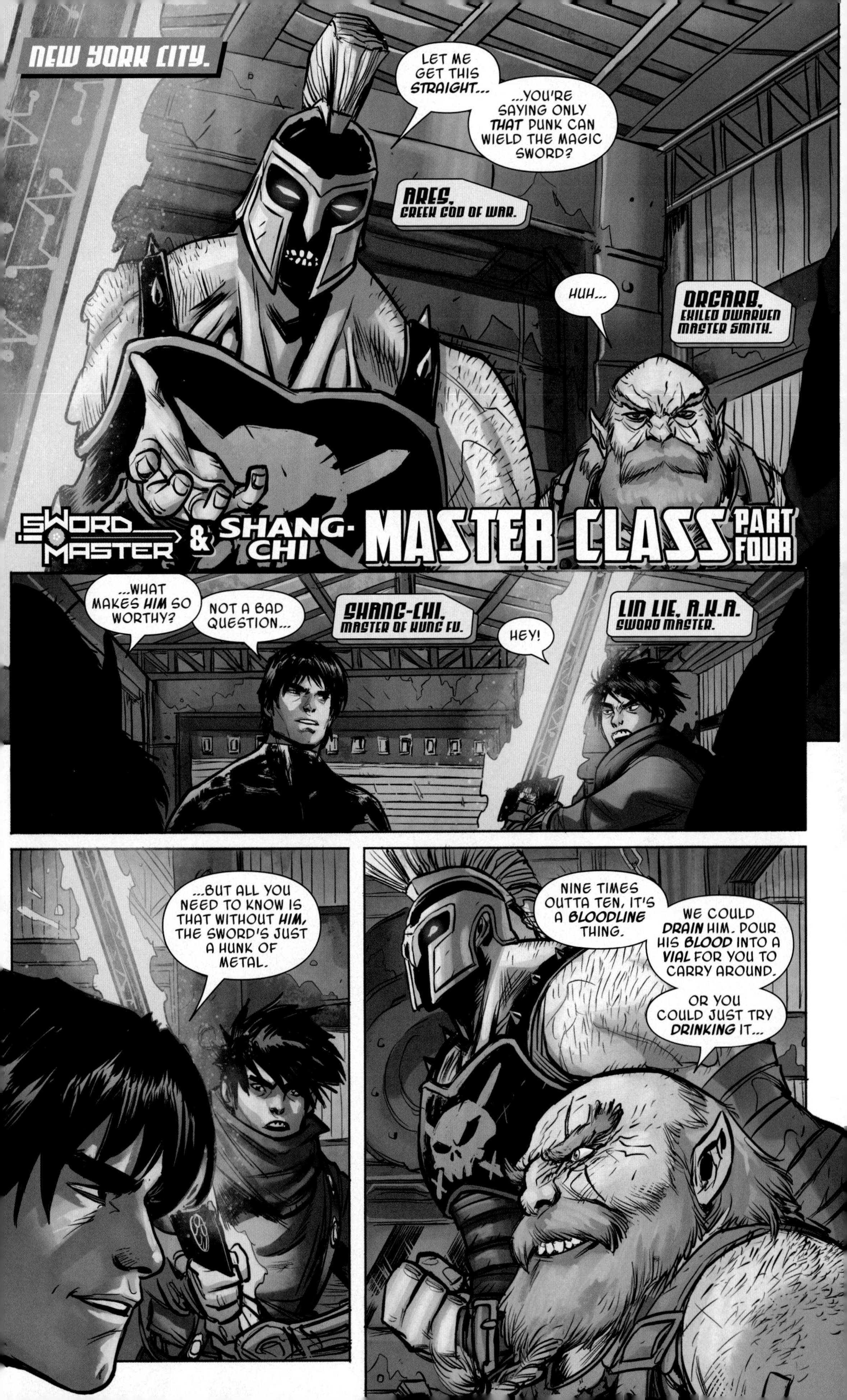
NEW YORK CITY.
LET ME GET THIS STRAIGHT...
...YOU'RE SAYING ONLY THAT PUNK CAN WIELD THE MAGIC SWORD?
ARES, GREEK GOD OF WAR.
HUH...
ORCARB, EXILED DWARVEN MASTER SMITH.
SWORD MASTER & SHANG-CHI
MASTER CLASS PART FOUR
...WHAT MAKES HIM SO WORTHY?
NOT A BAD QUESTION...
SHANG-CHI, MASTER OF KUNG FU.
HEY!
LIN LIE, A.K.A. SWORD MASTER.
...BUT ALL YOU NEED TO KNOW IS THAT WITHOUT HIM, THE SWORD'S JUST A HUNK OF METAL.
NINE TIMES OUTTA TEN, IT'S A BLOODLINE THING.
WE COULD DRAIN HIM. POUR HIS BLOOD INTO A VIAL FOR YOU TO CARRY AROUND.
OR YOU COULD JUST TRY DRINKING IT...

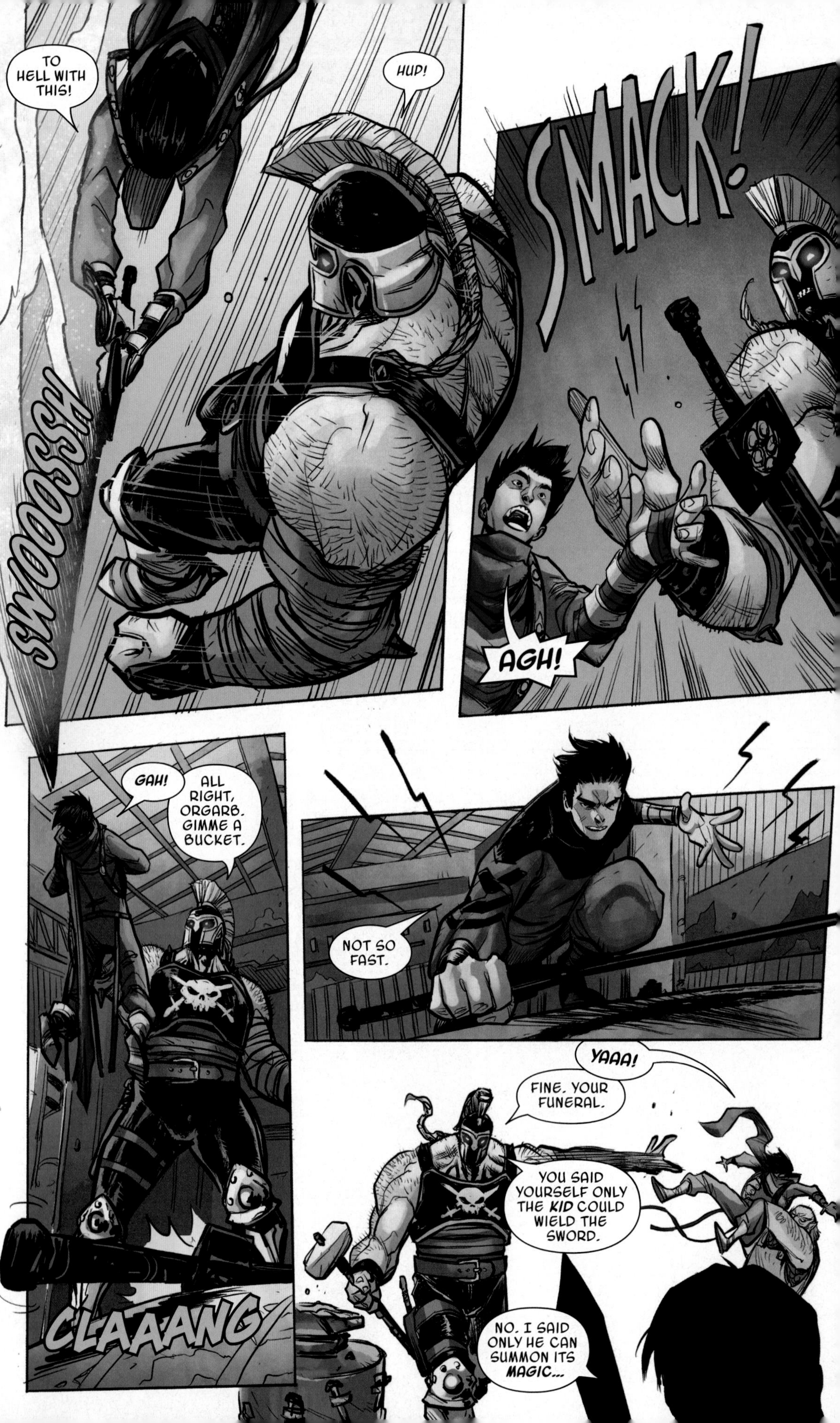
TO HELL WITH THIS!
HUP!
SWOOOSSH
SMACK!
AGH!
GAH!
ALL RIGHT, ORGARB. GIMME A BUCKET.
CLAAANG
NOT SO FAST.
YAAA!
FINE. YOUR FUNERAL.
YOU SAID YOURSELF ONLY THE KID COULD WIELD THE SWORD.
NO. I SAID ONLY HE CAN SUMMON ITS MAGIC...

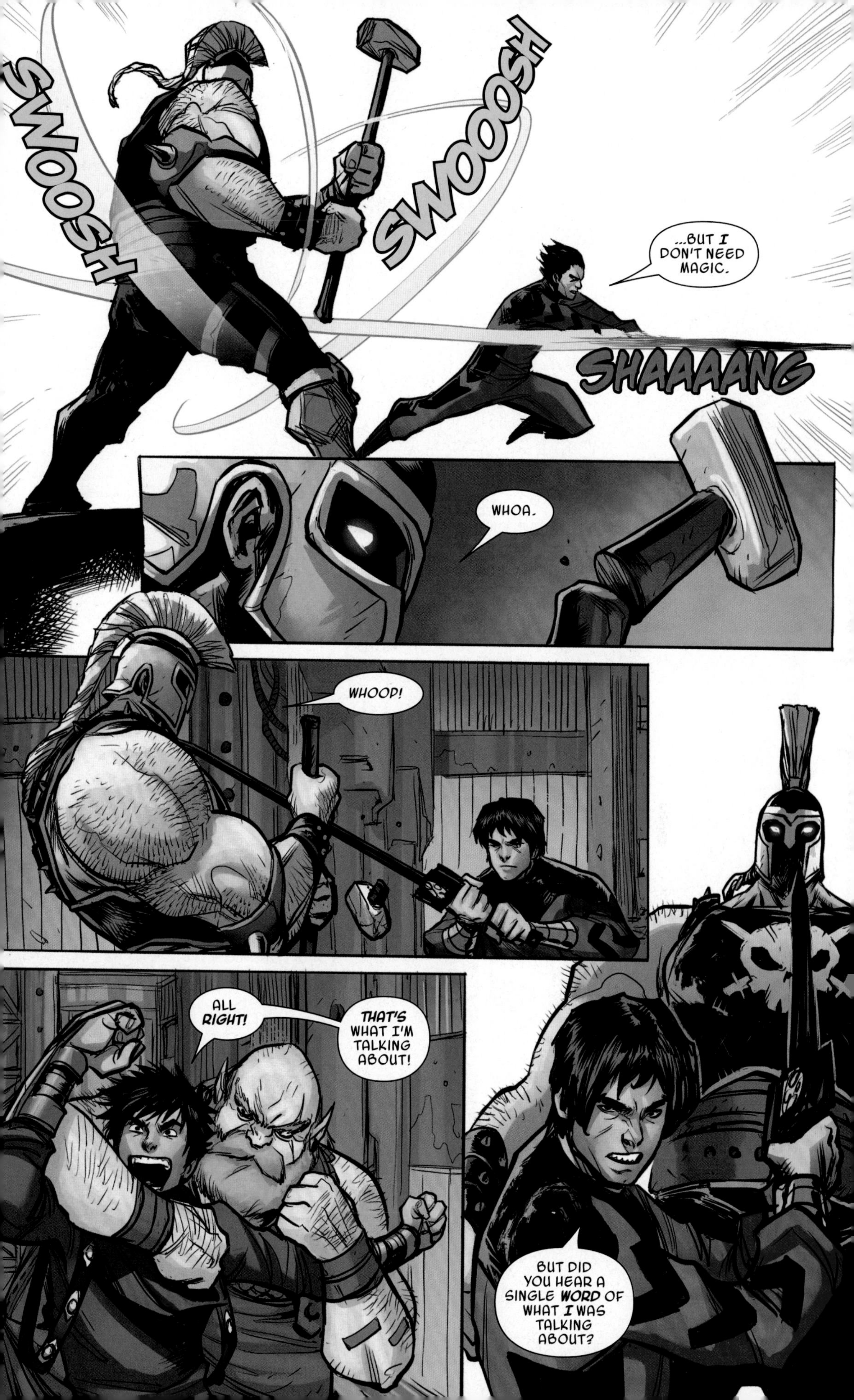
SWOOSH
SWOOOSH
...BUT I DON'T NEED MAGIC.
SHAAAANG
WHOA.
WHOOP!
ALL RIGHT!
THAT'S WHAT I'M TALKING ABOUT!
BUT DID YOU HEAR A SINGLE WORD OF WHAT I WAS TALKING ABOUT?

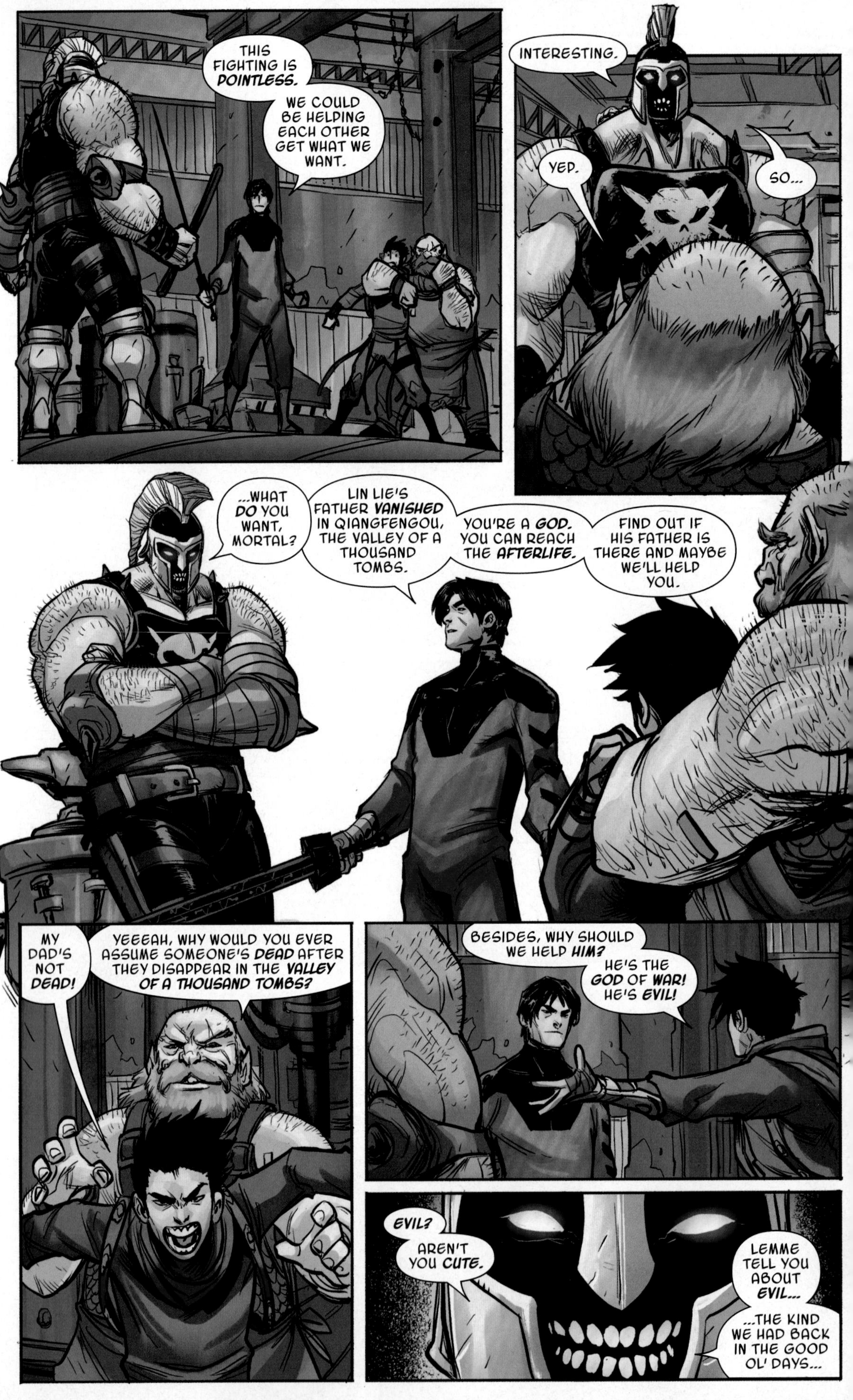
THIS FIGHTING IS POINTLESS.
WE COULD BE HELPING EACH OTHER GET WHAT WE WANT.
INTERESTING.
YEP.
SO...
...WHAT DO YOU WANT, MORTAL?
LIN LIE'S FATHER VANISHED IN QIANGFENGOU, THE VALLEY OF A THOUSAND TOMBS.
YOU'RE A GOD. YOU CAN REACH THE AFTERLIFE.
FIND OUT IF HIS FATHER IS THERE AND MAYBE WE'LL HELP YOU.
MY DAD'S NOT DEAD!
YEEEAH, WHY WOULD YOU EVER ASSUME SOMEONE'S DEAD AFTER THEY DISAPPEAR IN THE VALLEY OF A THOUSAND TOMBS?
BESIDES, WHY SHOULD WE HELP HIM?
HE'S THE GOD OF WAR! HE'S EVIL!
EVIL?
AREN'T YOU CUTE.
LEMME TELL YOU ABOUT EVIL...
...THE KIND WE HAD BACK IN THE GOOD OL' DAYS...

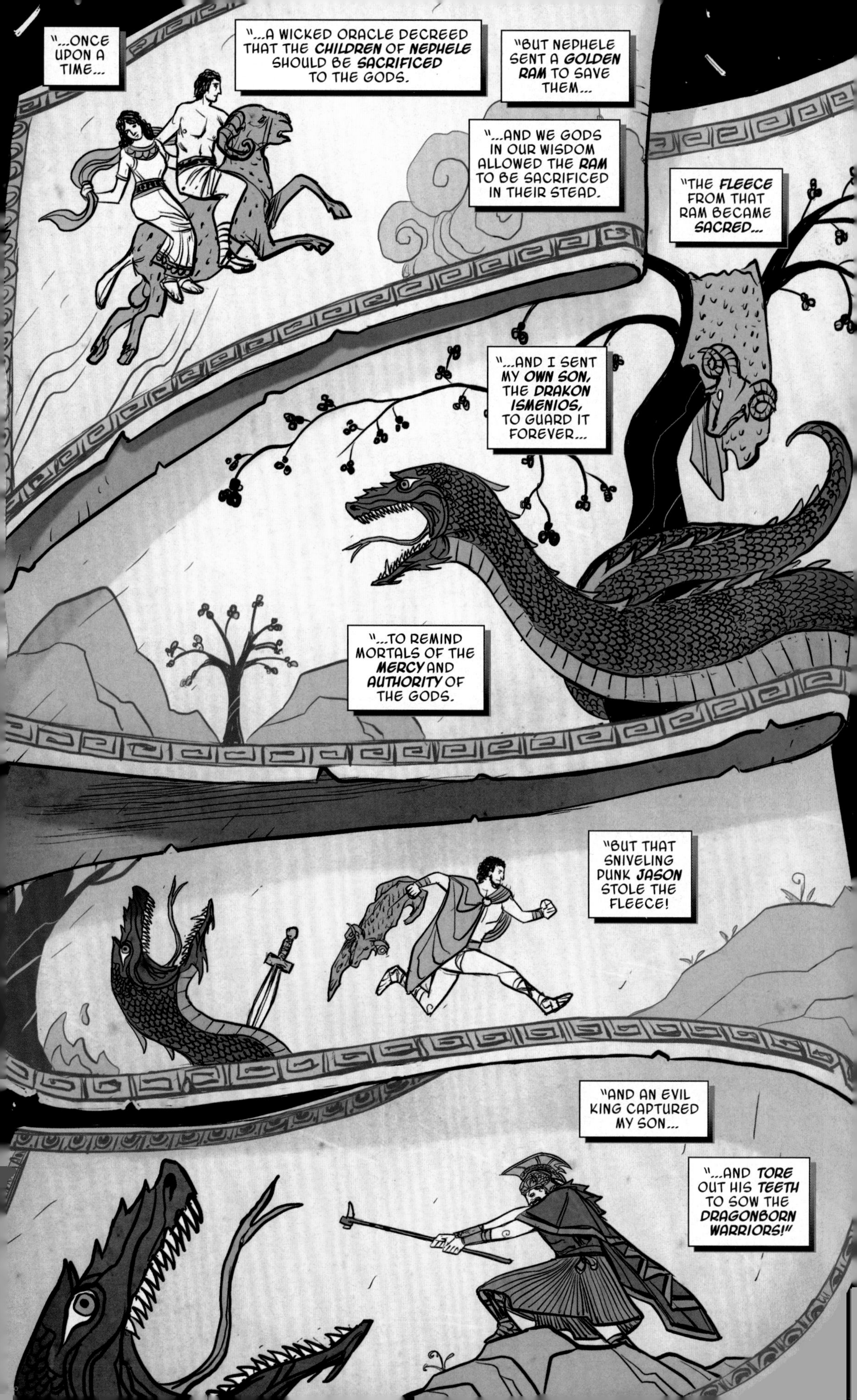
"...ONCE UPON A TIME...
"...A WICKED ORACLE DECREED THAT THE CHILDREN OF NEPHELE SHOULD BE SACRIFICED TO THE GODS.
"BUT NEPHELE SENT A GOLDEN RAM TO SAVE THEM...
"...AND WE GODS IN OUR WISDOM ALLOWED THE RAM TO BE SACRIFICED IN THEIR STEAD.
"THE FLEECE FROM THAT RAM BECAME SACRED...
"...AND I SENT MY OWN SON, THE DRAKON ISMENIOS, TO GUARD IT FOREVER...
"...TO REMIND MORTALS OF THE MERCY AND AUTHORITY OF THE GODS.
"BUT THAT SNIVELING PUNK JASON STOLE THE FLEECE!
"AND AN EVIL KING CAPTURED MY SON...
"...AND TORE OUT HIS TEETH TO SOW THE DRAGONBORN WARRIORS!"

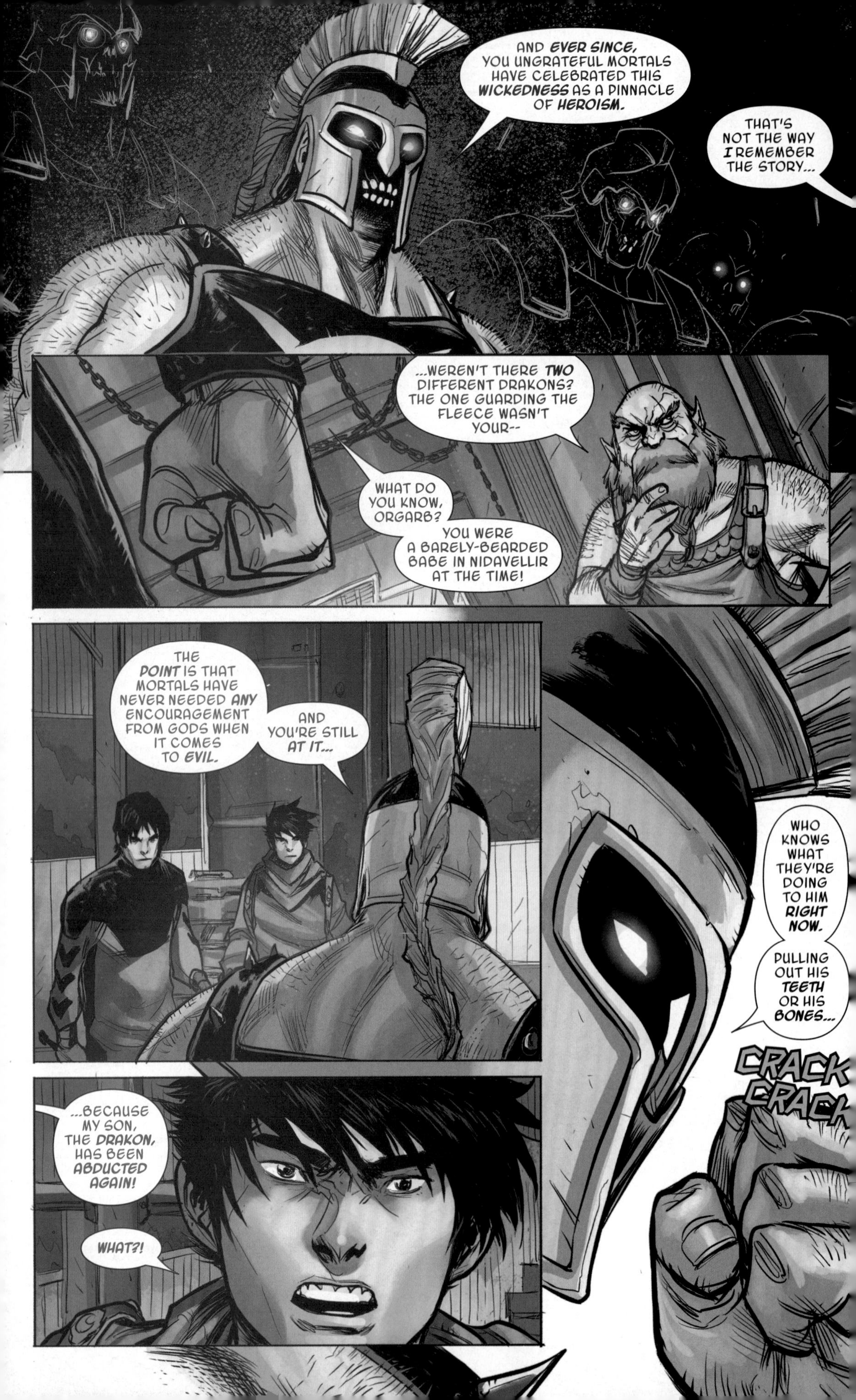

AND EVER SINCE, YOU UNGRATEFUL MORTALS HAVE CELEBRATED THIS WICKEDNESS AS A PINNACLE OF HEROISM.
THAT'S NOT THE WAY I REMEMBER THE STORY...
...WEREN'T THERE TWO DIFFERENT DRAKONS? THE ONE GUARDING THE FLEECE WASN'T YOUR--
WHAT DO YOU KNOW, ORGARB?
YOU WERE A BARELY-BEARDED BABE IN NIDAVELLIR AT THE TIME!
THE POINT IS THAT MORTALS HAVE NEVER NEEDED ANY ENCOURAGEMENT FROM GODS WHEN IT COMES TO EVIL.
AND YOU'RE STILL AT IT...
WHO KNOWS WHAT THEY'RE DOING TO HIM RIGHT NOW.
PULLING OUT HIS TEETH OR HIS BONES...
CRACK
CRACK
...BECAUSE MY SON, THE DRAKON, HAS BEEN ABDUCTED AGAIN!
WHAT?!

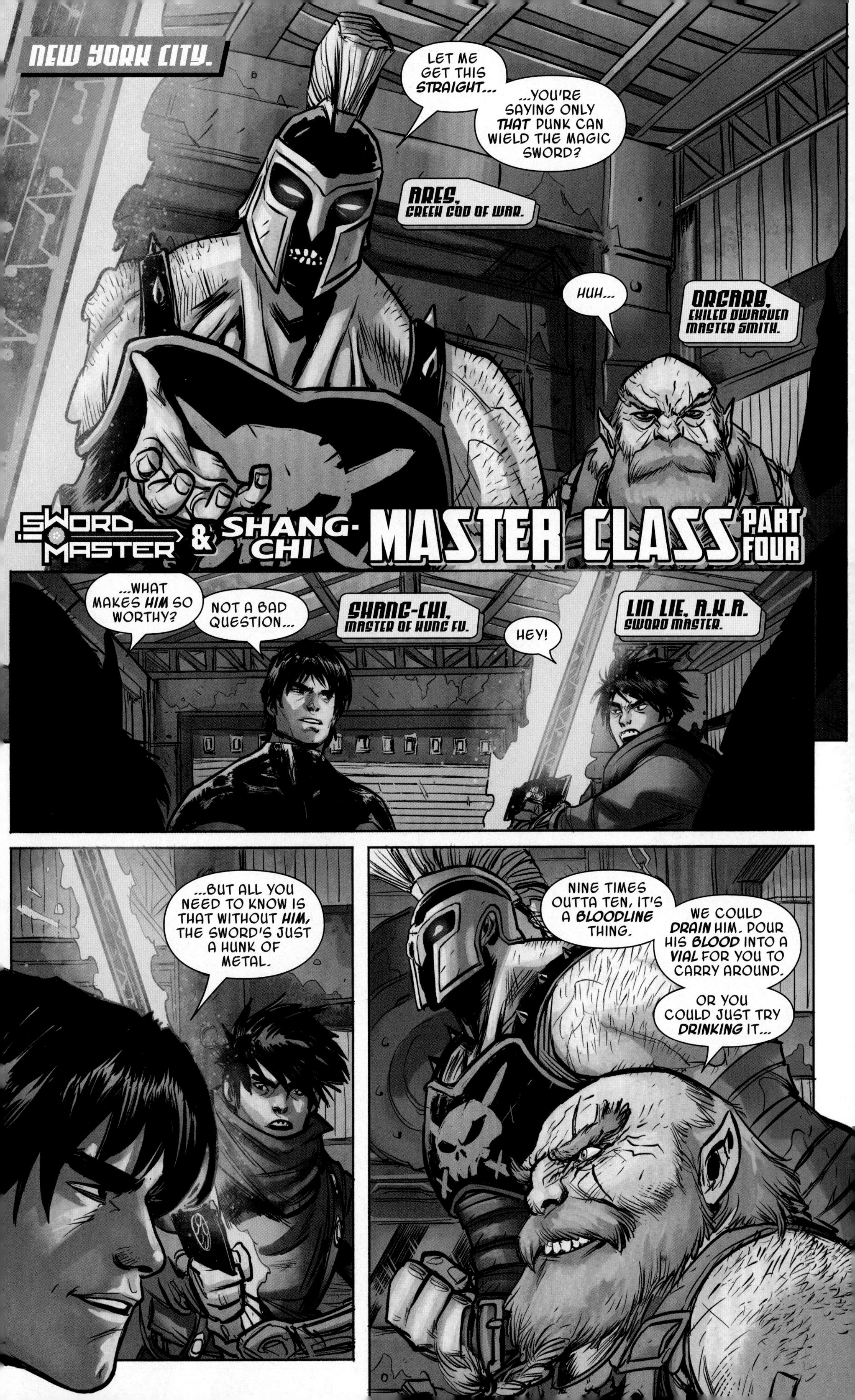
NEW YORK CITY.
LET ME GET THIS STRAIGHT...
...YOU'RE SAYING ONLY THAT PUNK CAN WIELD THE MAGIC SWORD?
ARES, GREEK GOD OF WAR.
HUH...
ORGARB, EXILED DWARVEN MASTER SMITH.
SWORD MASTER & SHANG-CHI
MASTER CLASS PART FOUR
...WHAT MAKES HIM SO WORTHY?
NOT A BAD QUESTION...
SHANG-CHI, MASTER OF KUNG FU.
HEY!
LIN LIE, A.K.A. SWORD MASTER.
...BUT ALL YOU NEED TO KNOW IS THAT WITHOUT HIM, THE SWORD'S JUST A HUNK OF METAL.
NINE TIMES OUTTA TEN, IT'S A BLOODLINE THING.
WE COULD DRAIN HIM. POUR HIS BLOOD INTO A VIAL FOR YOU TO CARRY AROUND.
OR YOU COULD JUST TRY DRINKING IT...

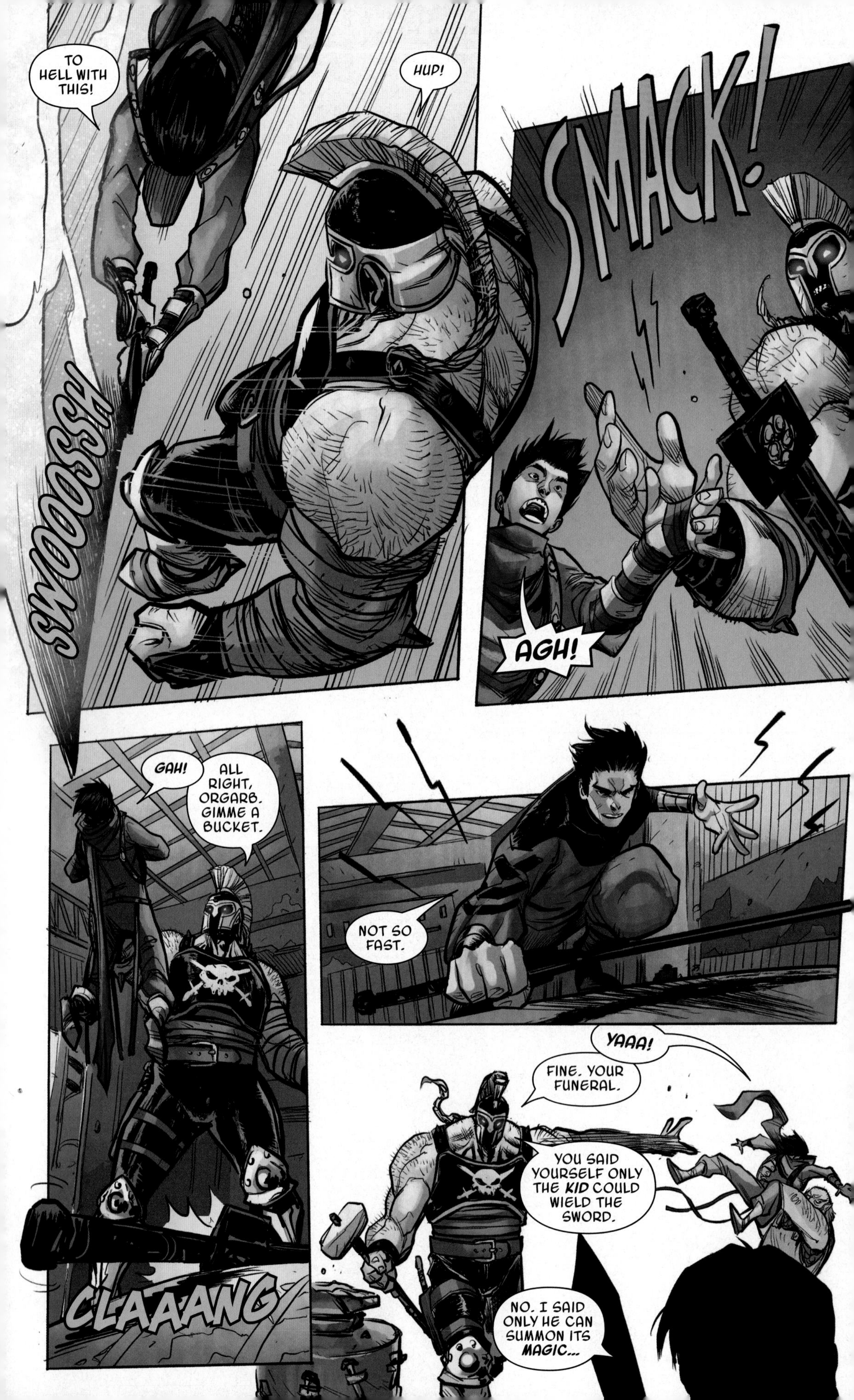
TO HELL WITH THIS!
HUP!
SWOOOSH
SMACK!
AGH!
GAH!
ALL RIGHT, ORGARB. GIMME A BUCKET.
CLAAANG
NOT SO FAST.
YAAA!
FINE. YOUR FUNERAL.
YOU SAID YOURSELF ONLY THE KID COULD WIELD THE SWORD.
NO. I SAID ONLY HE CAN SUMMON ITS MAGIC...

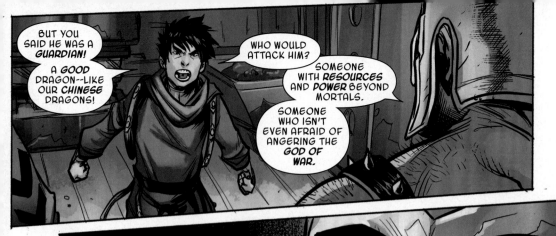

BUT YOU SAID HE WAS A *GUARDIAN!* A *GOOD* DRAGON--LIKE OUR *CHINESE* DRAGONS!

WHO WOULD ATTACK HIM?

SOMEONE WITH *RESOURCES* AND *POWER* BEYOND MORTALS.

SOMEONE WHO ISN'T EVEN AFRAID OF ANGERING THE *GOD OF WAR.*

I'M GONNA FREE MY SON AND MAKE THAT SOMEONE *PAY.*

WHICH MEANS I GUESS I NEED *YOU.*

SO I NEED A *WEAPON* STRONG ENOUGH TO KILL *ANYTHING*--EVEN A *GOD.*

YOU HELP ME GET MY SON BACK...

...AND I'LL HELP YOU FIND YOUR *FATHER.*

WHETHER HE'S *DEAD* OR *NOT.*

WHAT DO YOU THINK?

I ALREADY SAID WE SHOULD WORK TOGETHER.

WHAT DO *YOU* THINK?

I DON'T *TRUST* HIM...

...BUT IF SOMEONE *IS* ABDUCTING GOOD DRAGONS, THEN WE HAVE A RESPONSIBILITY TO STOP THEM.

COME ON, THEN. NO TIME TO LOSE!

JUST REMEMBER THAT NOT ALL DRAGONS ARE AS *BENEVOLENT* AS THE ONES BACK HOME IN CHINA.

SO STAY *WATCHFUL.* OR IN YOUR *CASE...*

I KNOW! I FOUGHT OFF THOSE *WYVERNS* IN PAN JUST LIKE YOU!*

*IN *AGENTS OF ATLAS* #1, NATCH! --METICULOUS MARK

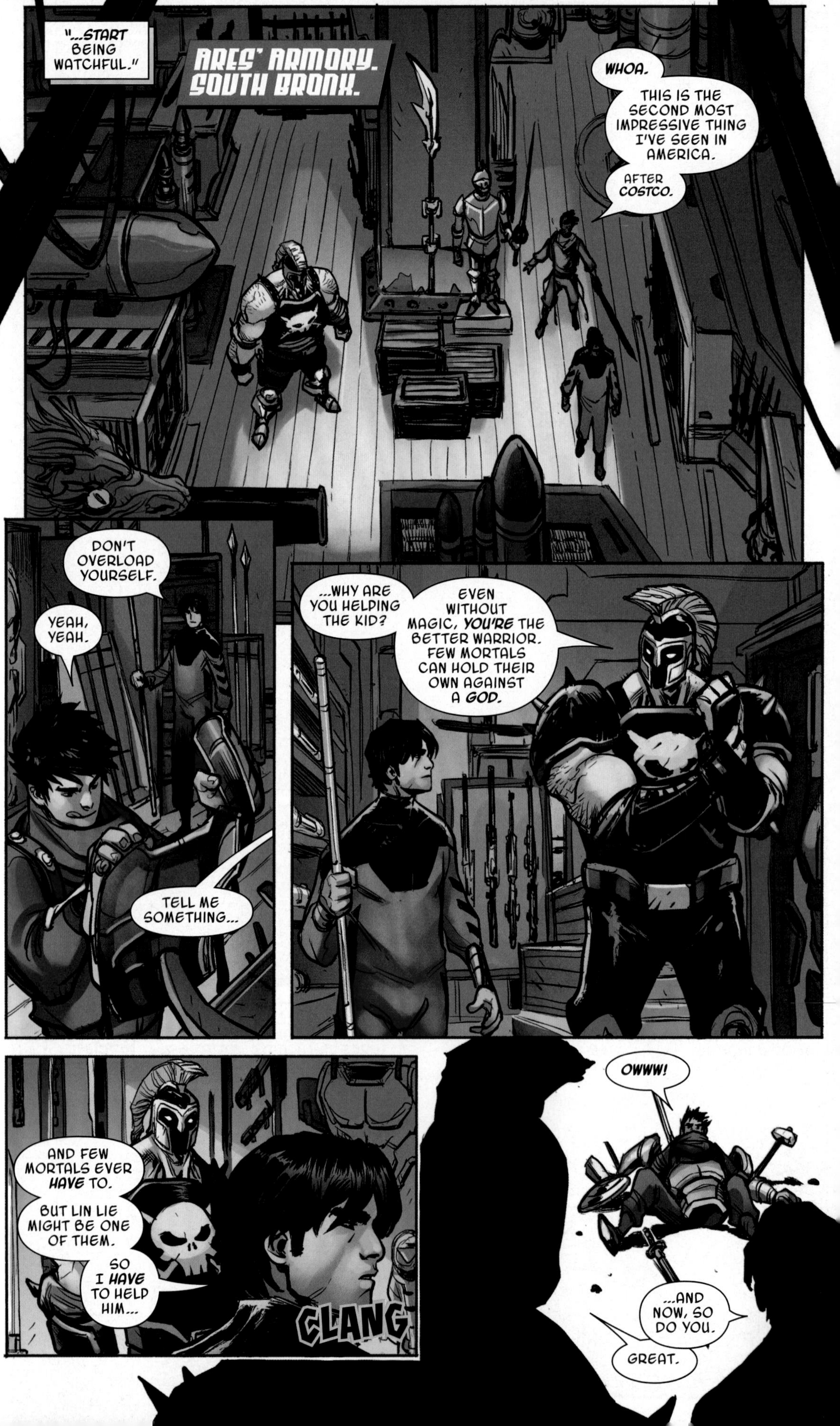
"...START BEING WATCHFUL."
ARES' ARMORY. SOUTH BRONX.
WHOA.
THIS IS THE SECOND MOST IMPRESSIVE THING I'VE SEEN IN AMERICA.
AFTER COSTCO.
DON'T OVERLOAD YOURSELF.
YEAH, YEAH.
TELL ME SOMETHING...
...WHY ARE YOU HELPING THE KID?
EVEN WITHOUT MAGIC, YOU'RE THE BETTER WARRIOR. FEW MORTALS CAN HOLD THEIR OWN AGAINST A GOD.
AND FEW MORTALS EVER HAVE TO.
BUT LIN LIE MIGHT BE ONE OF THEM.
SO I HAVE TO HELP HIM...
CLANG
OWWW!
...AND NOW, SO DO YOU.
GREAT.

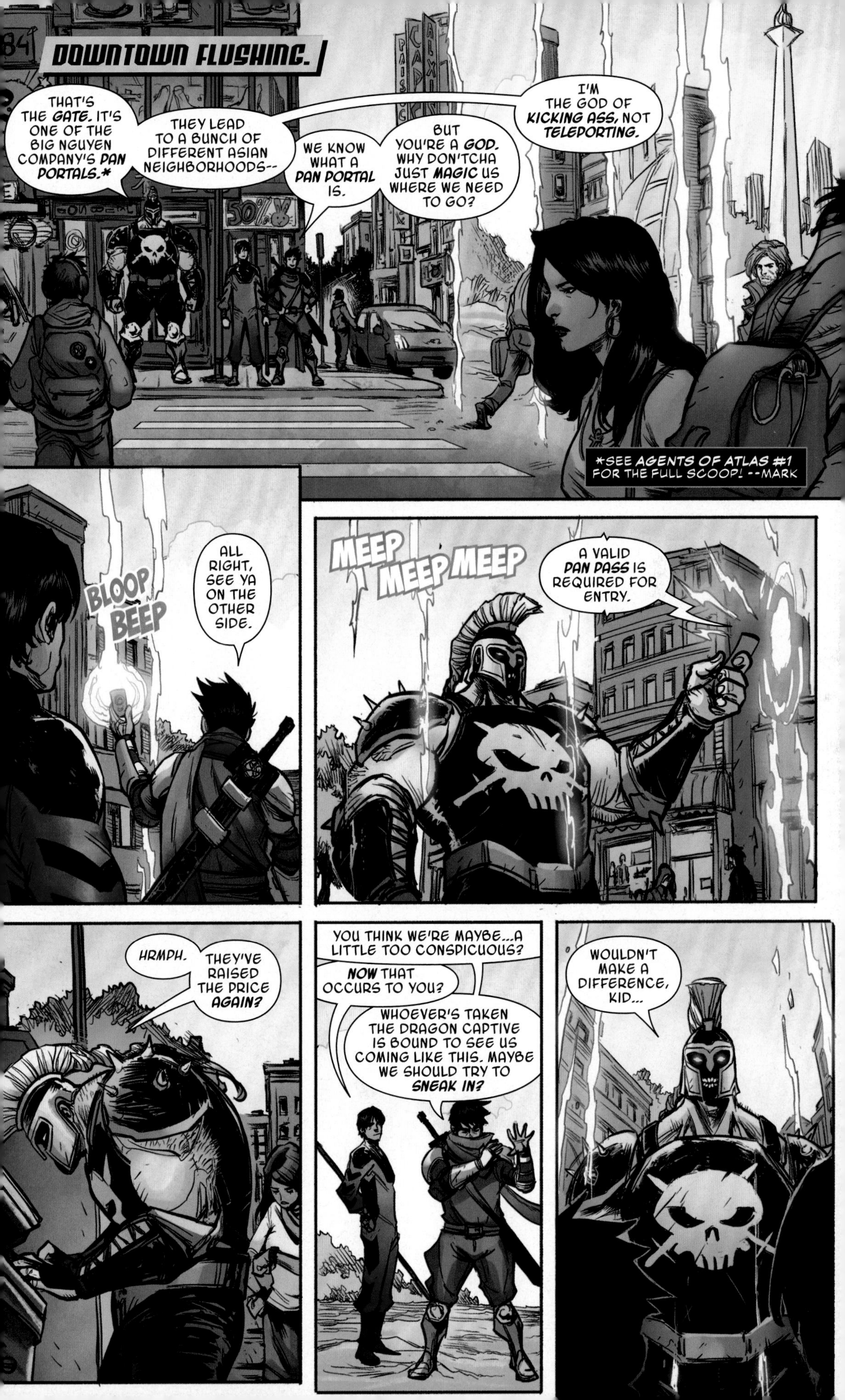
DOWNTOWN FLUSHING.
THAT'S THE GATE. IT'S ONE OF THE BIG NGUYEN COMPANY'S PAN PORTALS.*
THEY LEAD TO A BUNCH OF DIFFERENT ASIAN NEIGHBORHOODS--
WE KNOW WHAT A PAN PORTAL IS.
BUT YOU'RE A GOD. WHY DON'TCHA JUST MAGIC US WHERE WE NEED TO GO?
I'M THE GOD OF KICKING ASS, NOT TELEPORTING.
*SEE AGENTS OF ATLAS #1 FOR THE FULL SCOOP! --MARK
BLOOP BEEP
ALL RIGHT, SEE YA ON THE OTHER SIDE.
MEEP MEEP MEEP
A VALID PAN PASS IS REQUIRED FOR ENTRY.
HRMPH.
THEY'VE RAISED THE PRICE AGAIN?
YOU THINK WE'RE MAYBE...A LITTLE TOO CONSPICUOUS?
NOW THAT OCCURS TO YOU?
WHOEVER'S TAKEN THE DRAGON CAPTIVE IS BOUND TO SEE US COMING LIKE THIS. MAYBE WE SHOULD TRY TO SNEAK IN?
WOULDN'T MAKE A DIFFERENCE, KID...

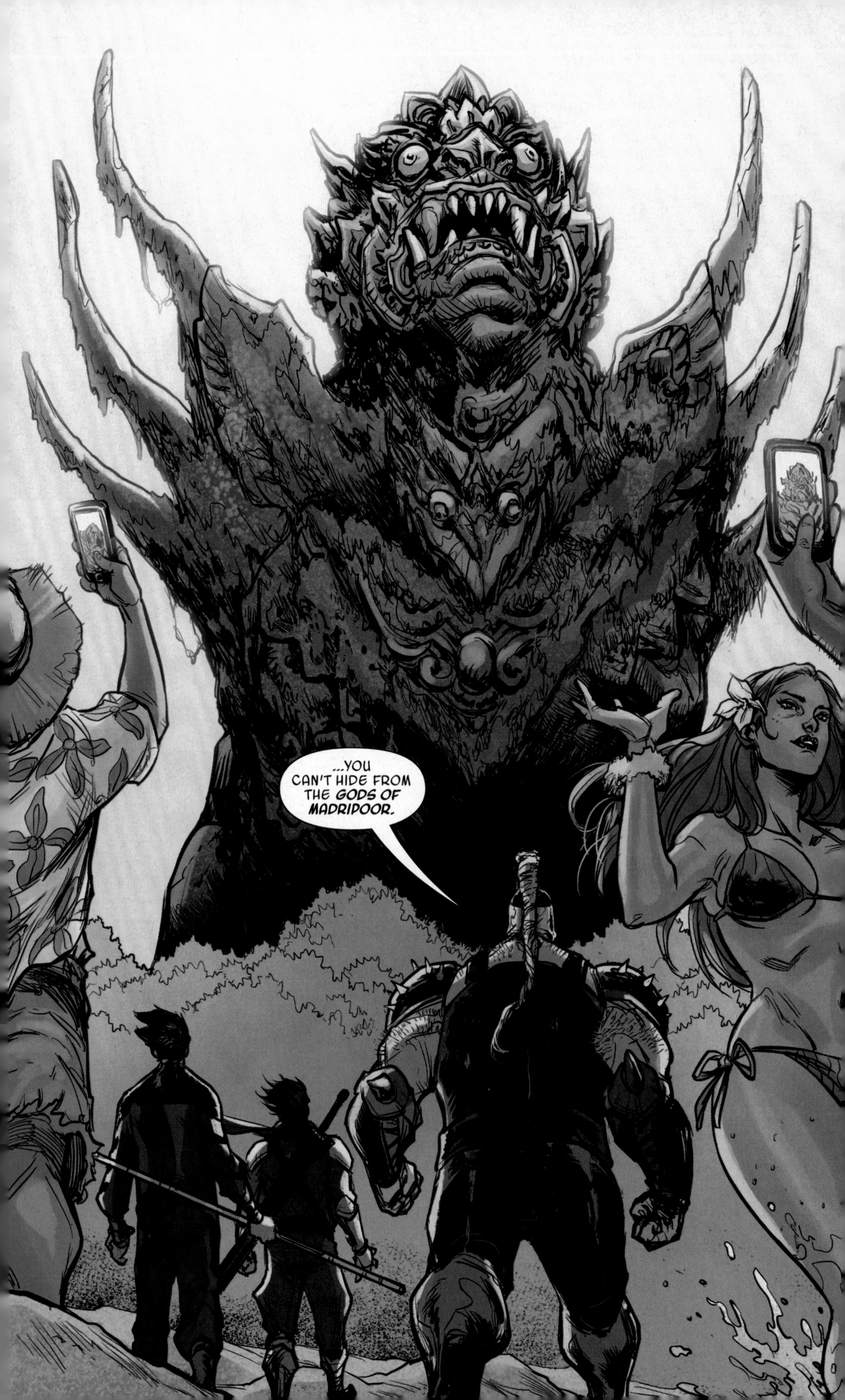
...YOU CAN'T HIDE FROM THE *GODS OF MADRIPOOR*.

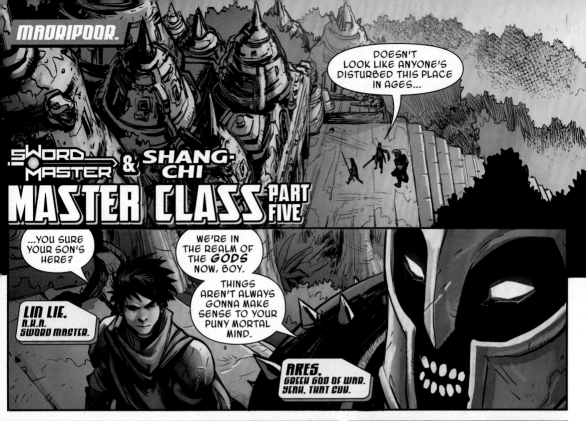

SWORD MASTER & SHANG-CHI

MASTER CLASS PART FIVE

DOESN'T LOOK LIKE ANYONE'S DISTURBED THIS PLACE IN AGES...

...YOU SURE YOUR SON'S HERE?

WE'RE IN THE REALM OF THE **GODS** NOW, BOY. THINGS AREN'T ALWAYS GONNA MAKE SENSE TO YOUR **PUNY MORTAL MIND.**

LIN LIE, A.K.A. SWORD MASTER.

ARES, GREEK GOD OF WAR. YEAH, THAT GUY.

WHY WOULD THE GODS OF **MADRIPOOR** ABDUCT YOUR SON, ANYWAY?

SHANG-CHI, MASTER OF KUNG FU.

WHAT DID I JUST SAY ABOUT **PUNY MORTAL MINDS?**

YOU UP FOR THAT, PUNK?

AS LONG AS YOU KEEP UP **YOUR** END OF THE BARGAIN, I'M UP FOR...

WE CAN'T HELP YOU IF YOU DON'T TELL US WHAT YOU KNOW, ARES.

YOU DON'T HAVE TO **KNOW** ANYTHING 'CAUSE YOU DON'T HAVE TO **DO** ANYTHING, SHANG-CHI.

I JUST NEED THE **KID** HERE TO SWING HIS **MAGIC SWORD** AT THE RIGHT TIME.

RRRRRRRRRR

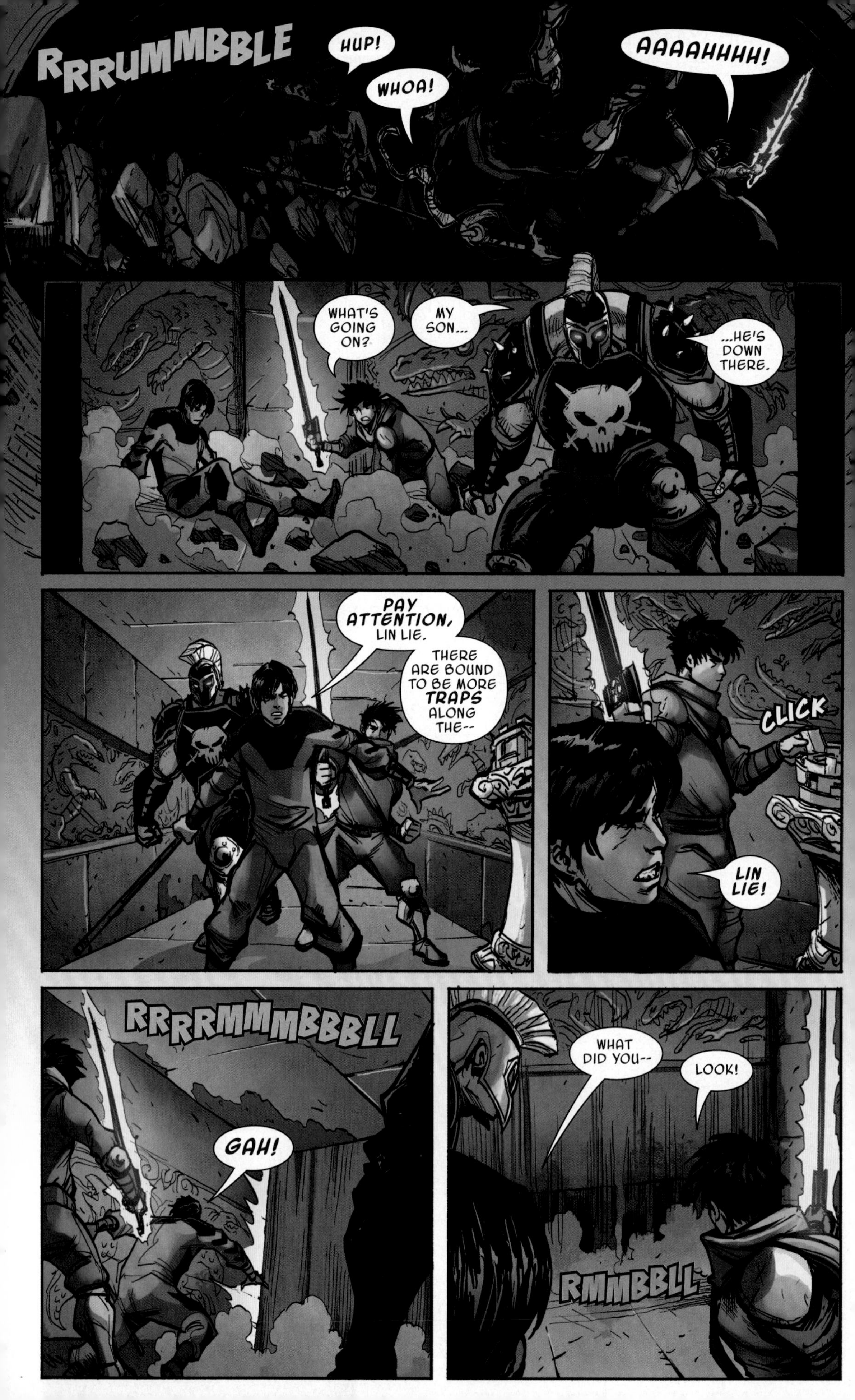
RRRUMMBBLE
HUP!
WHOA!
AAAAHHHH!
WHAT'S GOING ON?
MY SON...
...HE'S DOWN THERE.
PAY ATTENTION, LIN LIE.
THERE ARE BOUND TO BE MORE TRAPS ALONG THE--
CLICK
LIN LIE!
RRRRMMMMBBBLL
GAH!
WHAT DID YOU--
LOOK!
RMMBBLL

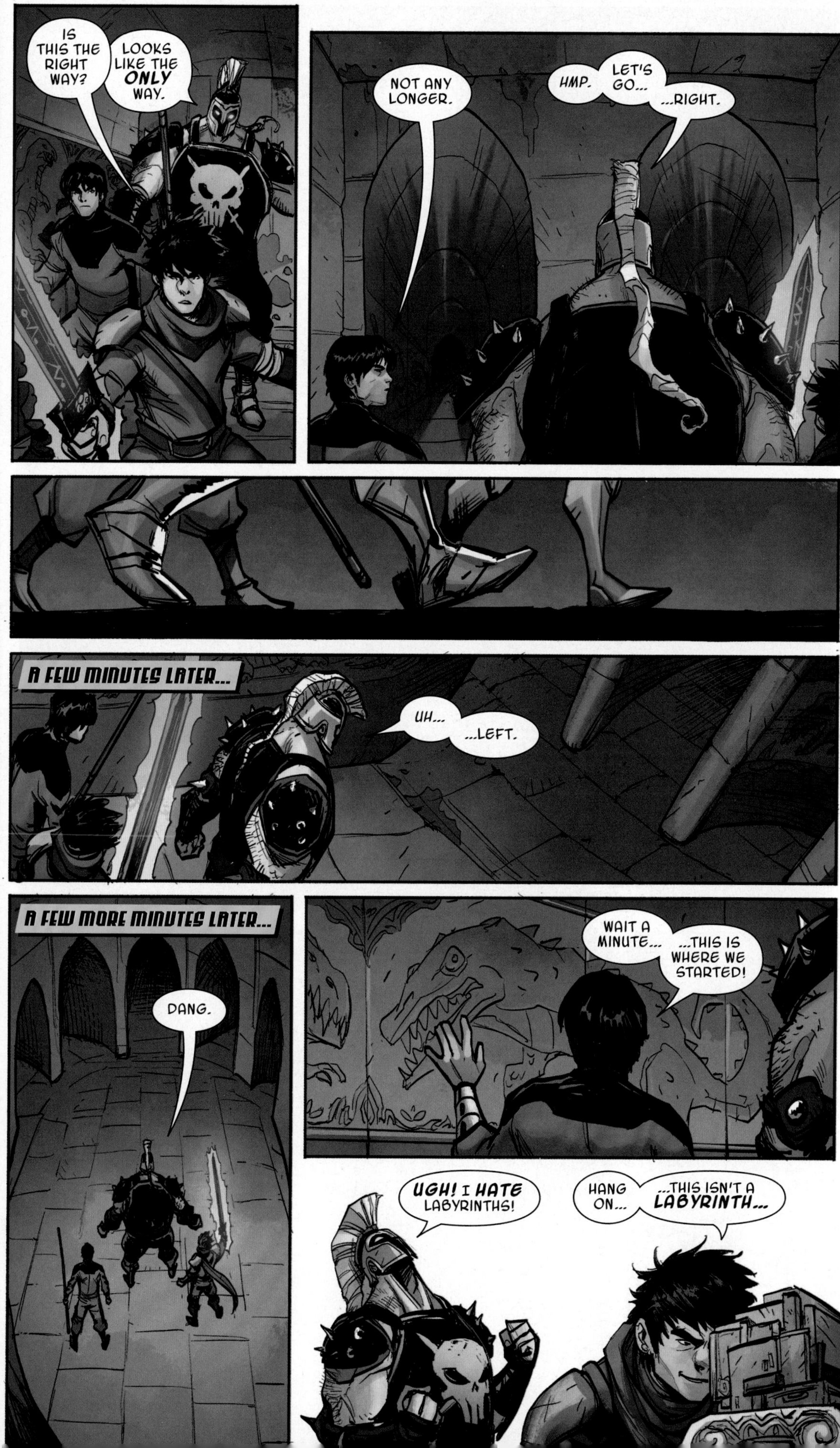
IS THIS THE RIGHT WAY?
LOOKS LIKE THE ONLY WAY.
NOT ANY LONGER.
HMP.
LET'S GO...
...RIGHT.
A FEW MINUTES LATER...
UH...
...LEFT.
A FEW MORE MINUTES LATER...
DANG.
WAIT A MINUTE...
...THIS IS WHERE WE STARTED!
UGH! I HATE LABYRINTHS!
HANG ON...
...THIS ISN'T A LABYRINTH...

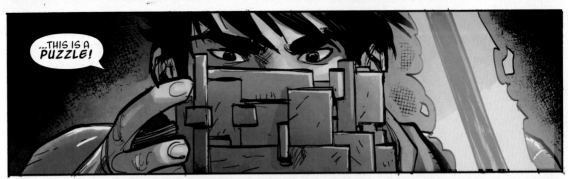

...THIS IS A PUZZLE!

BE CAREFUL!

SHUNK SHAKK

DON'T WORRY. I KNOW WHAT I'M--

RRRMMMBBLLLL

LIN LIE!

SHANK SHUK SHAAKK

RRRMMMMMBBBLL

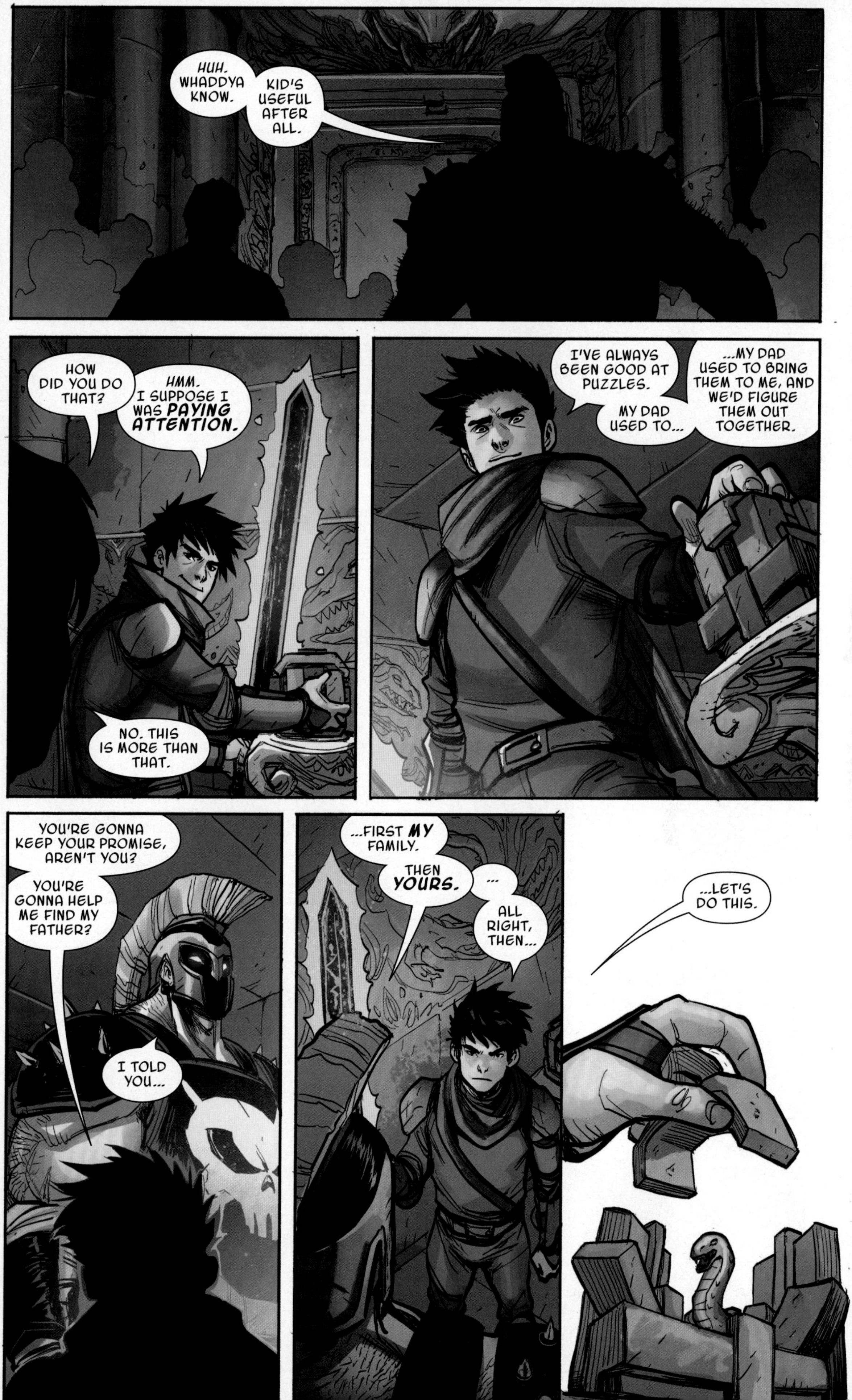
HUH. WHADDYA KNOW.
KID'S USEFUL AFTER ALL.
HOW DID YOU DO THAT?
HMM. I SUPPOSE I WAS **PAYING ATTENTION.**
NO. THIS IS MORE THAN THAT.
I'VE ALWAYS BEEN GOOD AT PUZZLES.
MY DAD USED TO...
...MY DAD USED TO BRING THEM TO ME, AND WE'D FIGURE THEM OUT TOGETHER.
YOU'RE GONNA KEEP YOUR PROMISE, AREN'T YOU?
YOU'RE GONNA HELP ME FIND MY FATHER?
I TOLD YOU...
...FIRST **MY** FAMILY.
THEN **YOURS.**
...
ALL RIGHT, THEN...
...LET'S DO THIS.

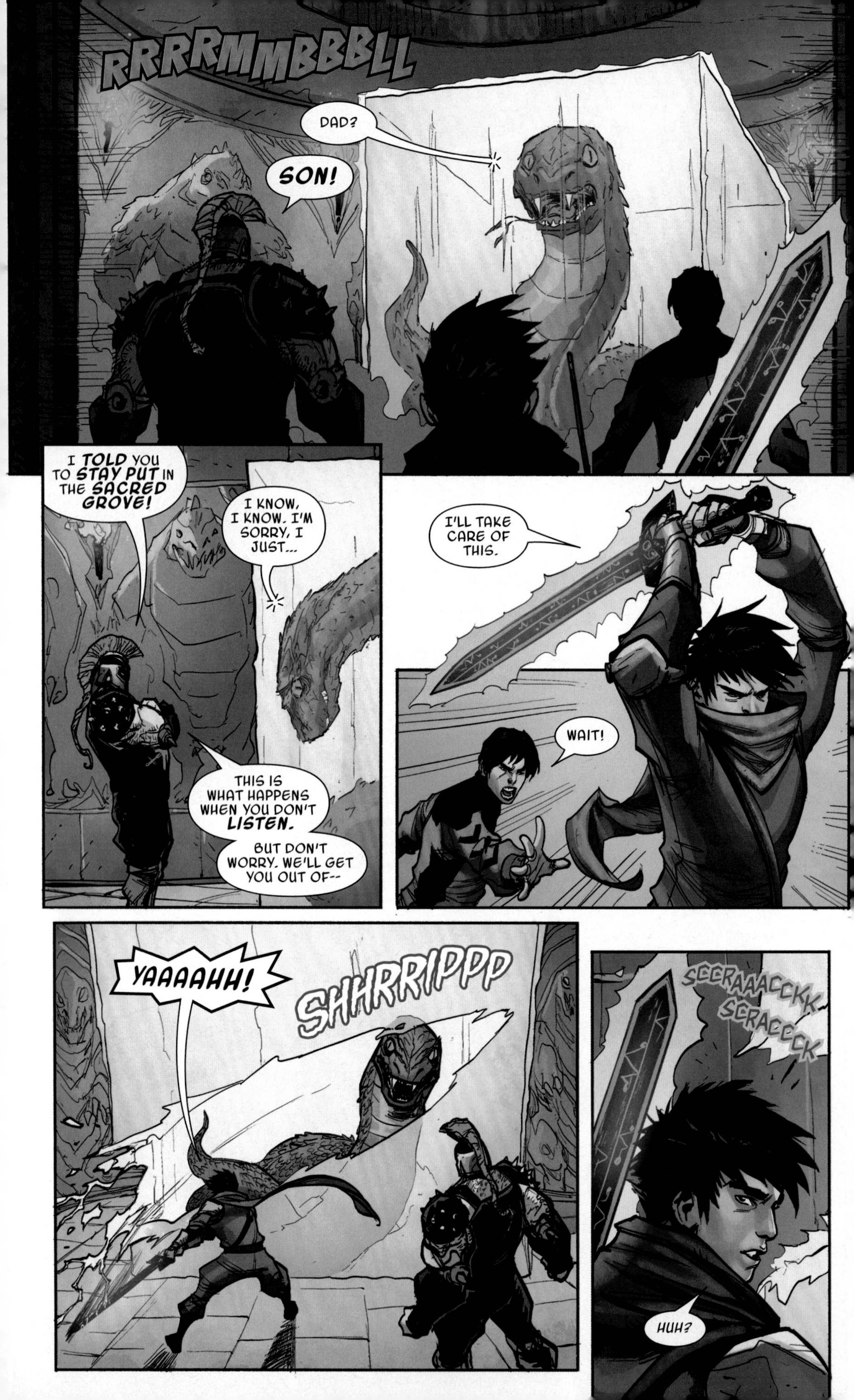
RRRRMMBBBLL
DAD?
SON!
I TOLD YOU TO STAY PUT IN THE SACRED GROVE!
I KNOW, I KNOW. I'M SORRY, I JUST...
THIS IS WHAT HAPPENS WHEN YOU DON'T LISTEN.
BUT DON'T WORRY. WE'LL GET YOU OUT OF--
I'LL TAKE CARE OF THIS.
WAIT!
YAAAAHH!
SHHRRIPPP
SCCRAAACCKK
SCRACCCCK
HUH?

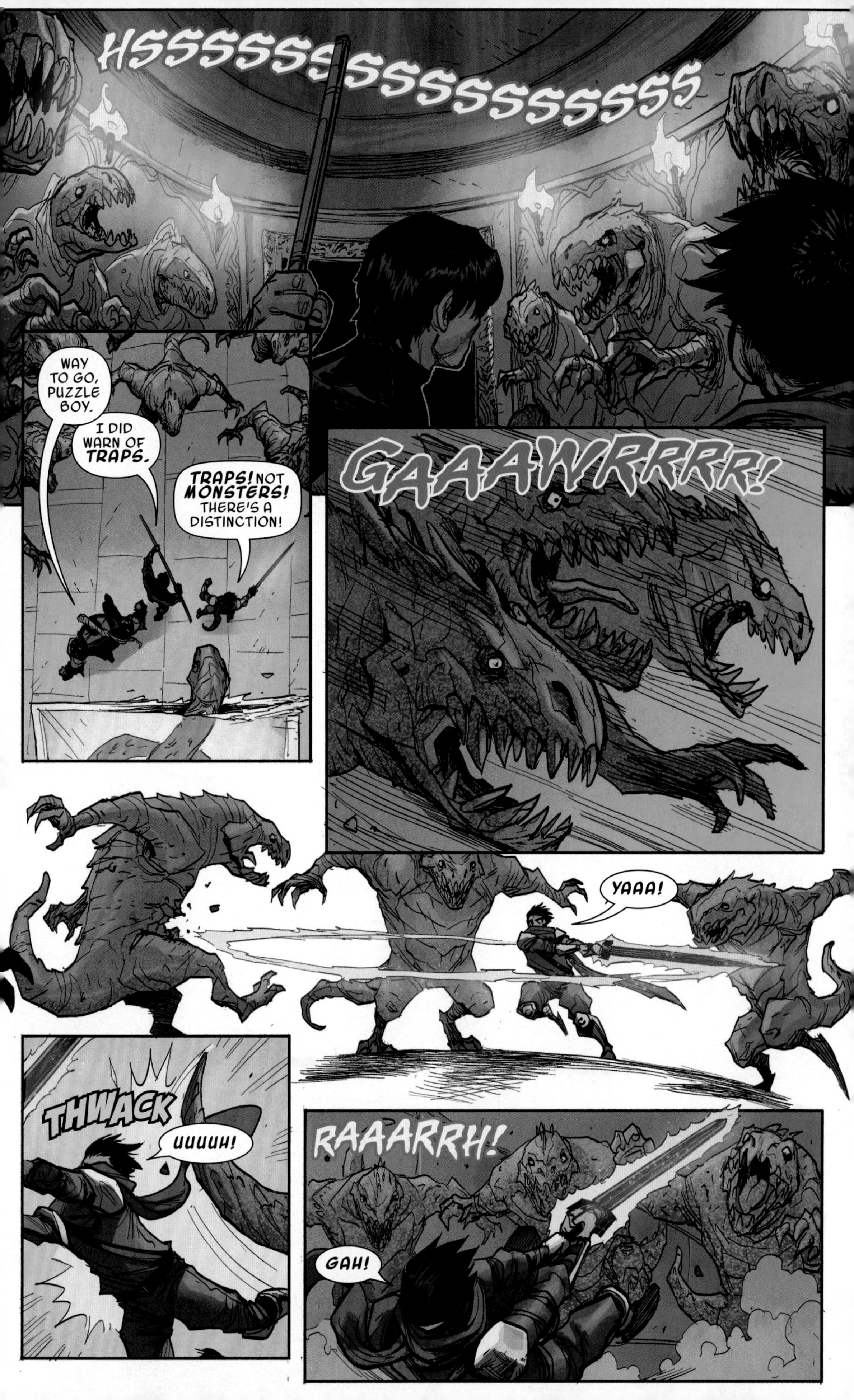
HSSSSSSSSSSSSSSSSS
WAY TO GO, PUZZLE BOY.
I DID WARN OF TRAPS.
TRAPS! NOT MONSTERS! THERE'S A DISTINCTION!
GAAAWRRRR!
YAAA!
THWACK
UUUUH!
RAAARRH!
GAH!

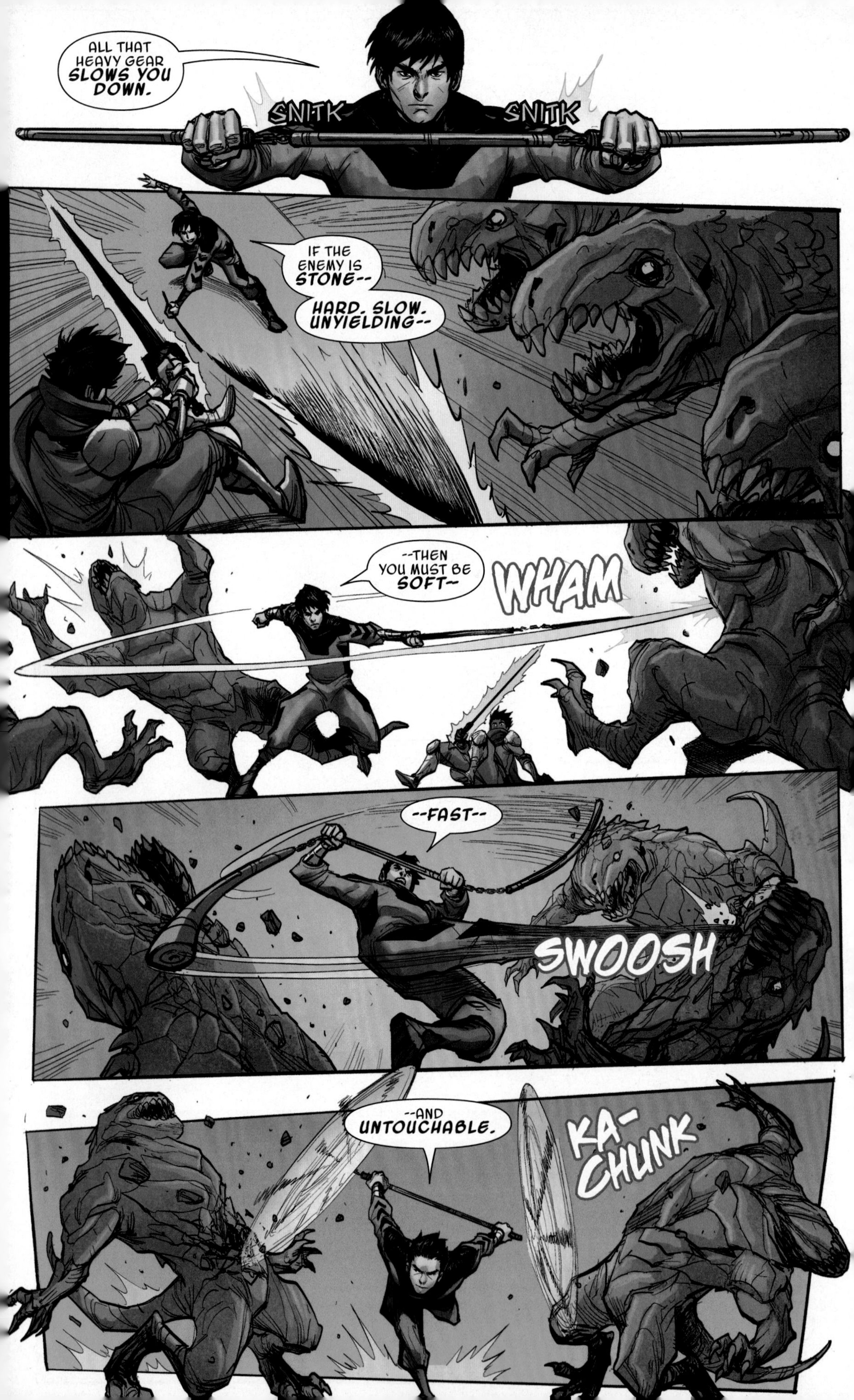
ALL THAT HEAVY GEAR SLOWS YOU DOWN.
SNITK
SNITK
IF THE ENEMY IS STONE--
HARD. SLOW. UNYIELDING--
--THEN YOU MUST BE SOFT--
WHAM
--FAST--
SWOOSH
--AND UNTOUCHABLE.
KA-CHUNK

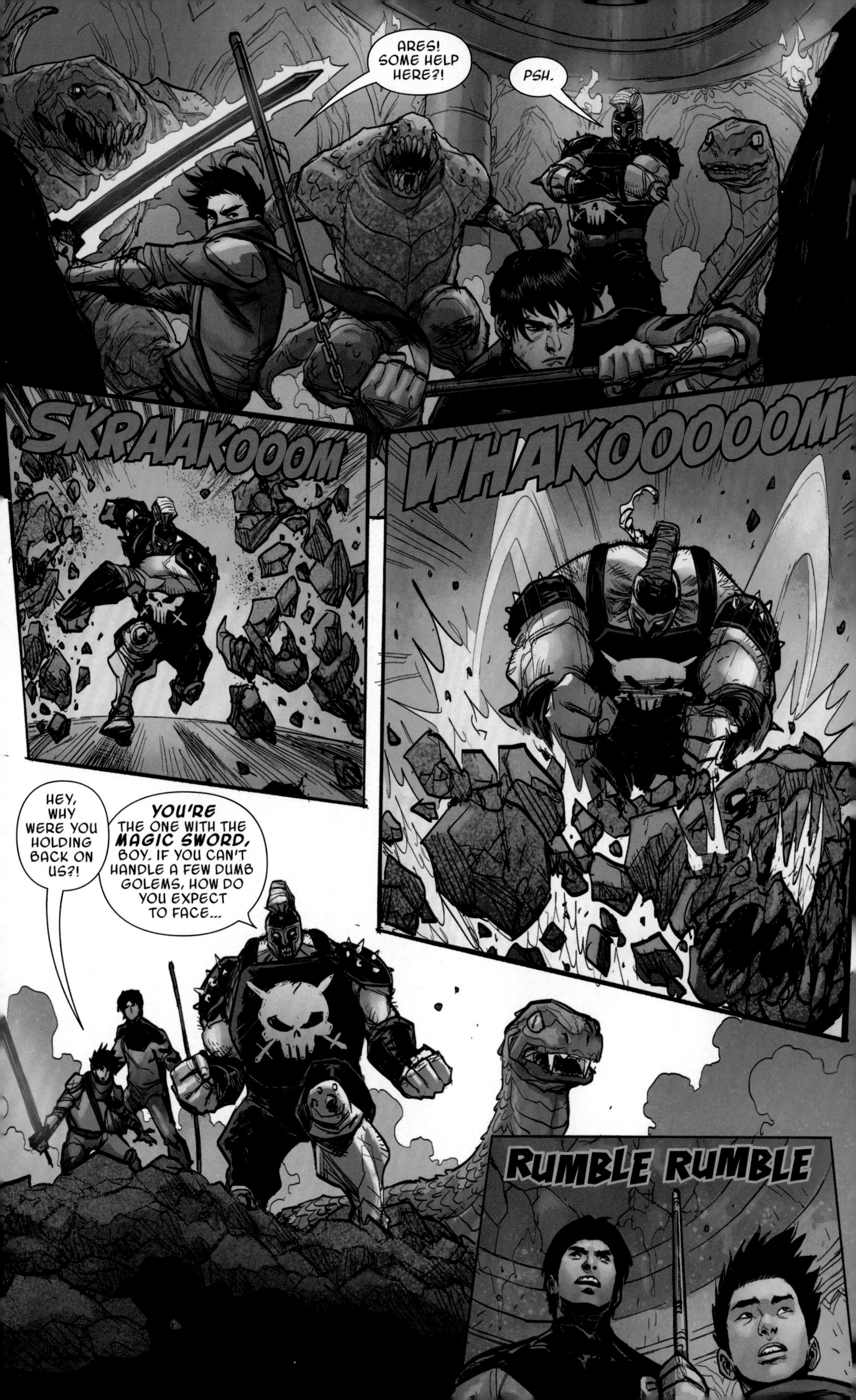
ARES! SOME HELP HERE?!
PSH.
SKRAAKOOOM
WHAKOOOOOM
HEY, WHY WERE YOU HOLDING BACK ON US?!
YOU'RE THE ONE WITH THE MAGIC SWORD, BOY. IF YOU CAN'T HANDLE A FEW DUMB GOLEMS, HOW DO YOU EXPECT TO FACE...
RUMBLE RUMBLE

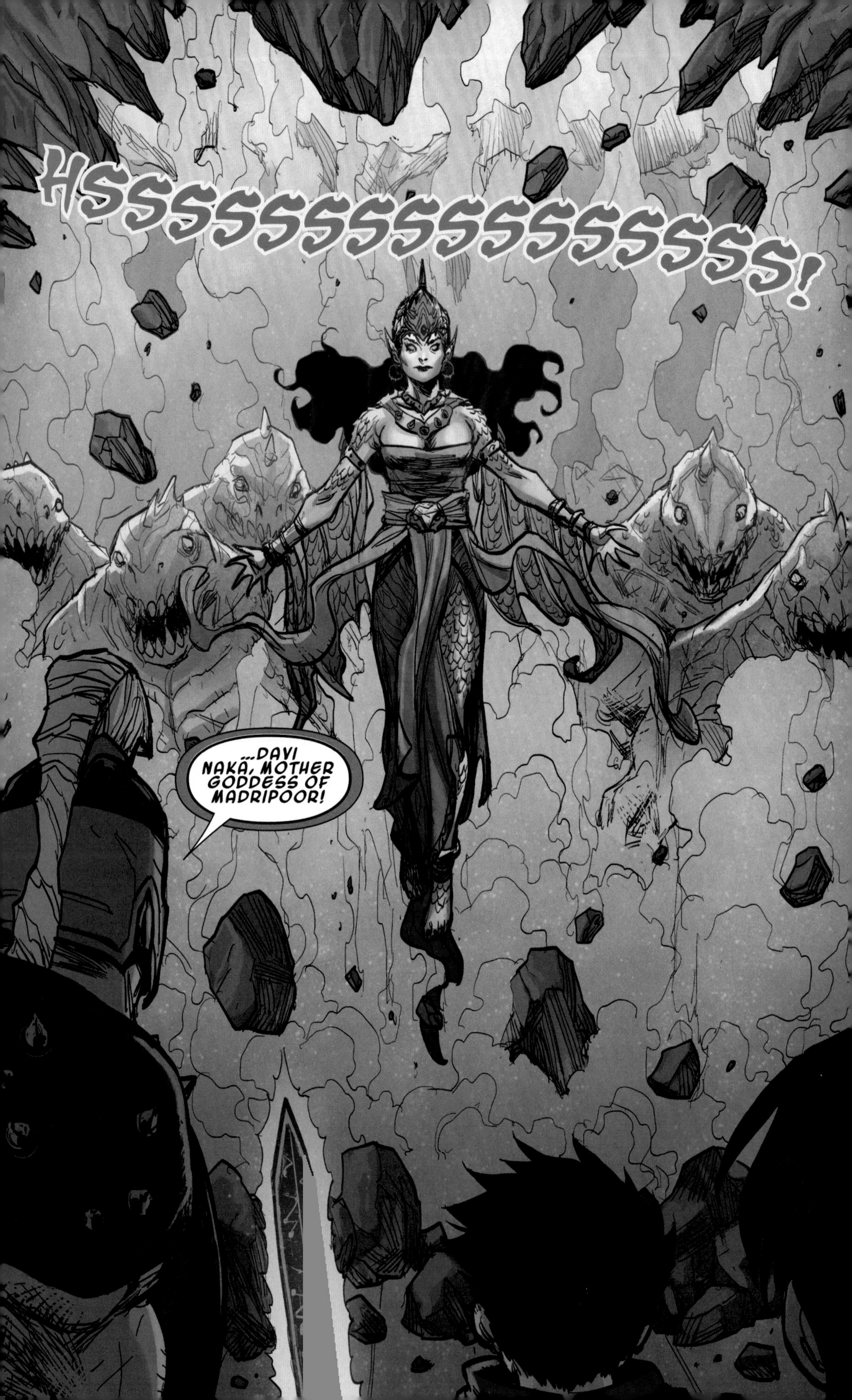
HSSSSSSSSSSSSSSSSS!
...DAVI NAKÂ, MOTHER GODDESS OF MADRIPOOR!

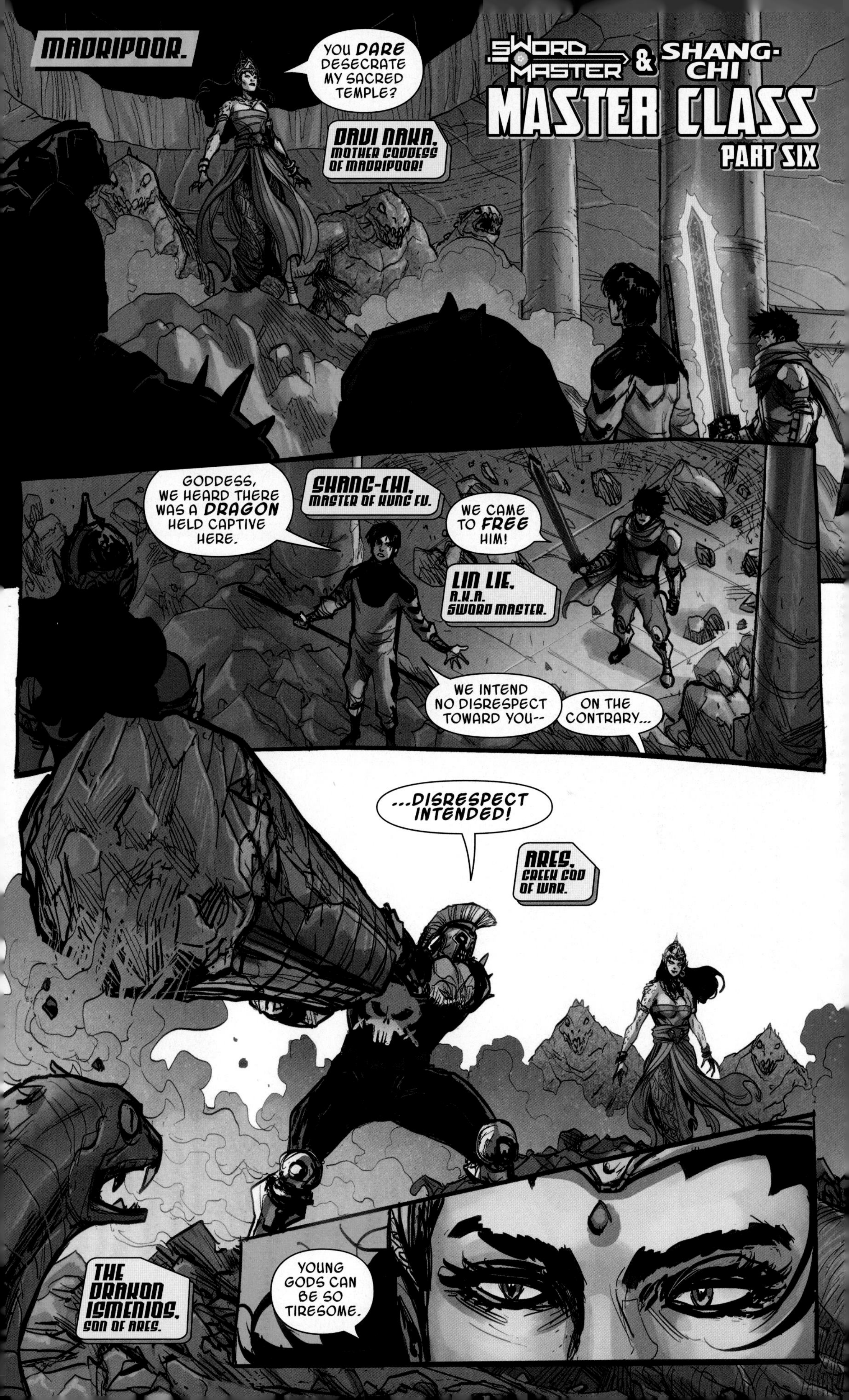

MADRIPOOR.
YOU DARE DESECRATE MY SACRED TEMPLE?
DAVI NAKA, MOTHER GODDESS OF MADRIPOOR!
SWORD MASTER & SHANG-CHI
MASTER CLASS
PART SIX
GODDESS, WE HEARD THERE WAS A DRAGON HELD CAPTIVE HERE.
SHANG-CHI, MASTER OF KUNG FU.
WE CAME TO FREE HIM!
LIN LIE, A.K.A. SWORD MASTER.
WE INTEND NO DISRESPECT TOWARD YOU--
ON THE CONTRARY...
...DISRESPECT INTENDED!
ARES, GREEK GOD OF WAR.
THE DRAKON ISMENIOS, SON OF ARES.
YOUNG GODS CAN BE SO TIRESOME.

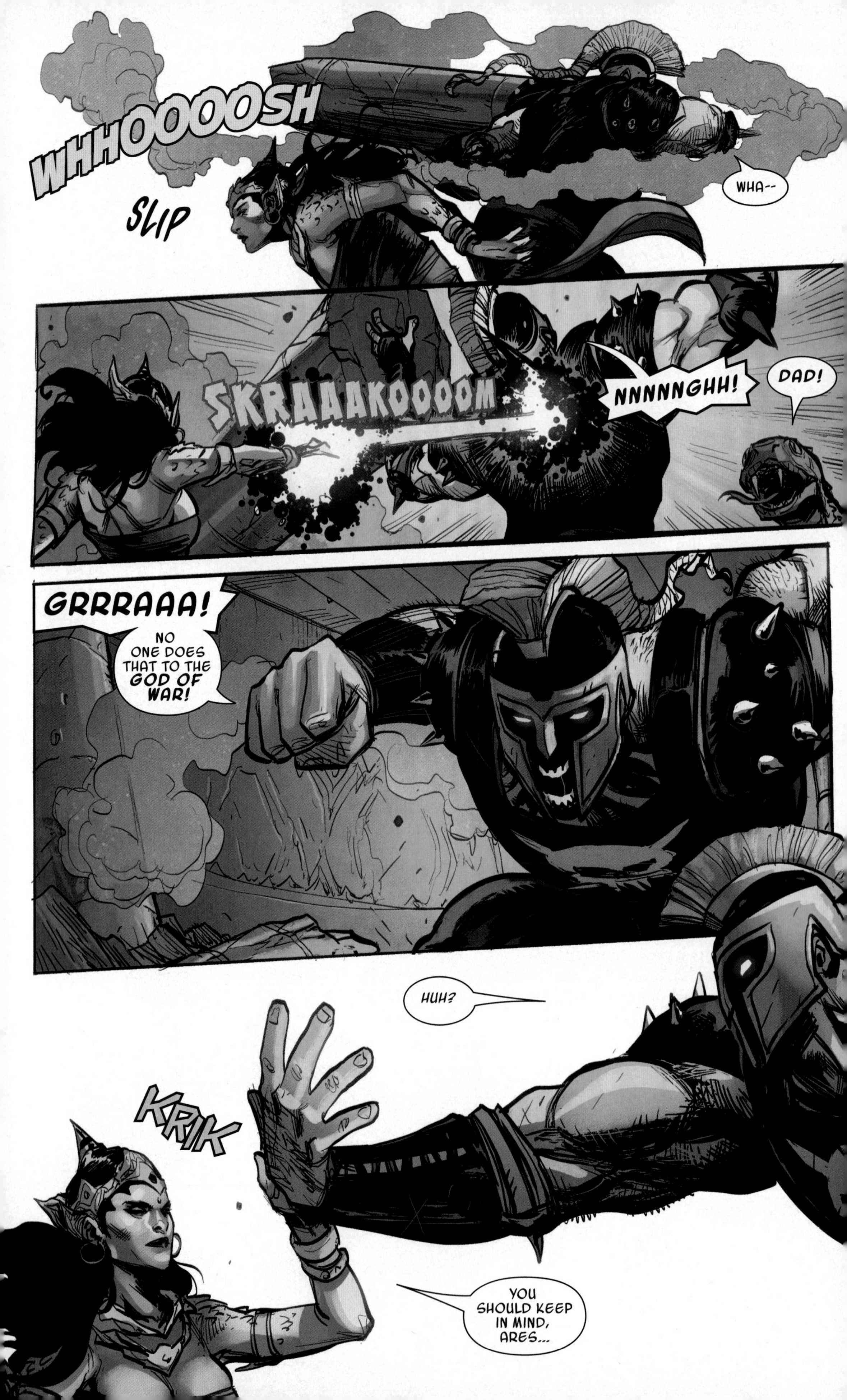
WHHOOOOSH
SLIP
WHA--
SKRAAAKOOOOM
NNNNNGHH!
DAD!
GRRRAAA!
NO ONE DOES THAT TO THE GOD OF WAR!
HUH?
KRIK
YOU SHOULD KEEP IN MIND, ARES...

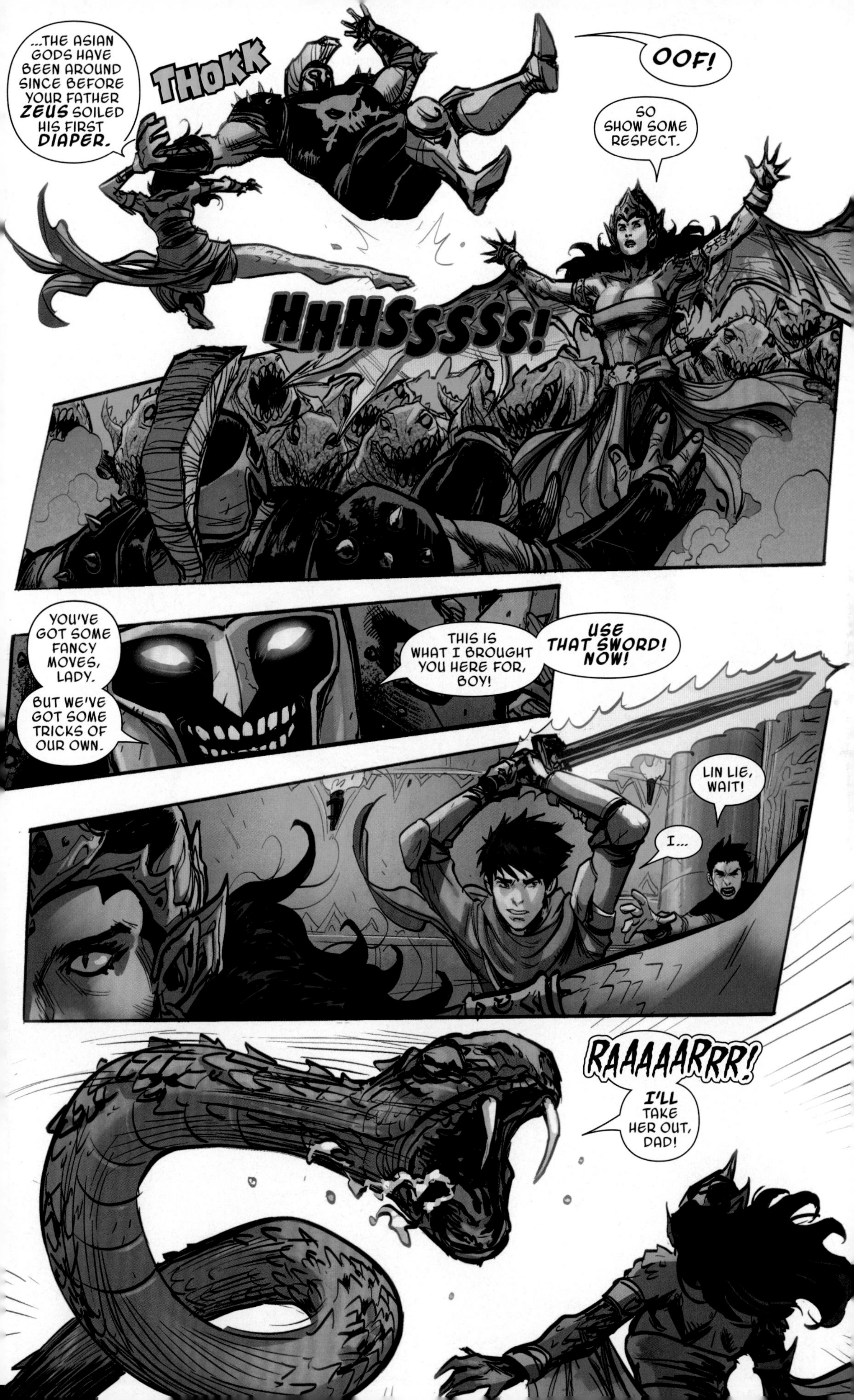
...THE ASIAN GODS HAVE BEEN AROUND SINCE BEFORE YOUR FATHER ZEUS SOILED HIS FIRST DIAPER.
THOKK
OOF!
SO SHOW SOME RESPECT.
HHHSSSSS!
YOU'VE GOT SOME FANCY MOVES, LADY.
BUT WE'VE GOT SOME TRICKS OF OUR OWN.
THIS IS WHAT I BROUGHT YOU HERE FOR, BOY!
USE THAT SWORD! NOW!
LIN LIE, WAIT!
I...
RAAAAARRR!
I'LL TAKE HER OUT, DAD!

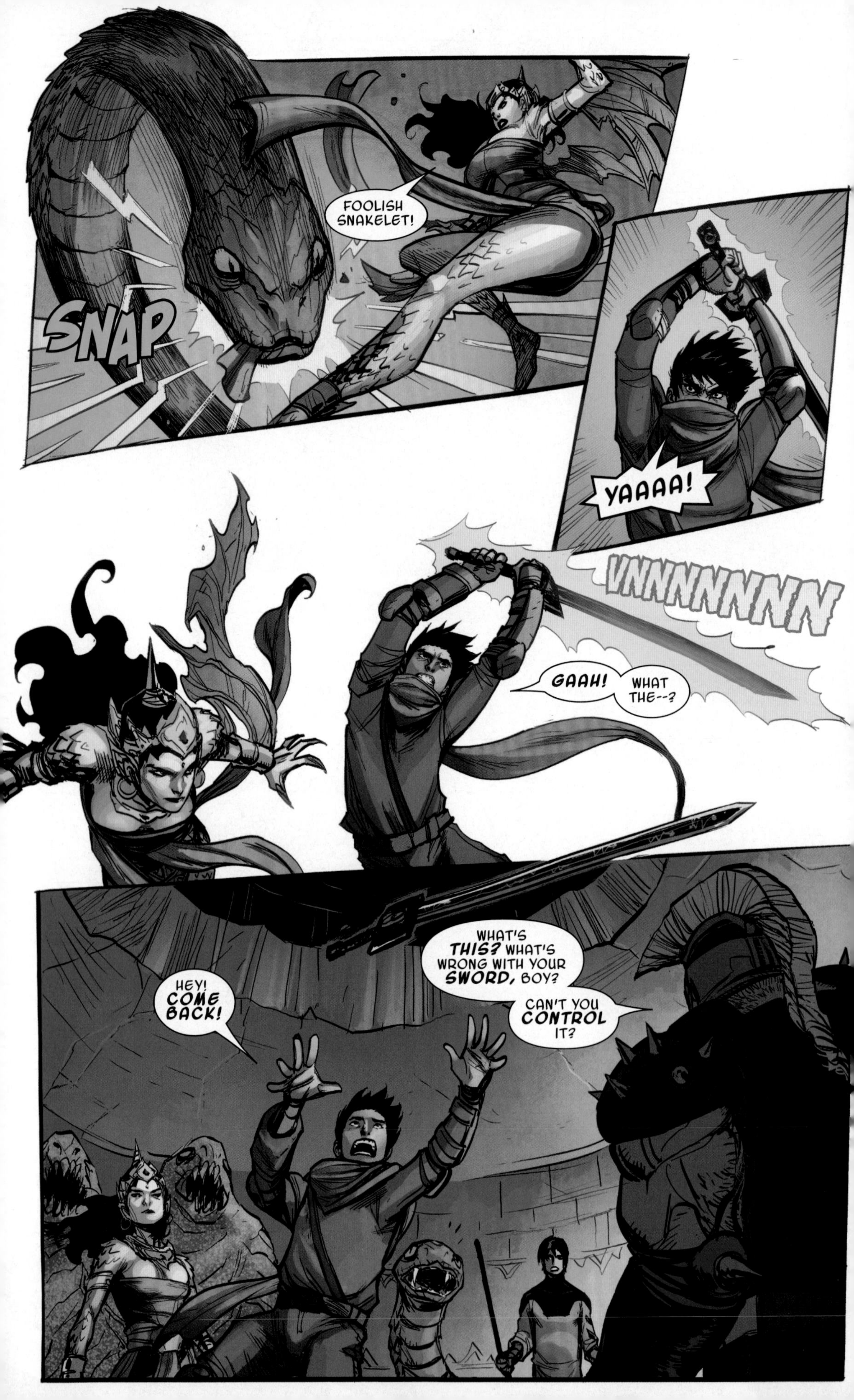
FOOLISH SNAKELET!
SNAP
YAAAA!
VNNNNNNNN
GAAH!
WHAT THE--?
WHAT'S THIS? WHAT'S WRONG WITH YOUR SWORD, BOY?
CAN'T YOU CONTROL IT?
HEY! COME BACK!

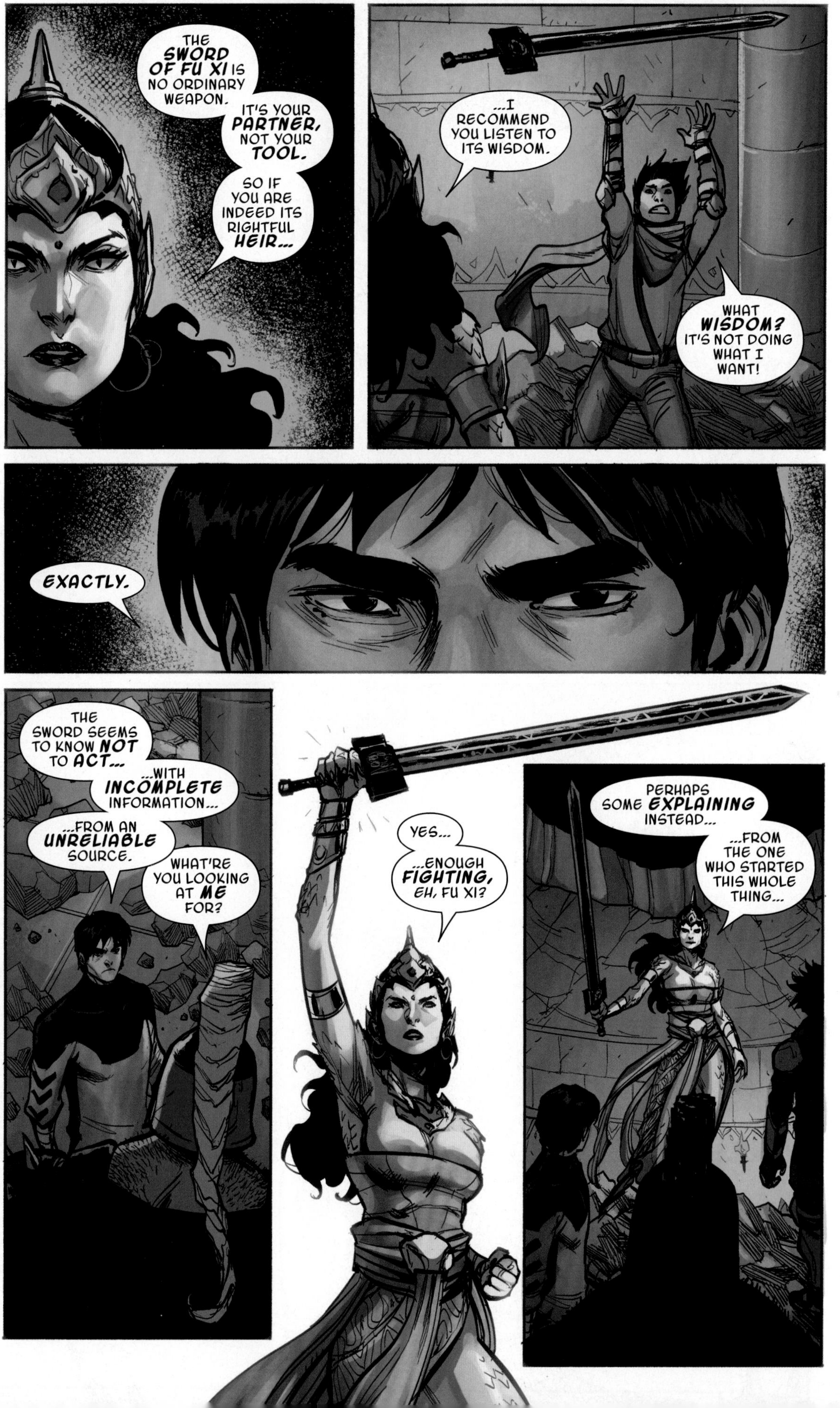
THE SWORD OF FU XI IS NO ORDINARY WEAPON.
IT'S YOUR PARTNER, NOT YOUR TOOL.
SO IF YOU ARE INDEED ITS RIGHTFUL HEIR...
...I RECOMMEND YOU LISTEN TO ITS WISDOM.
WHAT WISDOM? IT'S NOT DOING WHAT I WANT!
EXACTLY.
THE SWORD SEEMS TO KNOW NOT TO ACT...
...WITH INCOMPLETE INFORMATION...
...FROM AN UNRELIABLE SOURCE.
WHAT'RE YOU LOOKING AT ME FOR?
YES...
...ENOUGH FIGHTING, EH, FU XI?
PERHAPS SOME EXPLAINING INSTEAD...
...FROM THE ONE WHO STARTED THIS WHOLE THING...

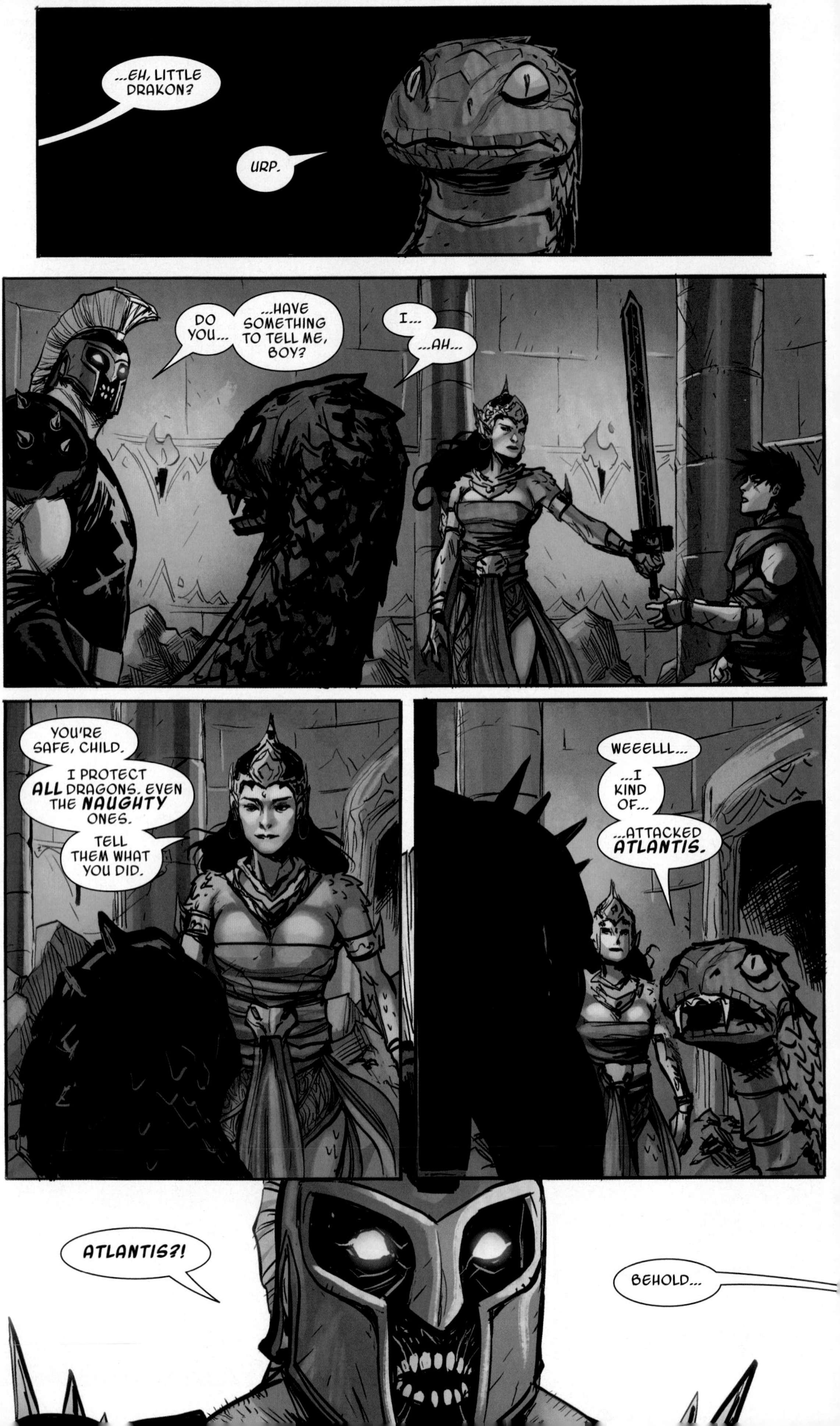
...EH, LITTLE DRAKON?
URP.
DO YOU...
...HAVE SOMETHING TO TELL ME, BOY?
I...
...AH...
YOU'RE SAFE, CHILD.
I PROTECT ALL DRAGONS. EVEN THE NAUGHTY ONES.
TELL THEM WHAT YOU DID.
WEEELLL...
...I KIND OF...
...ATTACKED ATLANTIS.
ATLANTIS?!
BEHOLD...

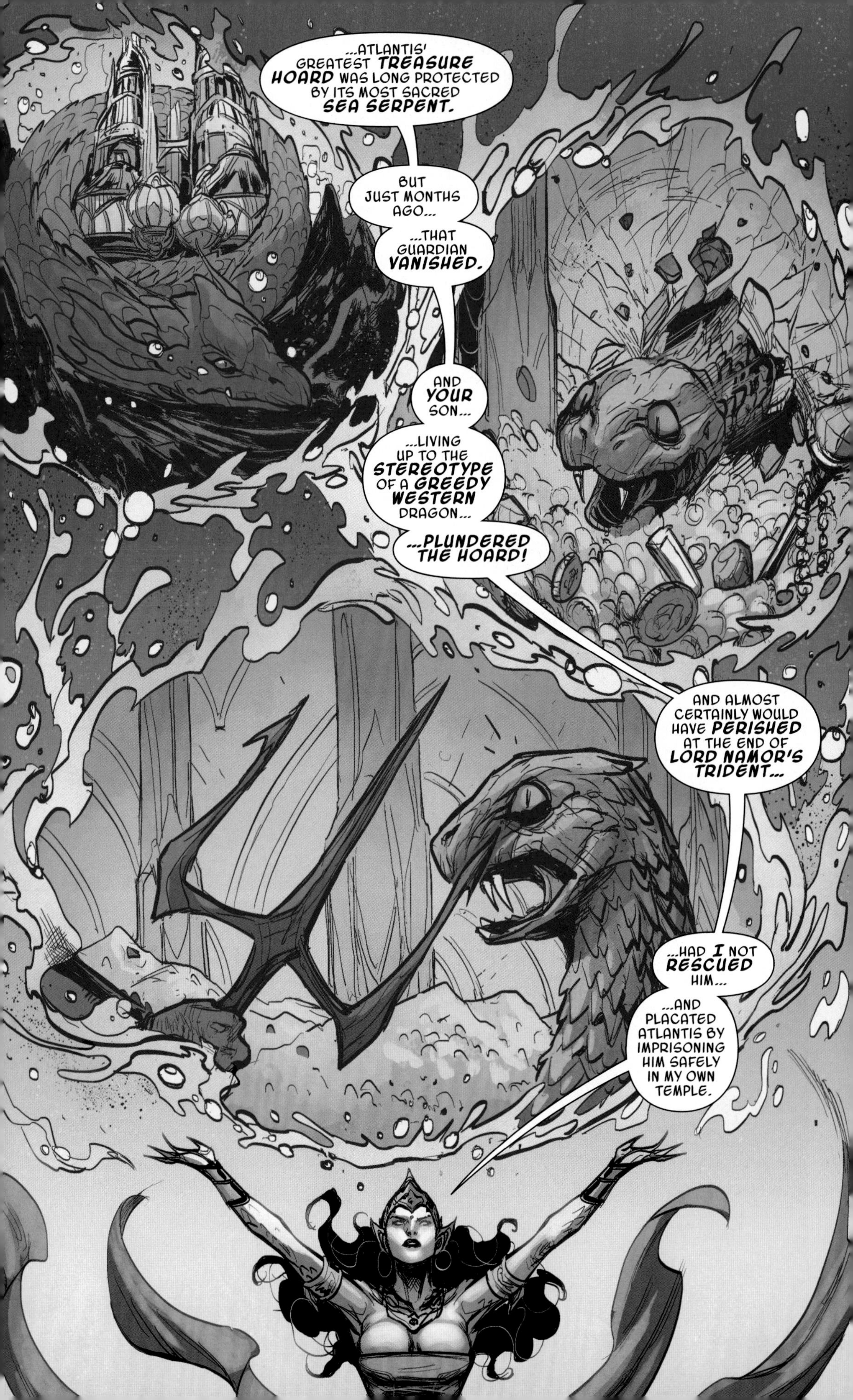
...ATLANTIS' GREATEST TREASURE HOARD WAS LONG PROTECTED BY ITS MOST SACRED SEA SERPENT.
BUT JUST MONTHS AGO...
...THAT GUARDIAN VANISHED.
AND YOUR SON...
...LIVING UP TO THE STEREOTYPE OF A GREEDY WESTERN DRAGON...
...PLUNDERED THE HOARD!
AND ALMOST CERTAINLY WOULD HAVE PERISHED AT THE END OF LORD NAMOR'S TRIDENT...
...HAD I NOT RESCUED HIM...
...AND PLACATED ATLANTIS BY IMPRISONING HIM SAFELY IN MY OWN TEMPLE.

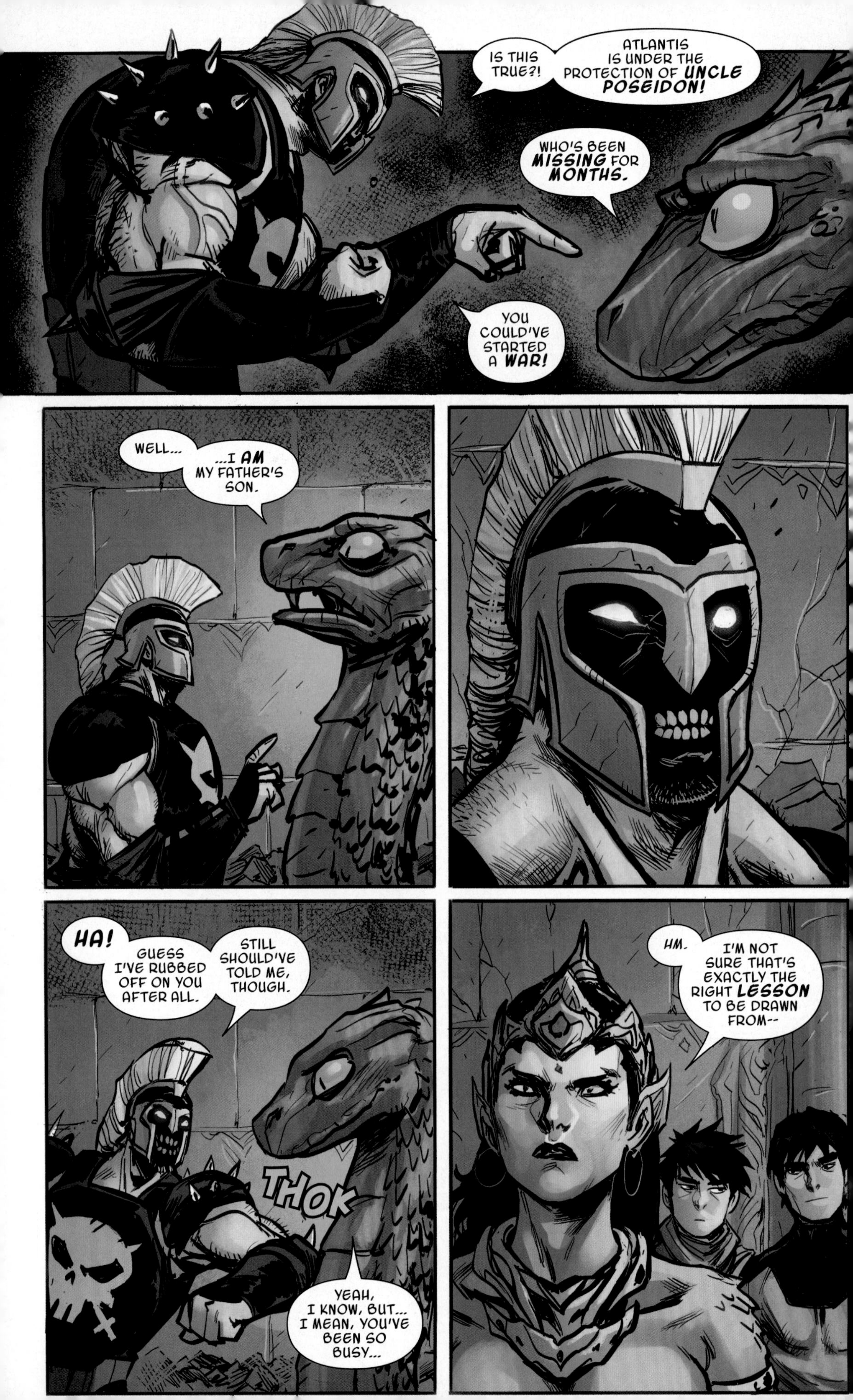

IS THIS TRUE?!
ATLANTIS IS UNDER THE PROTECTION OF UNCLE POSEIDON!
WHO'S BEEN MISSING FOR MONTHS.
YOU COULD'VE STARTED A WAR!
WELL...
...I AM MY FATHER'S SON.
HA!
GUESS I'VE RUBBED OFF ON YOU AFTER ALL.
STILL SHOULD'VE TOLD ME, THOUGH.
THOK
YEAH, I KNOW, BUT... I MEAN, YOU'VE BEEN SO BUSY...
HM.
I'M NOT SURE THAT'S EXACTLY THE RIGHT LESSON TO BE DRAWN FROM--

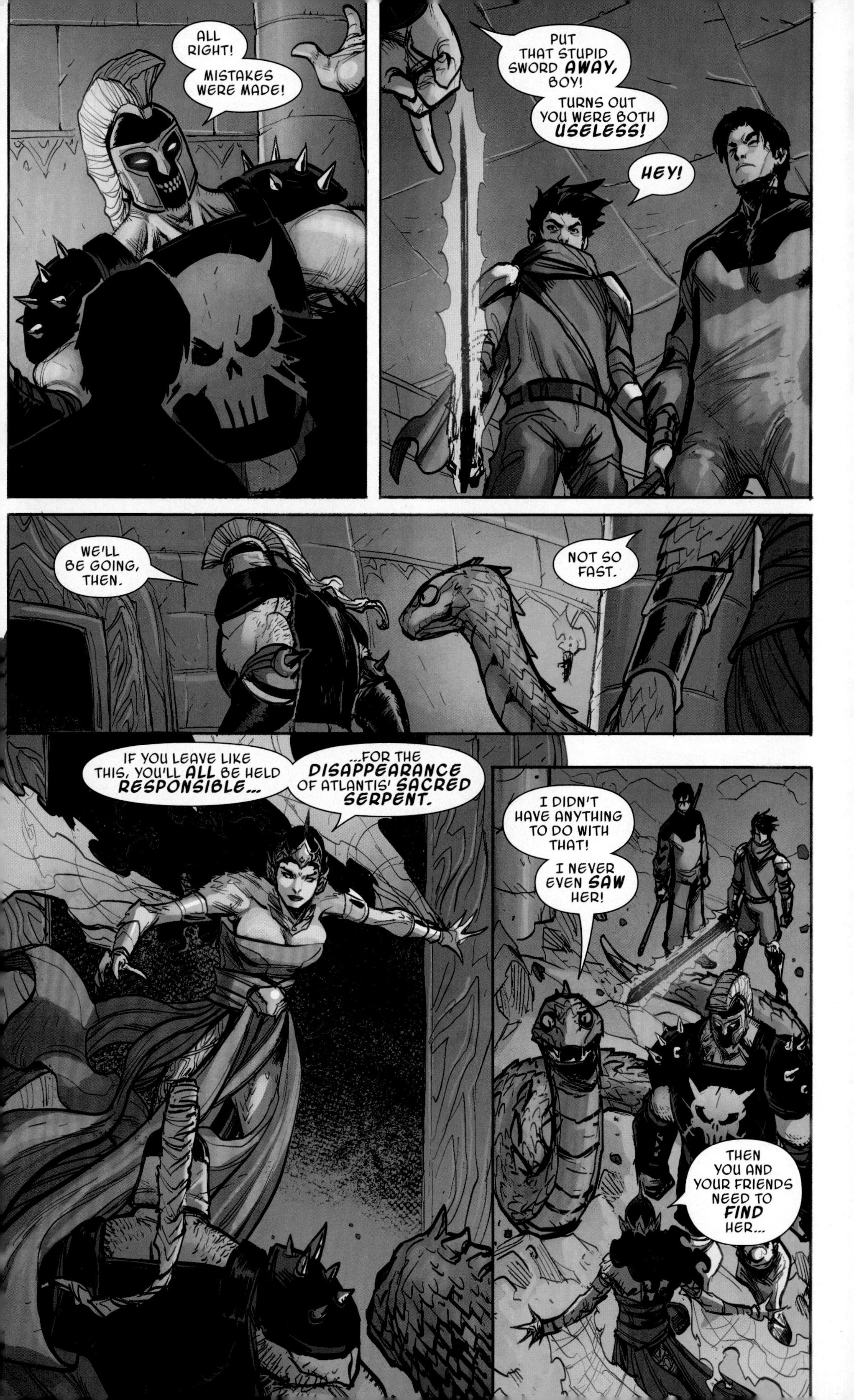
ALL RIGHT!
MISTAKES WERE MADE!
PUT THAT STUPID SWORD AWAY, BOY!
TURNS OUT YOU WERE BOTH USELESS!
HEY!
WE'LL BE GOING, THEN.
NOT SO FAST.
IF YOU LEAVE LIKE THIS, YOU'LL ALL BE HELD RESPONSIBLE...
...FOR THE DISAPPEARANCE OF ATLANTIS' SACRED SERPENT.
I DIDN'T HAVE ANYTHING TO DO WITH THAT!
I NEVER EVEN SAW HER!
THEN YOU AND YOUR FRIENDS NEED TO FIND HER...

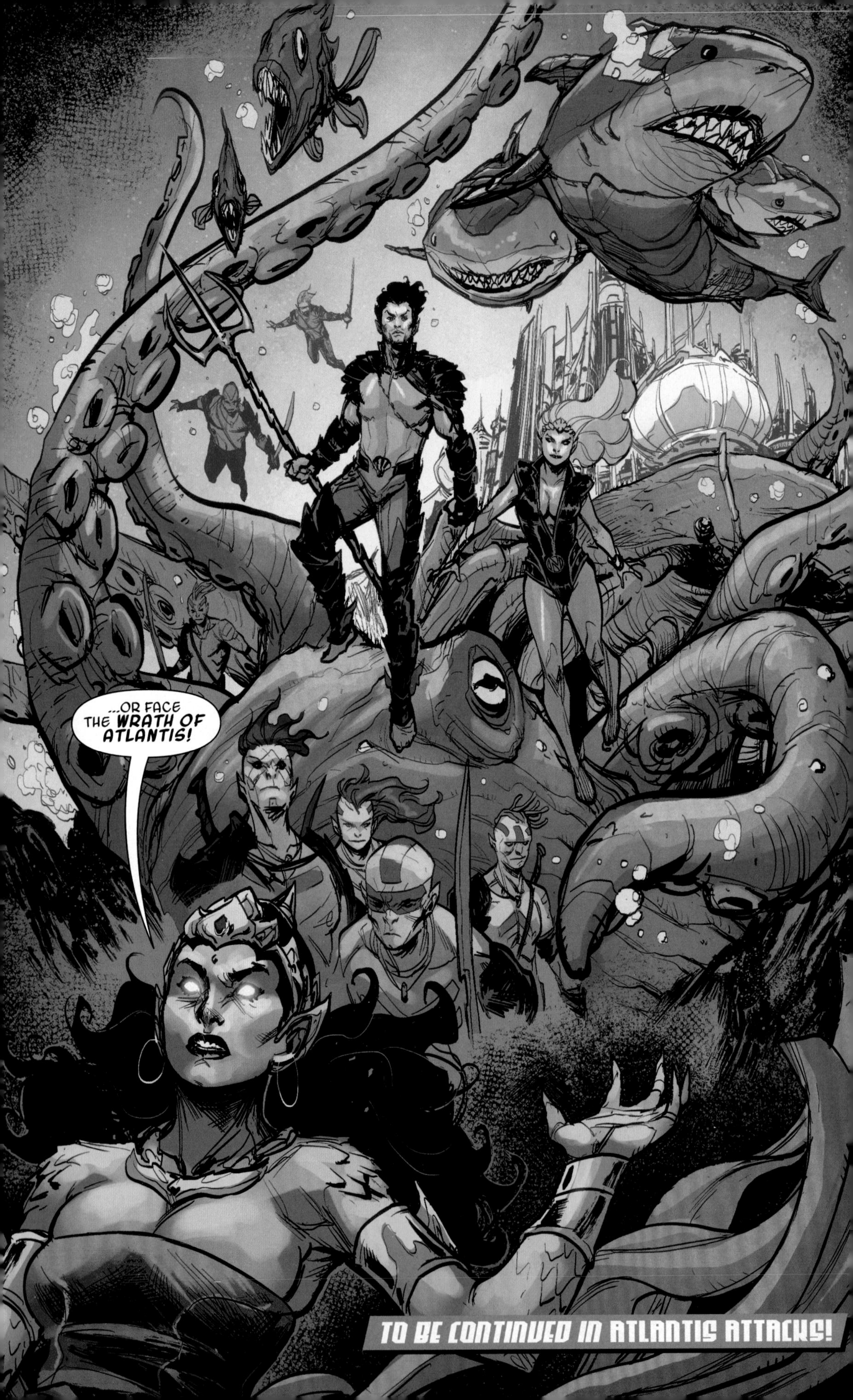
...OR FACE THE WRATH OF ATLANTIS!
TO BE CONTINUED IN ATLANTIS ATTACKS!

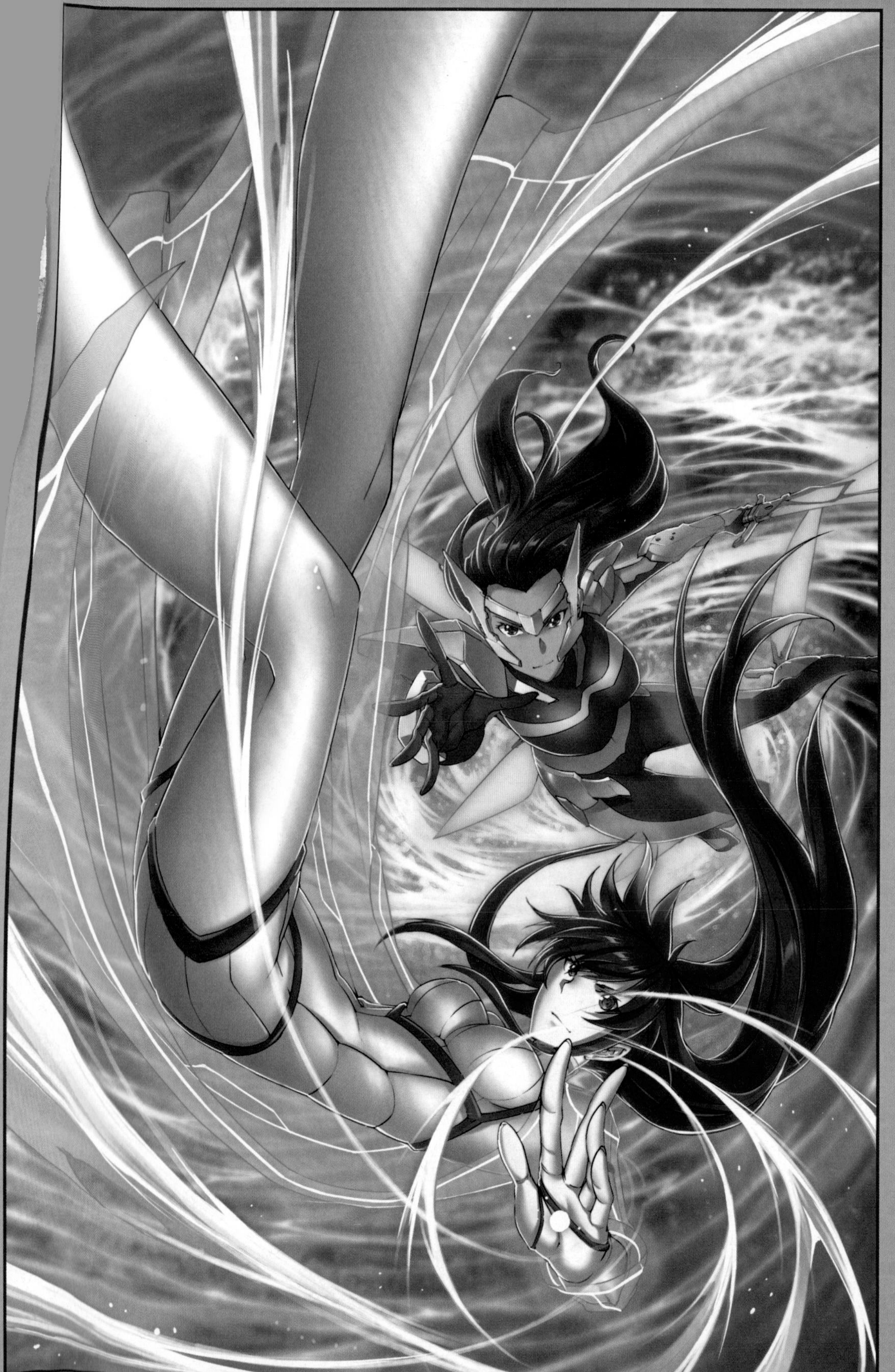

AERO #6 COVER BY
KENG